MORE THAN A DOCTRINE

The Eisenhower Era in the Middle East

RANDALL FOWLER

Foreword by MARTIN J. MEDHURST

Potomac Books

AN IMPRINT OF THE UNIVERSITY OF NEBRASKA PRESS

Portions of this book were originally published as
"Lion's Last Roar, Eagle's First Flight: Eisenhower and
the Suez Crisis of 1956," in *Rhetoric & Public Affairs* 20,
no. 1 (Spring 2017): 33–67.

Map created by United States Army Map Service.
Retrieved from the Library of Congress,
https://www.loc.gov/item/2013593016/.

Library of Congress Cataloging-in-Publication Data
Names: Fowler, Randall, author.
Title: More than a doctrine: the Eisenhower era
in the Middle East / Randall Fowler; foreword
by Martin J. Medhurst.
Description: Lincoln: Potomac Books, an imprint of
the University of Nebraska Press, 2018. | Includes
bibliographical references and index.
Identifiers: LCCN 2017036454 (print)
LCCN 2017037982 (ebook)
ISBN 9781612349978 (cloth: alk. paper)
ISBN 9781640120419 (epub)
ISBN 9781640120426 (mobi)
ISBN 9781640120433 (pdf)
Subjects: LCSH: Middle East—Foreign relations—
United States. | United States—Foreign
relations—Middle East. | United States—Foreign
relations—1953–1961.
Classification: LCC DS63.2.U5 (ebook)
LCC DS63.2.U5 F69 2018 (print)
DDC 327.7305609/045—dc23
LC record available at https://lccn.loc.gov/2017036454

Set in Scala OT by E. Cuddy.

For my parents, Mark and Kayla

CONTENTS

Foreword ix

Acknowledgments xi

Introduction xiii

Eisenhower Doctrine Address 1

1. The Eisenhower Doctrine: A Species of Containment 13

2. Operation Ajax: Eisenhower's Rhetoric of Misdirection 41

3. From Baghdad to Cairo: The Limits of Rhetorical Surreption . . . 73

4. Lion's Last Roar, Eagle's First Flight: Eisenhower at Suez 105

5. The Doctrine Applied: Intervention in Lebanon and the
   Rhetoric of Justification 135

Conclusion 167

Notes 183

Bibliography 205

Index 223

TABLES

1. Events of Operation Ajax 53
2. Events of Operation Blue Bat 147

FOREWORD

MARTIN J. MEDHURST

When one thinks of Dwight D. Eisenhower many images come to mind: the conquering general, who mingled with the troops prior to the D-Day invasion; the charismatic candidate, whose endless grin and arms thrust high in a V-for-victory sign exuded confidence; the Cold War president, who guided the nation with a steady hand and a determined philosophy that "the future shall belong to the free." These were the public images of "Ike," a man we felt we knew and a leader we believed we could trust. Although time has not eroded these images, it has complicated them. Ike, we now know, was not the simple soldier he often made himself out to be. Instead, he was a strategic thinker, a cold warrior of the first rank, a determined projector of American power and influence around the globe, and a crafty backstage operator who did not hesitate to use martial, sometimes even lethal means of achieving his ends. He was, from first to last, General Ike.

This book deals with this more complicated Ike, the one who understood the great stakes of the post–World War II world and purposed to position the United States to be victorious in peace just as it had been in war. In no arena was this strategic positioning more acute than in the Middle East. Randall Fowler takes the reader inside the Eisenhower administration as Ike and his lieutenants debate the fate of nations: Iran, Egypt, Syria, and Lebanon, chief among them. The lens through which Fowler follows these actions is presidential rhetoric. Eisenhower, in this account, was not a great orator, but he was a strategic communicator, one who knew precisely what he wanted to accomplish and chose his language, images, and arguments to give effect to those goals. Ike's words were selected with an end in mind; he knew what he was doing and why he was doing it. Rhetoric was his instrument.

In the case of Eisenhower and the Middle East, presidential rhetoric was used to displace the traditional European powers—Great Britain and France—and to reposition the United States as the chief hegemon in the region. Eventually taking the form of the Eisenhower Doctrine, this rhetoric was the vehicle by which the United States assumed responsibility for the region and projected its power. Anyone wondering why the United States is still knee-deep in Middle Eastern politics could do no better than to start with this book. Rhetoric does have consequences, especially when its purely instrumental uses outpace the values, morals, and ethical actions the rhetoric was meant to serve.

ACKNOWLEDGMENTS

This book would not have come to be without the generous assistance of numerous people. As a native of Abilene, Texas, I grew up far removed from the Middle East, and I therefore have many people to thank who opened my eyes to the region, its richness, and its complexities. To Randy Turner, Drew Young, Jason and Amanda McCall, William Baker, my Arabic professor Abjar Bahkou, Alain McNamara, and countless others, I owe a great deal of gratitude for introducing me to the Middle East. I likewise offer my sincerest thanks to friends, students, and colleagues who have challenged, encouraged, and inspired me. These relationships have deepened my understanding of the region and the rhetorical forces that shape it.

I owe much to the scholarly guidance of my former advisor, Martin J. Medhurst, whose study of Cold War and presidential rhetoric paved the way for future scholarly investigations on these subjects, including my own; as such, this book very much seeks to build on his foundational studies of Eisenhower's presidential rhetoric. This study also would not have been possible without the groundbreaking work of Kenneth Osgood, Shawn Parry-Giles, Ned O'Gorman, Ira Chernus, Robert Ivie, Stephen Ambrose, Fred Greenstein, Meena Bose, Salim Yaqub, David Zarefsky, and others. I am greatly indebted to Samuel Perry for his steady support throughout my time at Baylor University and for his help from this project's earliest iterations. My thanks go out to Mark Long as well; my work has greatly benefited from his unique perspective and thoughtful comments.

Many others also deserve thanks. The staff of the Dwight D. Eisenhower Presidential Library in Abilene, Kansas, especially

Kevin Bailey, rendered invaluable assistance during my visit to their archives and continued to offer their help over the course of this project's evolution. My gratitude also extends to David Schlueter and the Baylor Communication Department for making such a trip possible. I also wish to thank my colleagues in the Baylor Interdisciplinary Core and the Binational Fulbright Commission of Jordan. Without the opportunities provided by these organizations I would not have been able to conduct this study.

On a personal note, I would also like to thank my family and friends who have supported me throughout the drafting of this book. Your constant encouragement and prayers—not to mention an editorial insight or two—played a large role in bringing this project to completion. To my mother and father in particular I am grateful, and I am proud to dedicate this book to you both. To all those who kept me going, I have but one thing to say: thank you. I am truly blessed.

INTRODUCTION

On June 12, 2014, comedian Jon Stewart of *The Daily Show* resurrected his long-running recurring segment titled "Mess O'Potamia" to report the fall of Mosul to the Islamic State, or isis. Labeling the terrorist organization a group of "militant overachievers," Stewart proceeded to provide his standard repertoire of quips, cable news excerpts, and clever remarks as he lamented the lack of any good information to report. Displaying a still image of President George W. Bush giving his infamous "Mission Accomplished" speech aboard the uss *Ronald Reagan*, Stewart finished the segment by sardonically shouting: "Yes! We did it! We finally got it so that Iraq will now greet us as liberators!" The episode aptly captured the shock many felt at the Islamic State's stunningly successful military offensive.[1]

Perhaps it is odd to begin a book about President Dwight Eisenhower with an anecdote about Jon Stewart. The scathingly liberal twenty-first-century late-night comedian has little to do with Eisenhower on the surface. Yet Stewart's reliance on a single governing comedic metaphor—"Mess O'Potamia"—to explain the complicated events taking place in the Middle East, from Operation Iraqi Freedom to the post–Arab Spring, speaks not only to Americans' inability to knowledgeably interpret the events of the region but also to the pervasive power of presidential rhetoric to structure American perceptions of the Middle East. Both trends, as I hope to show, are not new phenomena.

The Middle East is a difficult place for Americans to understand. Since the earliest days of Anglo North American settlement, in which Cotton Mather praised the return of captured New England sailors from the "Hellish Moors" of North Africa and the young

United States waged a series of wars against the Barbary States, Americans have struggled to accurately comprehend the intricacies of a region whose complexity has more often than not bedeviled them.[2] Whether drawn to the region by the pursuit of power, faith, or profit—or all three—Americans of all stripes have visited the Middle East throughout their nation's history. A U.S. consulate graced the region as early as 1835.[3] And as long as Americans have journeyed there, they have returned to share their (mis)interpretations of the region. American depictions of the Middle East have ranged from romantic to violent, barbaric to enlightened, but all share one common quality: they are periphrastic reconstructions of a region far removed from this nation's shores, and as such, they are very much the products of rhetorical invention. In other words they all provide a story, telling us who "we" are, who "they" are, and what the United States and the Middle East are to each other.

• • •

All these elements converge in the presidency of Dwight David Eisenhower, or Ike. As he did in many aspects of modern life, Eisenhower deeply influenced American policy and conceptions of the Middle East. Though perhaps better known for his numerous other feats—ending the Korean War, enforcing integration at Little Rock, incorporating West Germany into NATO, creating the Interstate Highway system, and, most significantly, avoiding nuclear war—Ike also oversaw a substantial expansion of America's presence in the Middle East. In a way more popularly reminiscent of his successors, Eisenhower brokered peace deals, toppled governments, formed alliances, accelerated decolonization, and deployed U.S. military forces to Arab lands during his eight years in office. It is Ike's rhetoric that anticipated, authorized, and attended to this shift in American Middle East policy that comprises the subject of this book.

Eisenhower came into office promising to prioritize the Middle East. Although the Truman administration did much to shape events in the region—securing the Dardanelles and Iran from Soviet interference, granting recognition to Israel, announcing the Truman Doctrine to support Greece and Turkey, and issuing the 1950 Tripartite Declaration with Britain and France—the president himself did not speak much of or seemingly devote much attention to the Middle East. This presidential inattention changed during Ike's 1952 campaign. Eisenhower told the electorate that, in terms of pure territory, there was "no more strategically important area in the world."[4] His secretary of state John Foster Dulles undertook a tour of the Middle East soon after his appointment and declared that it was "high time that the United States government paid more attention to the Near East and South Asia."[5] Moreover, Ike delivered on these promises. From the Iranian coup to the deployment of troops to Lebanon, amid quiet support for American oil companies and an Arab-Israeli settlement, the Eisenhower administration can be said, in the words of Steven Spiegel, to have been "the first presidency to view the Middle East as a prime region of foreign policy concern."[6]

But while Ike's interest in the region was more or less unchanging, the way in which he chose to communicate the Middle East's importance to the American public shifted dramatically throughout his presidency. His rhetoric swung from totally denying and downplaying U.S. regional involvement—declaring the Iranian shah's 1953 return to power a purely "internal" matter—to strident oratory demanding from Congress virtually unlimited authority to fight any regional threat from "International Communism," in the 1957 Eisenhower Doctrine speech. And as with all things Eisenhower, his rhetoric was a strategic choice, often ambiguous and always purposeful. He rarely, if ever, let slip information he did not want known or gave an impression he did not wish to give, and the way he managed American relations with the Middle East was no exception. His treatment of the region was, from his first inaugural to his farewell address, a consummately rhetorical performance.

The Power of Presidential Rhetoric

Missionaries, oilmen, diplomats, explorers, and even literary figures such as Herman Melville and Mark Twain have all written about the Middle East and influenced American perceptions of it. Long-form journalism, entertainment media, and cable news dispatches often serve the same epistemic function in our present age, providing accounts—veritable or not—that inform and educate the American populace of what to think about the latest events in Riyadh, Tehran, Tel Aviv, Cairo, Damascus, Abu Dhabi, or Baghdad. Public discourse in a liberal democracy such as the United States draws from a variety of sources, and thus political knowledge (or ignorance) springs from many wells.[7]

Yet for all the influence these accounts may wield, few sources can match the rhetorical power possessed by the president of the United States to shape public discourse and, therefore, affect public perception. Since the groundbreaking publication of Jeffrey Tulis's *The Rhetorical Presidency*, many scholars have commented on the chief executive's unique ability to establish and influence the parameters of public life. As David Zarefsky contends, the president often serves "as the chief inventor and broker of the symbols of American politics," his rhetoric producing, pushing, and policing the boundaries of what may be considered political at any given moment.[8] By virtue of his attention, the president designates an issue as political; as head of state and chief citizen (not to mention his other roles), the president is by definition the symbolic representation of the people. Thus as Martin J. Medhurst argues, even mundane aspects of presidential activity, such as embracing a child, signing a bill into law, or greeting visitors to the White House, "can be construed as aspects of rhetorical leadership if given the proper framing and definition."[9] Stated otherwise, the president, as the symbolic leader of the nation, exercises an exclusive mode of rhetorical power in American political life and is therefore uniquely capable of influencing public debate.

This rhetorical power is manifested in several different ways. Presidential speech has long been associated with the bully pulpit, or the president's ability to circumvent legislative constraints by appealing to the electorate directly. By openly addressing the people, the president can create public pressure on Congress to institute particular items on the president's agenda. As a large legislative body with members continually up for reelection, Congress is often sensitive to localized political pressure in a way that the president is not, and thus the bully pulpit bestows on the president a certain degree of coercive power in its application. Presidents can, furthermore, also redirect public attention by using their platform as an agenda-setting device, as Donald Trump's ability to capture a news cycle with a single tweet well illustrates.

In addition to the bully pulpit and the symbolic import of his speech, much of the president's rhetorical power also derives from the act of speaking itself. While few members of the general public studiously inspect the actual words a president utters, his "dramatic visual performance" of giving them—coupled with the direct and instantaneous communication enabled by mass-media technologies—works to generate a "public impression" that can then be used for political purposes.[10] This condition applies to foreign policy no less than to other areas of presidential politics. Cases in point, many Americans remember George W. Bush donning a flight suit to give his "Mission Accomplished" address or Barrack Obama's announcement that SEAL Team Six killed Osama bin Laden, but far fewer remember the presidents' actual words. These utterances elucidate both the importance of presidential rhetoric to enduringly shape public perception *and* the rhetorical effect the president's performance of speaking can have.

With all that in mind, I contend that presidential rhetoric can be understood as functioning in four distinct ways, with significant implications for Eisenhower's Middle East rhetoric.[11] First, *presidential rhetoric is a strategic choice*. While some, following Plato, consider the term "rhetoric" analogous to trickery or deception, such a definition would have seemed limited to classical rhetoricians like Isocrates, Aristotle, or Cicero. These thinkers viewed rhetoric not merely as a theory of persuasion but also as a way of understanding problems in the world and responding appropriately to them. They taught their students how to diagnose situations and adapt to different audiences as well as how to argue effectively and orate eloquently; their pupils included expert speakers in addition to statesmen and generals, including Alexander the Great. This rhetorical tradition embodies what Medhurst defines as "rhetorical leadership," or "the ability to conceptualize and use language and symbols to help achieve specific goals with particular audiences."[12] Rhetoric in this sense consists of a method of evaluating a situation, knowing when to speak, inventing compelling arguments, and the deftness to deliver one's case forcefully to the appropriate audience.

Viewed from this vantage, rhetoric comes into existence as a response to exigences, or imperfections, in the world. To be effective, speakers must know when, why, in what way, and how best to respond to the situations with which they are confronted. Skilled rhetors hone these abilities and are better able to identify moments when their rhetorical leadership might be successful. In other words rhetoric encompasses not only the ability to proffer persuasive arguments but also the ability to know *when* such arguments are needed, to *whom* they need to be delivered, and *how* to identify problems requiring redress as well as how to navigate the constraints of a situation so that one may craft a practicable rhetorical response.[13]

This conception of rhetoric, Medhurst goes on to note, "is a helpful starting point for considering the rhetorical leadership of a president, for it parallels the political situation faced by all presidents who must daily deal with people, events, objects, and relationships and the various problems or exigences they present."[14] Presidents use rhetoric as a means of achieving an objective, responding to a problem, or analyzing a situation, and therefore presidential rhetoric should be viewed as far more than the simple occasion of a president opening his mouth. Rather it should be seen as a calculated, strategic decision concerned with achieving some end. According to the thinkers noted here, presidents engage in rhetoric as a response to the bewildering amount of exigences with which they are daily faced; that is, they use rhetoric to accomplish the aims and goals inherent in their office.

Eisenhower, as a strategist par excellence, knew well how to employ rhetoric as a component of leadership. As the supreme commander of the Allied Expeditionary Forces in Europe during World War II, Ike demonstrated a penchant for managing the wildly disparate personalities and agendas of his generals, deploying his rhetorical skill to alternatively cajole, discipline, motivate, and direct his subordinates to victory. After the war, as Ira Chernus notes, Eisenhower concealed his anxiety regarding the Soviet Union with public accolades of rapport and appreciation, intentionally using his public rhetoric to de-escalate tensions and thereby lower the risk of World War III.[15] Whether he was managing relationships, hiding his true intentions, or developing a popular public persona, rhetoric was a key instrument in Eisenhower's strategic toolbox. Therefore, I contend his uses of rhetoric as president—before all else—should be critically examined as deliberate and strategic choices.

Second, *presidential rhetoric can be understood as a means of changing the orientation of the polity toward a policy or group.* Modern presidents often engage in public rhetoric to persuade voters to support a particular policy item or agenda. From Woodrow Wilson's Western Tour to generate public backing for the League of Nations Treaty to Barrack Obama's series of speeches and town hall meetings in support of the Affordable Care Act, presidents frequently campaign to generate public approval for their policies. These attempts to shape opinion directly through the bully pulpit frequently involve commending or castigating certain political groups. In Wilson's case he attempted to associate opposition to the League of Nations Treaty as an act of collaboration with the defeated Germany, in this manner exploiting lingering anti-German sentiment after World War I.[16] A more successful example of a president using rhetoric to publicly condemn his enemies might be Franklin Roosevelt, who wielded invective against his domestic opponents like John L. Lewis and William Randolph Hearst in devastating fashion. He attacked their actions in clearly identifiable but indirect terms, thus maintaining the moral high ground while still heaping scorn on them—all of which enabled him to promote his agenda with less interference.[17]

Nowhere can this aspect of presidential rhetoric be seen more clearly than in foreign policy. For the United States, a nation deeply suspicious of foreign entanglements ever since George

Washington's admonition to "steer clear of permanent alliances with any portion of the foreign world," the need to habilitate allies and demonize enemies has been especially pronounced.[18] Such maneuvers are complex and often take time. For example, in the prelude to both World Wars the president embarked on a program of attacking the Germans rhetorically as enemies before the United States entered the conflict, so as to make war a more palatable political option.[19] For Woodrow Wilson this required establishing a hard contrast between democracy, metonymically represented by the United States, and autocracy, symbolized by the kaiser's Germany, before moving on to make his case that "the world must be made safe for democracy."[20] Franklin Roosevelt, on the other hand, slowly began "the long process of education" to coax the American polity out of its isolationist stance through rhetorical performances like his "Quarantine," "Arsenal of Democracy," and 1941 Navy Day addresses.[21]

A similar effort can be seen in regard to the Soviet Union. In the immediate aftermath of World War I, the Russian Communists were viewed as enemies, and the United States—working in tandem with Britain, Japan, Greece, and other nations—sent expeditionary forces to occupy Russian port cities and aid their opponents. Throughout the 1920s and 1930s, the newly minted Soviet Union was a pariah state. After the Soviet attack on Poland and Finland in 1939, Roosevelt declared Stalin's "dictatorship as absolute as any other dictatorship in the world" and even threatened to cut off diplomatic relations with Moscow for its collaboration with the Nazis. But once the United States entered the war against Germany alongside the Soviets, that all changed. Roosevelt needed to rehabilitate the Soviet Union to justify the sending of American lend-lease equipment to Moscow. Less than three weeks after Pearl Harbor, he publicly praised the Russians, declaring them to have "shown a power of resiliency, a gift of modern warfare under their leader, Stalin, which ha[d] rendered immense service to the world cause."[22] Before long, propaganda posters appeared across America with pictures of a Russian soldier declaring, "This man is your FRIEND."[23] In short presidential rhetoric—alongside domestic propaganda—was employed as a means of influencing American attitudes toward the Soviet Union, both positive and negative, as dictated by U.S. foreign policy objectives.

As these examples show, the political demands of governing within a liberal democracy create challenges for presidents in their dealings with other nations. Alliances or agreements may be entered into for any number of geopolitical reasons, reasons that may not make sense to the average member of the electorate. This leads to problems for the president in a representative system of government, who might end up pursuing sound foreign-policy goals that are nevertheless unpopular. In such conditions presidents often use their rhetorical platform in attempts to reorient or persuade the public in regard to a certain policy or group. However, these attempts just as commonly reveal the impotence of the president to meaningfully shift public opinion, as Barack Obama's failure to pass the Trans-Pacific Trade Pact during his last year in office well demonstrates. And when confronted by the limits of their rhetoric, presidents may be tempted to use other means to prosecute their foreign-policy objectives.

Eisenhower, as a president both firmly dedicated to containing the Soviet Union and with an affinity for CIA action, habitually employed covert methods in his approach to the Middle East during his years in office. In doing so he circumvented the normally constraining influence of public opinion on American foreign policy. In the chapters that follow, I show how his decision to engage in clandestine activity in the Middle East can be understood as a fundamentally rhetorical strategy born from his analysis of the situations he faced. By using secret means to achieve his goals, he avoided having to make a public case to the American people for his Middle East policy—with ultimately disastrous results for America's allies.

Third, *presidential rhetoric is constitutive of the political world.* Presidential rhetoric can function as a pedagogical device by which the public develops a new understanding of political events. Sometimes this happens because the president makes known information to which he is privy but the public is not; when Barrack

Obama announced the death of Osama bin Laden, for example, his rhetoric worked to alter Americans' conception of the War on Terror, 9/11, and Al Qaeda by offering new facts pertaining to these political events and entities. At other points presidential rhetoric functions constitutively by encouraging Americans to understand public knowledge in a particular way. While virtually all Americans learned quickly of the Japanese bombing of Pearl Harbor in World War II, for instance, Franklin Roosevelt's characterization of December 7, 1941, as "a day that will live in infamy" advanced a new understanding of the attack; by invoking a mythic historical lens, Roosevelt's rhetoric elevated the conflict's importance and pointed forward to a day when Americans could look back on the attack as an event of the past, not as the awful present reality. In similar fashion Eisenhower's rhetoric worked to constitute the Middle East as a region of political importance to the American public, and he did so in ways that broke from previous presidential rhetorical precedent.

By "constitutive" I do not mean that Eisenhower's rhetoric functioned to call forth his audience into being in the way that Maurice Charland described in his analysis of the *peuple québécois*—my analysis does not seek to explain how Americans came to understand themselves as such. I do not mean that Eisenhower's words, following the formulation of Louis Althusser, interpellated his audience into a newly created subject position (although Ike's Middle East rhetoric does have important implications for American identity).[24] Rather, I mean "constitutive" in the sense that James Farr uses the term when he states that "political concepts . . . *constitute*, and so make possible, the beliefs of political actors."[25] Rhetoric works constitutively by populating the conceptual world of political actors, including the electorate.

Stated otherwise, presidential rhetoric is a powerful mechanism for conceptual reconstitution within the political life of the nation. By reconstituting concepts with discursive circulation (such as "equality" or "torture" or "special relationship"), presidents can work to expand, contract, or completely alter the existing meanings of ideas, places, persons, or groups. Lincoln, for example, altered the meaning of the Civil War through the Gettysburg Address and his second inaugural; rather than representing the nation's end, the war, as he envisioned it, constituted America's rebirth and rededication to "the proposition that all men are created equal." Presidential rhetoric works to articulate and rearticulate—and thereby constantly reconstitute—the ideas that animate American politics.

Eisenhower oversaw such a conceptual shift in the United States' treatment of the Middle East. For American policy makers—particularly those involved in intelligence and defense planning—the region had taken priority almost immediately following World War II. Yet this shift in concern was not reflected in the public rhetoric of Ike's predecessors. Therefore, like many other aspects of American politics, over the course of Eisenhower's presidency he rhetorically reconstituted what the Middle East meant in the context of American politics and foreign policy. Because Eisenhower often incorporated his public utterances into larger strategic programs of psychological warfare, a focus on the rhetorical effects of Ike's foreign-policy rhetoric could be warranted for any region of the world. The Middle East, as an area few Americans knew well in the 1950s, would appear to be especially apt for this kind of analysis given the outsized role that Eisenhower played in shaping Americans' perception of the region.

Fourth, *presidential rhetoric produces argument fields that can then be redeployed.* Classical Greek and Roman rhetoricians argued over the nature and extent of their art extensively, culminating with Quintilian's first-century codification of rhetoric into five canons.[26] Invention, the first of these canons, concerned the ability to generate lines of argument, and it involved much more than simply developing *ethos, pathos,* or *logos* appeals. Invention included being able to apply *stasis* theory to determine whether parties disagreed at the level of fact, definition, value, or policy, and an aptitude for *kairos,* or knowing the most effective time to speak. In addition to their own arguments, pupils were encouraged to develop effective *refutatio,* or refutations of their opponents' appeals. These lines of argument cohered into topoi, or "places" of invention, which

Aristotle categorized into special and common types. Common topoi included arguments one can make regarding cause and effect, definitions, comparisons, or circumstance.

What these rhetoricians pointed out, and what is more important for this study, is that rhetorical appeals often cohere into argument fields. Rhetorical invention builds on previously successful arguments; effective arguments invite their own appropriation, and this borrowing frequently occurs in innovative and unexpected ways. As Jerome Dean Mahaffey points out in his book *Preaching Politics*, for example, political cases for American independence drew heavily from the arguments produced and disseminated by Christian revival preachers such as George Whitefield and Gilbert Tennent during the Great Awakening. Put forth most famously in the sermon "The Danger of an Unconverted Ministry," one of this movement's most compelling arguments was to analogize the American clergy to the New Testament Pharisees, thus spurring the laity to seek spiritual regeneration through the teaching of the revivalists. This was an argument field other kinds of revolutionaries would find easy to replicate. Mahaffey writes:

> The critical eye turned toward British governance can be linked with the new vistas provided by blended republican and religious discourse. Tellingly, these writers employed arguments invented by Whitefield that drew upon the Awakening conceptual system for intelligibility and force. . . . This pattern of thought—that one's qualifications for office depended upon one's ability and faithfulness in the execution of duty to the people—functioned as an inventional resource for anyone who wished to argue against corrupt leadership. Arguments generated by this resource sought to uncover behavioral and ideological inconsistencies, not just among unconverted ministers but public servants as well.[27]

Like the claims of Reverends Whitefield and Tennent, successful presidential appeals create new fields of argument that can then be applied to other political arenas or built on by future presidents. Rhetorical performances such as FDR's first inaugural, Lincoln's Gettysburg Address, and Kennedy's inaugural address create new constellations of arguments that can then be replicated or adapted for use by future presidents: even today, decades after their utterance, the phrases "the only thing we have to fear is fear itself," "that government of the people, by the people, for the people shall not perish from the earth," and "ask not what your country can do for you, but what you can do for your country" permeate our political culture.[28] More recently, Hillary Clinton, in the Roosevelt Island speech opening her 2016 presidential campaign, imitated FDR's "Four Freedoms" address by announcing her "Four Fights" for the American people. As commonly understood rhetorical artifacts, renowned presidential speeches such as these lend themselves to invention and appropriation in the present.

Thus the Eisenhower Doctrine Address—as a speech that clearly broke from previously articulated rationales for American engagement with the Middle East and stringently promoted an ethic of intervention—should also be understood as an act of rhetorical invention, and therefore as creating a new field of arguments from which subsequent presidents have drawn to justify their own forays into the Arab world. In short, the Eisenhower administration, driven by the exigences of the Cold War, generated new constellations of argument in its rhetoric surrounding a region of supreme importance to American foreign policy and the globe. It is the goal of this book to explore the ways in which this process occurred.

• • •

With the preceding discussion in mind, it is also important to note what presidential rhetoric does *not* do. As George C. Edwards III and others point out, presidential rhetoric is not always effective as a method of passing specific legislation.[29] Individual presidential speeches rarely correlate directly with an immediate shift in public attitudes toward a given topic. Presidential rhetoric resists efforts to track from it clear cause-and-effect relationships. And even the most oratorically gifted presidents can fall flat on their face no matter their persuasiveness, as the Iran-Contra scandal, the Monica Lewinsky affair, and the Obama administration's handling of the 2012 attack on the U.S. embassy in Benghazi demonstrate. There are clear limits to what presidential rhetoric can do. Even so, much criticism of this type seems to confuse the rhetorical presidency with a kind of wizardry. Franklin Roosevelt did not cast a spell over the electorate to get the United States into World War II. He did, however, use his position as president to frame and interpret world events so as to make American entry into the conflict more politically palatable. Eisenhower similarly employed presidential rhetoric in the ways outlined above to redefine the United States' relationship to the Middle East to enduring political effect. Edwards and others' criticism notwithstanding, as the following chapters show, presidential speech can very much generate and provide its own warrants for major policy changes—including military action.[30] Presidential rhetoric matters.

Of course, the president is but one member of the executive branch, a body that has grown ever larger to include cabinet members, chiefs of staff, press secretaries, and, most notably for students of rhetoric, speech- or ghostwriters. Presidential staffs now regularly boast multiple writers for the president, a practice that began after Woodrow Wilson departed the oval office.[31] As Campbell and Jamieson note, "ghostwriting has been part and parcel of the presidency throughout its history," so we should view the presidency as "an aggregate of people, as a corporate entity . . . a syndicate generating the actions associated with the head of state, including those deeds done in words."[32] This view certainly holds true for Eisenhower, who frequently dispatched special representatives and employed surrogates to speak on his behalf. He likewise carefully coordinated his public statements concerning foreign policy with Secretary of State John Foster Dulles, usually as a means to pursue some strategic end. Thus my working assumption is that the presidency includes more actors than simply the president alone. The words a president utters—including those written by another or words that an explicitly authorized subordinate utters on his behalf—assume the authorial imprint of the

chief executive once voiced, and given Ike's hidden-hand procliv-
ities, this condition applies especially to the Eisenhower administration. As Shawn Parry-Giles notes, "Eisenhower's rhetorical
powers and the covert channels extended beyond the bully pulpit
to include messages delivered by rhetorical surrogates over overt
and covert propaganda media."[33] Ike maintained messaging control over all his subordinates.

Consequently, this book examines the utterances of Eisenhower
and the members of his administration regarding the Middle East
during the years 1952–58 for the purpose of tracking the changing ways in which Ike articulated the United States' relationship
to the Middle East. Undergirding my analysis is a belief in the
scholarly importance of presidential rhetoric for the insights it
provides about American political life. If, as Mary Stuckey argues,
"presidential words matter" and that even "when presidents speak
instrumentally, that rhetoric may still have constitutive consequences," then it is worth investigating how presidents use their
power of definition to constitute certain realities for their audiences, regardless of their immediate instrumental aims.[34] In this
case that means studying how Eisenhower's Cold War rhetoric
helped change the frame by which Americans understood the Middle East. Although much of this study will be devoted to analyzing
Ike's strategic use of rhetoric, my underlying aim is to investigate
how Eisenhower articulated the Middle East to the American public during a period in which the United States of America's role
in the region underwent a dramatic transformation.

Eisenhower, Containment, and the Middle East

Like much of American foreign policy in the early Cold War, the
words, actions, and rhetorical strategies I examine were an outgrowth of the overarching doctrine of "containment" of the Soviet
Union and Communist power. The Eisenhower-Dulles team came
into office asserting the need for a more robust conception of this
strategy. In his famous *Life* magazine article, Dulles argued that
America needed to eschew the passivity of containment for an
active policy of "liberation" aimed at rolling back Soviet influence

in the satellite states.[35] While significantly more restrained in his rhetoric, in his first inaugural address Eisenhower also gave voice to the global need for universal liberty: "Conceiving the defense of freedom, like freedom itself, to be one and indivisible, we hold all continents and peoples in equal regard and honor. We reject any insinuation that one race or another, one people or another, is in any sense inferior or expendable."[36] America, as the exemplar of such freedom, had a special role to play in defending it from Soviet totalitarianism. Under Ike the containment doctrine sanctioned halting any perceived Communist expansion through the aggressive use of military and covert means.

The complex way in which this doctrine was applied and expressed to the public can be seen most clearly in the Eisenhower administration's treatment of the Middle East. The Eisenhower Doctrine speech, perhaps the clearest articulation of containment in the entire Eisenhower presidency, set forth the logic of containment in a way that was easily accessible to the American public. It also won congressional approval for a robust policy of intervention, and its subject matter was not Eastern Europe, Korea, or Southeast Asia, but the Middle East. This fact has profound ramifications, as the Eisenhower Doctrine speech fundamentally altered the way in which the region is conceived in presidential rhetoric and American political discourse more generally.

In brief I wish to demonstrate the following claims: The foreign-policy rhetoric of the early Cold War and Eisenhower's first years in office positioned the Middle East as a region that was important to the West but not a direct American concern. Eisenhower's rhetoric of misdirection, most clearly demonstrated in the Iran coup, worked to conceal the growing level of authority that the United States was assuming in the region as its power displaced that of the British and the French. The Eisenhower administration maintained this approach to the Middle East over the course of Ike's first term by deploying strategies of rhetorical surreption, through which American interests were secured by covert means without publicly challenging the regional status quo. When Britain and France, in coordination with Israel, initiated the Suez crisis, Eisenhower broke from this rhetorical strategy and chose instead to make a case for the United States' unique responsibility to maintain peace in the region. Enacting this principle Ike then proclaimed what quickly became known as the Eisenhower Doctrine, an open-ended American commitment to active interventionism in the Middle East to prevent Communism from taking root. In 1958 Ike chose to apply the Eisenhower Doctrine and intervene in Lebanon. Although observer groups in Lebanon found no evidence of Communist instigation of the conflict, Eisenhower characterized the turmoil in Lebanon as Soviet-inspired and declared that the United States had a moral duty to protect the Lebanese through occupation.[37] By announcing an American obligation for Middle East security and backing up this claim with several thousand marines, Eisenhower established an American rhetoric of responsibility for the region that has not been repudiated by any subsequent president. Since Eisenhower the United States, not Europe, has become the regional hegemon at which the buck stops.

The central focus of my analysis concerns the Eisenhower Doctrine speech, which constituted a major shift in presidential rhetoric regarding the Middle East. The transcript of the address has been reprinted in full between the introduction and the next chapter. However, limiting my analysis only to this obvious and eminently rhetorical situation would not effectively contextualize Eisenhower's rhetorical redefinition of the relationship between the United States and the Middle East. Thus the scope of this book includes the buildup to the Eisenhower Doctrine address and a rhetorical analysis of the doctrine's application in Lebanon so as to better demonstrate the evolution of Ike's rhetoric throughout his presidency.

I believe alongside Jeff Bass that, like metaphors, themes, identity construction, or other schemata by which presidential rhetoric can be analyzed, the official "interpretations" of certain regions of the world, which guide "the relationship between such regions and the . . . United States," are worthy of scholarly study.[38] That is, I hold that a sustained examination of presidential rhetoric on a specific subject, in this case America's relationship to the region known as the Middle East during the mid-1950s, will yield academic insight. By expanding my analytical frame beyond the Eisenhower Doctrine address itself, I hope to facilitate a more comprehensive view of the shift in presidential rhetoric concerning the Middle East that occurred under Ike, the effects of which we are still living with today.

Method of Criticism

According to Medhurst rhetoric is "a power that operates from history and in history to make history," and for this reason this study draws from a number of sources that could be characterized as historical in nature: memoirs, biographies, diplomatic papers, intelligence briefings, cabinet meeting minutes, secondary accounts, and regional histories.[39] However, my primary texts for analysis consist of the public utterances of Eisenhower and members of his administration regarding the Middle East during the years 1952–58. I also draw from the rich tradition of Eisenhower scholarship that exists within the fields of rhetoric, history, and Middle East studies to aid in my criticism. While many excellent works exist in these fields (many of which I reference in this volume), what is missing is a work that links them. This book seeks to address that omission.

The act of rhetorical criticism is inherently subjective, and I am sure that my selection of texts will undoubtedly exclude those that some might find more pertinent for this study. My aim is not to exhaustively examine every utterance of Eisenhower on the Middle East—such a project would be far beyond the scope of this book—but rather to provide snapshots of a rhetorical transition in motion and to give a sense of what Ike accomplished through his rhetoric. My central goal is to chart the changing ways in which Eisenhower redefined America's stake in the Middle East. In doing so I have sought to insert myself as little as possible into the analysis and strive for as much objectivity as can be attained; as Edwin Black reminds us, "the critical methodology that minimizes the personal responses, peculiar tastes, and singularities of the critic will be superior to one that does not."[40] In examining the various exigences and strategic aims that shaped Eisenhower's Middle East rhetoric, then, I wish to analyze Ike and his subordinates in light of their own contextual frame. In this manner I hope to provide a baseline that enables future scholars to better situate the rhetorical context of presidential discourse regarding the Middle East.

As with any major figure, the process of determining just what to make of Eisenhower is ongoing and ever changing; what seemed important yesterday might not be today, so fresh analyses such as this one are always beneficial. This point becomes increasingly salient when one considers the important role that scholarly revisionism has played regarding Eisenhower specifically. At the end of his second term, Eisenhower was widely considered to have been a passive, genteel president: "He is moved by forces," declared journalist Marquis Childs in his 1958 book *Eisenhower: Captive Hero*. "He does not undertake to move them himself."[41] Since then substantial reevaluations of Ike's time in office have been made, initially by Eisenhower himself and later by scholars such as Stephen Ambrose, Fred Greenstein, Richard Immerman, Martin Medhurst, Ira Chernus, and Kenneth Osgood. By revisiting Ike's actions and rhetoric in the Middle East—and doing so from an explicitly rhetorical perspective—I hope to add to the process of Eisenhower reevaluation while addressing an important area of concern that has not garnered the attention it deserves: Ike's Middle East rhetoric.

Preview of Book

The first part of this study concerns the Eisenhower Doctrine address, starting with the text of the speech itself and including the next full chapter. Specifically, chapter 1 considers the academic work that has been done concerning the Eisenhower Doctrine and contextualizes the speech historically and rhetorically. Here I discuss the rhetorical context of the address and the Eisenhower administration's evolutionary understanding of containment. Having contextualized the speech, the rest of the chapter consists of a rhetorical analysis of the address, with the primary focus on the domestic audiences. I conclude the chapter by discussing how the Eisenhower Doctrine speech was not given in a vacuum but was both a historical and a rhetorical development with origins at the start of the Eisenhower presidency, setting up the next four chapters to demonstrate this claim.

Chapters 2 through 5 proceed chronologically, respectively dealing with the Iran coup (Operation Ajax), the remainder of Ike's first term, the Suez crisis, and the intervention in Lebanon. The second chapter draws on existing rhetorical scholarship of Eisenhower by emphasizing the rhetorical strategies that accompanied his hidden-hand leadership and predilection for clandestine intervention. Central to my analysis are the concepts of polyvalence, rhetorical surrogacy, and strategic ambiguity. Specifically, I show how the Eisenhower administration employed the rhetoric of misdirection to downplay the nature and level of the U.S. government's activity in the Middle East. This strategy worked to mask the changing realities of power in the Middle East, namely, the United States' assumption of the role of senior partner in the region to make up for the weaknesses of the European imperial powers. Eisenhower's rhetoric thus worked to misdirect not only the American public but also the nation's allies insofar as they did not adjust their policies to account for this new status quo.

Until October 1956 the Eisenhower administration largely continued the rhetorical strategy of downplaying America's military and diplomatic investment in the Middle East established during Operation Ajax. In chapter 3 I provide an overview of the ways in which this strategy, which I label rhetorical surreption, was prosecuted over the course of Ike's first term. Eisenhower's rhetorical surreption was characterized by a public display of benign impartiality to the Middle East, the use of surrogates and ostensible goodwill ambassadors, and reliance on covert activity to secure American interests. These strategies continued to mask the level of American security involvement in the Middle East, and they were also consistent with the larger Cold War rhetorical campaigns launched during Eisenhower's first term (Open Skies, Atoms for Peace, New Look, Chance for Peace). As Ike's term progressed, however, this rhetorical approach to the region began to break down along with the European colonial order. Using Operation Straggle, the sending of CIA advisors to Egypt, the secret Project Alpha peace talks, and the development of the Baghdad Pact as case studies, I conclude this chapter by demonstrating how Eisenhower's strategy of rhetorical surreption failed to successfully address major U.S. policy concerns. This rhetorical approach therefore set the stage for Suez by allowing a dangerous discrepancy to exist between the United States' perceived role in the Middle East and the nation's actual status as the dominant foreign power in the region.

The fourth chapter deals with the Suez crisis. I build on Richard Gregg's work analyzing Eisenhower's address of October 31, 1956, by showing how this speech worked to rhetorically position the United States as the primary world power in the Middle East.[42] Drawing from the work of Robert Ivie, Ned O'Gorman, and Edward Said, I show in this chapter how Eisenhower gave the first comprehensive case for a uniquely American responsibility to maintain order and safeguard the Middle East independently of other powers. Whereas earlier Ike had sought to misdirect, at Suez he publicly announced American responsibility and intent to end the conflict, and he enforced the U.S.-proposed UN peace resolution even over the stringent objections of the nation's allies. By doing so he inaugurated a new public understanding of the region within American political discourse and established a new precedent of American responsibility for the Middle East's security within presidential rhetoric.

In the fifth chapter I investigate how Ike applied the Eisenhower Doctrine. He boldly made material the rhetorical shift that had occurred in the relationship between the United States and the Middle East by authorizing Operation Blue Bat, the American occupation of Lebanon in 1958. In the eyes of many Arabs, after this action "it became much easier for Lebanese and Arab peoples to think and speak of the U.S. in imperial terms."[43] In this chapter I examine exactly how Ike employed the rhetorical resources developed over his previous years in office to provide a warrant for a major intervention in a faraway country for reasons unclear to many Americans. By authorizing and rhetorically justifying Operation Blue Bat, Eisenhower made manifest the dramatic transition in United States–Middle East relations that had occurred under his presidency.

In the conclusion to this study, I recapitulate the overall arc of the book—the transformation of presidential rhetoric regarding the United States' relationship to the Middle East that occurred under Eisenhower—as well as the complicated legacy of the Eisenhower Doctrine. I offer several analytical frames by which to view Eisenhower's Middle East rhetoric, including comparisons to more-recent presidents and their rhetoric surrounding the Middle East. And while some scholars argue that the Eisenhower Doctrine ultimately failed as a policy, I show how the rhetorical shift it signified has continued to thrive long after the Eisenhower presidency ended.

Presidential rhetoric shapes and often structures the American political world, and it does not always do so in clear-cut or salutary ways. Marilyn J. Young argues that, "more than anywhere in the world, the Middle East has confounded presidential administrations and pushed the limits of presidential rhetoric."[44] If so this trend can trace much of its origin to Ike. Many Americans came to understand the Middle East as an entity of the American political universe via the rhetoric of Dwight D. Eisenhower. In examining the sometimes-conflicting ways he articulated American responsibility for the Middle East during the Cold War, I hope to provide profitable avenues for similar kinds of analyses devoted to other presidents and eras. There is still much to learn.

Today, at the dawn of the Trump presidency, the United States is as entrenched in the greater Middle East as at any point in American history. Across Afghanistan, Syria, and northern Iraq, U.S. soldiers by the thousands advise and assist their indigenous counterparts. American-controlled drones patrol the skies of Yemen, Somalia, and Libya, tracking persons of interest, gathering intelligence, and launching the occasional Hellfire missile. In Tehran Boeing executives and evangelical missionaries seek converts to their cause; in Dhahran businessmen and lawyers dispatched by U.S. firms arrive to parlay with Saudi Aramco. American tourists, reporters, students, and diplomats alike ply their trade in the cities of Israel, Egypt, Jordan, and Turkey as the United States Fifth Naval Fleet quietly safeguards the Arab Gulf states from its base in Bahrain. Despite this unprecedented level of American investment, persistent, extensive misperceptions continue to haunt relations between the population of the United States and those of the Middle East.[45] By examining the Eisenhower era, during which American policy—and more starkly, rhetoric—toward the region was utterly transformed, perhaps we can gain insight into our own tumultuous time.

MORE THAN A DOCTRINE

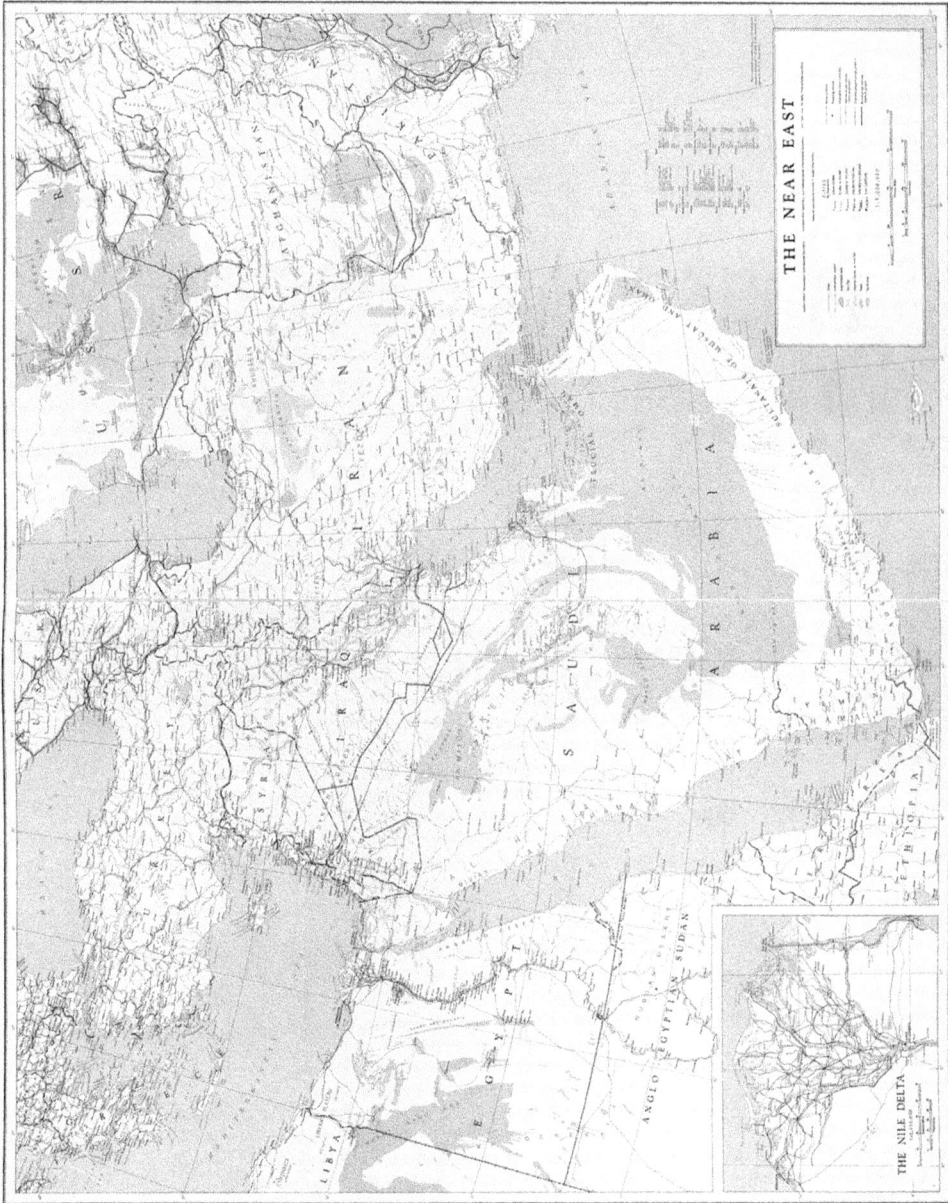

THE NEAR EAST

THE NILE DELTA

Eisenhower Doctrine Address

January 5, 1957

First may I express to you my deep appreciation of your courtesy in giving me, at some inconvenience to yourselves, this early opportunity of addressing you on a matter I deem to be of grave importance to our country.

In my forthcoming State of the Union Message, I shall review the international situation generally. There are worldwide hopes which we can reasonably entertain, and there are worldwide responsibilities which we must carry to make certain that freedom—including our own—may be secure.

There is, however, a special situation in the Middle East which I feel I should, even now, lay before you.

Before doing so it is well to remind ourselves that our basic national objective in international affairs remains peace—a world peace based on justice. Such a peace must include all areas, all peoples of the world if it is to be enduring. There is no nation, great or small, with which we would refuse to negotiate, in mutual good faith, with patience and in the determination to secure a better understanding between us. Out of such understandings must, and eventually will, grow confidence and trust, indispensable ingredients to a program of peace and to plans for lifting from us all the burdens of expensive armaments. To promote these objectives, our government works tirelessly, day by day, month by month, year by year. But until a degree of success crowns our efforts that will assure to all nations peaceful existence, we must, in the interests of peace itself, remain vigilant, alert and strong.

I.

The Middle East has abruptly reached a new and critical stage in its long and important history. In past decades many of the countries in that area were not fully self-governing. Other nations exercised considerable authority in the area and the security of the region was largely built around their power. But since the First World War there has been a steady evolution toward self-government and independence. This development the United States has welcomed and has encouraged. Our country supports without reservation the full sovereignty and independence of each and every nation of the Middle East.

The evolution to independence has in the main been a peaceful process. But the area has been often troubled. Persistent crosscurrents of distrust and fear with raids back and forth across national boundaries have brought about a high degree of instability in much of the Mid East. Just recently there have been hostilities involving Western European nations that once exercised much influence in the area. Also the relatively large attack by Israel in October has intensified the basic differences between that nation and its Arab neighbors. All this instability has been heightened and, at times, manipulated by International Communism.

II.

Russia's rulers have long sought to dominate the Middle East. That was true of the Czars and it is true of the Bolsheviks. The reasons are not hard to find. They do not affect Russia's security, for no one plans to use the Middle East as a base for aggression against Russia. Never for a moment has the United States entertained such a thought.

The Soviet Union has nothing whatsoever to fear from the United States in the Middle East, or anywhere else in the world, so long as its rulers do not themselves first resort to aggression.

That statement I make solemnly and emphatically.

Neither does Russia's desire to dominate the Middle East spring from its own economic interest in the area. Russia does not appreciably use or depend upon the Suez Canal. In 1955 Soviet traffic through the Canal represented only about three fourths of 1 percent of the total. The Soviets have no need for, and could provide no market for, the petroleum resources which constitute the principal natural wealth of the area. Indeed, the Soviet Union is a substantial exporter of petroleum products.

The reason for Russia's interest in the Middle East is solely that of power politics. Considering her announced purpose of Communizing the world, it is easy to understand her hope of dominating the Middle East.

This region has always been the crossroads of the continents of the Eastern Hemisphere. The Suez Canal enables the nations of Asia and Europe to carry on the commerce that is essential if these countries are to maintain well-rounded and prosperous economies. The Middle East provides a gateway between Eurasia and Africa.

It contains about two thirds of the presently known oil deposits of the world and it normally supplies the petroleum needs of many nations of Europe, Asia and Africa. The nations of Europe are peculiarly dependent upon this supply, and this dependency relates to transportation as well as to production! This has been vividly demonstrated since the closing of the Suez Canal and some of the pipelines. Alternate ways of transportation and, indeed, alternate sources of power can, if necessary, be developed. But these cannot be considered as early prospects.

These things stress the immense importance of the Middle East. If the nations of that area should lose their independence, if they were dominated by alien forces hostile to freedom, that would be both a tragedy for the area and for many other free nations whose economic life would be subject to near strangulation. Western Europe would be endangered just as though there had been no Marshall Plan, no North Atlantic Treaty Organization. The free nations of Asia and Africa, too, would be placed in serious jeopardy. And the countries of the Middle East would lose the markets upon which their economies depend. All this would have the most adverse, if not disastrous, effect upon our own nation's economic life and political prospects.

Then there are other factors which transcend the material. The Middle East is the birthplace of three great religions— Moslem, Christian and Hebrew. Mecca and Jerusalem are more than places on the map. They symbolize religions which teach that the spirit has supremacy over matter and that the individual has a dignity and rights of which no despotic government can rightfully deprive him. It would be intolerable if the holy places of the Middle East should be subjected to a rule that glorifies atheistic materialism.

International Communism, of course, seeks to mask its purposes of domination by expressions of good will and by superficially attractive offers of political, economic and military aid. But any free nation, which is the subject of Soviet enticement, ought, in elementary wisdom, to look behind the mask.

Remember Estonia, Latvia and Lithuania! In 1939 the Soviet Union entered into mutual assistance pacts with these then dependent countries; and the Soviet Foreign Minister, addressing the Extraordinary Fifth Session of the Supreme Soviet in October 1939, solemnly and publicly declared that "we stand for the scrupulous and punctilious observance of the pacts on the basis of complete reciprocity, and we declare that all the nonsensical talk about the Sovietization of the Baltic countries is only to the interest of our common enemies and of all anti-Soviet provocateurs." Yet in 1940, Estonia, Latvia and Lithuania were forcibly incorporated into the Soviet Union.

Soviet control of the satellite nations of Eastern Europe has been forcibly maintained in spite of solemn promises of a contrary intent, made during World War II.

Stalin's death brought hope that this pattern would change. And we read the pledge of the Warsaw Treaty of 1955 that the Soviet Union would follow in satellite countries "the principles of mutual respect for their independence and sovereignty and noninterference in domestic affairs." But we have just seen the subjugation of Hungary by naked armed force. In the aftermath of this Hungarian tragedy, world respect for and belief in Soviet promises have sunk to a new low. International Communism needs and seeks a recognizable success.

Thus, we have these simple and indisputable facts:

1. The Middle East, which has always been coveted by Rus-

sia, would today be prized more than ever by International Communism.

2. The Soviet rulers continue to show that they do not scruple to use any means to gain their ends.

3. The free nations of the Mid East need, and for the most part want, added strength to assure their continued independence.

III.

Our thoughts naturally turn to the United Nations as a protector of small nations. Its charter gives it primary responsibility for the maintenance of international peace and security. Our country has given the United Nations its full support in relation to the hostilities in Hungary and in Egypt. The United Nations was able to bring about a cease-fire and withdrawal of hostile forces from Egypt because it was dealing with governments and peoples who had a decent respect for the opinions of mankind as reflected in the United Nations General Assembly. But in the case of Hungary, the situation was different. The Soviet Union vetoed action by the Security Council to require the withdrawal of Soviet armed forces from Hungary. And it has shown callous indifference to the recommendations, even the censure, of the General Assembly. The United Nations can always be helpful, but it cannot be a wholly dependable protector of freedom when the ambitions of the Soviet Union are involved.

IV.

Under all the circumstances I have laid before you, a greater responsibility now devolves upon the United States. We have shown, so that none can doubt, our dedication to the principle that force shall not be used internationally for any aggressive purpose and that the integrity and independence of the nations of the Middle East should be inviolate. Seldom in history has a nation's dedication to principle been tested as severely as ours during recent weeks.

There is general recognition in the Middle East, as elsewhere, that the United States does not seek either political or economic domination over any other people. Our desire is a world environment of freedom, not servitude. On the other hand many, if not all, of the nations of the Middle East are aware of the danger that stems from International Communism and welcome closer cooperation with the United States to realize for themselves the United Nations goals of independence, economic well-being and spiritual growth.

If the Middle East is to continue its geographic role of uniting rather than separating East and West; if its vast economic resources are to serve the well-being of the peoples there, as well as that of others; and if its cultures and religions and their shrines are to be preserved for the uplifting of the spirits of the peoples, then the United States must make more evident its willingness to support the independence of the freedom-loving nations of the area.

V.

Under these circumstances I deem it necessary to seek the cooperation of the Congress. Only with that cooperation can we give the reassurance needed to deter aggression, to give courage and confidence to those who are dedicated to freedom and thus prevent a chain of events which would gravely endanger all of the free world.

There have been several Executive declarations made by the United States in relation to the Middle East. There is the Tripartite Declaration of May 25, 1950, followed by the Presidential assurance of October 31, 1950, to the King of Saudi Arabia. There is the Presidential declaration of April 9, 1956, that the United States will within constitutional means oppose any aggression in the area. There is our Declaration of November 29, 1956, that a threat to the territorial integrity or political independence of Iran, Iraq, Pakistan, or Turkey would be viewed by the United States with the utmost gravity.

Nevertheless, weaknesses in the present situation and the increased danger from International Communism convince me that basic United States policy should now find expression in joint action by the Congress and the Executive. Furthermore, our joint resolve should be so couched as to make it apparent that if need be our words will be backed by action.

VI.

It is nothing new for the President and the Congress to join to recognize that the national integrity of other free nations is directly related to our own security.

We have joined to create and support the security system of the United Nations. We have reinforced the collective security system of the United Nations by a series of collective defense arrangements. Today we have security treaties with 42 other nations which recognize that our peace and security are intertwined. We have joined to take decisive action in relation to Greece and Turkey and in relation to Taiwan.

Thus, the United States through the joint action of the President and the Congress, or, in the case of treaties, the Senate, has manifested in many endangered areas its purpose to support free and independent governments—and peace—against external menace, notably the menace of International Communism. Thereby we have helped to maintain peace and security during a period of great danger. It is now essential that the United States should manifest through joint action of the President and the Congress our determination to assist those nations of the Mid East area, which desire that assistance.

The action which I propose would have the following features.

It would, first of all, authorize the United States to cooperate with and assist any nation or group of nations in the general area of the Middle East in the development of economic strength dedicated to the maintenance of national independence.

It would, in the second place, authorize the Executive to undertake in the same region programs of military assistance and cooperation with any nation or group of nations which desires such aid.

It would, in the third place, authorize such assistance and cooperation to include the employment of the armed forces of the United States to secure and protect the territorial integrity and political independence of such nations, requesting such aid, against overt armed aggression from any nation controlled by International Communism.

These measures would have to be consonant with the treaty obligations of the United States, including the Charter of the United Nations and with any action or recommendations of the United Nations. They would also, if armed attack occurs, be subject to the overriding authority of the United Nations Security Council in accordance with the Charter.

The present proposal would, in the fourth place, authorize the President to employ, for economic and defensive military purposes, sums available under the Mutual Security Act of 1954, as amended, without regard to existing limitations.

The legislation now requested should not include the authorization or appropriation of funds because I believe that, under the conditions I suggest, presently appropriated funds will be adequate for the balance of the present fiscal year ending June 30. I shall, however, seek in subsequent legislation the authorization of $200,000,000 to be available during each of the fiscal years 1958 and 1959 for discretionary use in the area, in addition to the other mutual security programs for the area hereafter provided for by the Congress.

VII.

This program will not solve all the problems of the Middle East. Neither does it represent the totality of our policies for the area. There are the problems of Palestine and relations between Israel and the Arab States, and the future of the Arab refugees. There is the problem of the future status of the Suez Canal. These difficulties are aggravated by International Communism, but they would exist quite apart from that threat. It is not the purpose of the legislation I propose to deal directly with these problems. The United Nations is actively concerning itself with all these matters, and we are supporting the United Nations. The United States has made clear, notably by Secretary Dulles' address of August 26, 1955, that we are willing to do much to assist the United Nations in solving the basic problems of Palestine.

The proposed legislation is primarily designed to deal with the possibility of Communist aggression, direct and indirect. There is imperative need that any lack of power in the area should be made good, not by external or alien force, but by the increased vigor and security of the independent nations of the area.

Experience shows that indirect aggression rarely if ever succeeds where there is reasonable security against direct aggression; where the government disposes of loyal security forces, and where economic conditions are such as not to make Communism seem an attractive alternative. The program I suggest deals with all three aspects of this matter and thus with the problem of indirect aggression.

It is my hope and belief that if our purpose be proclaimed, as proposed by the requested legislation, that very fact will serve to halt any contemplated aggression. We shall have heartened the patriots who are dedicated to the independence of their nations. They will not feel that they stand alone, under the menace of great power. And I should add that patriotism is, throughout this area, a powerful sentiment. It is true that fear sometimes perverts true patriotism into fanaticism and to the acceptance of dangerous enticements from without. But if that fear can be allayed, then the climate will be more favorable to the attainment of worthy national ambitions.

And as I have indicated, it will also be necessary for us to contribute economically to strengthen those countries, or groups of countries, which have governments manifestly dedicated to the preservation of independence and resistance to subversion. Such measures will provide the greatest insurance against Communist inroads. Words alone are not enough.

VIII.

Let me refer again to the requested authority to employ the armed forces of the United States to assist to defend the territorial integrity and the political independence of any nation in the area against Communist armed aggression. Such authority would not be exercised except at the desire of the nation attacked. Beyond this it is my profound hope that this authority would never have to be exercised at all.

Nothing is more necessary to assure this than that our policy with respect to the defense of the area be promptly and clearly determined and declared. Thus the United Nations and all friendly governments, and indeed governments which are not friendly, will know where we stand.

If, contrary to my hope and expectation, a situation arose which called for the military application of the policy which I ask the Congress to join me in proclaiming, I would of course maintain hour-by-hour contact with the Congress if it were in session. And if the Congress were not in session, and if the situation had grave implications, I would, of course, at once call the Congress into special session.

In the situation now existing, the greatest risk, as is often the case, is that ambitious despots may miscalculate. If power-hungry Communists should either falsely or correctly estimate that the Middle East is inadequately defended, they might be tempted to use open measures of armed attack. If so, that would start a chain of circumstances which would almost surely involve the United States in military action. I am convinced that the best insurance against this dangerous contingency is to make clear now our readiness to cooperate fully and freely with our friends of the Middle East in ways consonant with the purposes and principles of the United Nations. I intend promptly to send a special mission to the Middle East to explain the cooperation we are prepared to give.

IX.

The policy which I outline involves certain burdens and indeed risks for the United States. Those who covet the area will not like what is proposed. Already, they are grossly distorting our purpose. However, before this Americans have seen our nation's vital interests and human freedom in jeopardy, and their fortitude and resolution have been equal to the crisis, regardless of hostile distortion of our words, motives and actions.

Indeed, the sacrifices of the American people in the cause of freedom have, even since the close of World War II, been measured in many billions of dollars and in thousands of the precious lives of our youth. These sacrifices, by which great areas of the world have been preserved to freedom, must not be thrown away.

In those momentous periods of the past, the President and the Congress have united, without partisanship, to serve the vital interests of the United States and of the free world.

The occasion has come for us to manifest again our national unity in support of freedom and to show our deep respect for the rights and independence of every nation—however great, however small. We seek not violence, but peace. To this purpose we must now devote our energies, our determination, ourselves.[1]

1

The Eisenhower Doctrine

A Species of Containment

You yourselves must be masters in your own land! You yourselves
must arrange your life as you yourselves see fit! You have the right
to do this for your fate is in your own hands. Comrades! Brothers!
Advance firmly and resolutely towards a just and democratic peace. We
inscribe the liberation of the oppressed peoples of the world on our
banners. Moslems of Russia! Moslems of the East! We look to you for
sympathy and support in the work of reconstructing the world.

—Vladimir Lenin and Joseph Stalin, December 3, 1917

The essentials of our global strategy are not too difficult to
understand. . . . Europe [first]. Next, the Middle East. That's half
of the oil resources. We can't let it go to Russia.

—Eisenhower, reply to Senator Robert Taft, April 30, 1953

Congress has no alternative but to go along with the President in this
program to prevent the Russians from taking over the whole strategic
Middle East. . . . The League of Nations collapsed without us,
and the United Nations could crumble if we falter.

—Harry S. Truman, newspaper op-ed, January 16, 1957

T
he United States to which Eisenhower announced his eponymous doctrine was a nation in the midst of great changes.
Consumerism, manifested by the advent of popular new
products like the refrigerator and the television set, was on the
upswing. Transportation patterns were disrupted by the widespread acquisition of the automobile. Debt, as well as marital
infidelity, was on the rise. Mainline Protestantism's domination
of America's public spiritual life would soon be undercut by the

fiery Manhattan crusade of Billy Graham. Massive migration to the South, school integration, and a nascent feminist labor movement all signified a society on the cusp of social upheaval. The political realm was full of tumult as well. The Korean conflict and Joseph McCarthy had been weathered, only to be replaced by the frightening specter of mutually assured destruction, the disintegration of the French and the British colonial empires, and the mass production of intercontinental ballistic missiles. Soviet tanks in Budapest crushed any hope that Communism's grip on Eastern Europe might be peacefully "rolled back," and in a few short months Sputnik would soar across the skies, taking with it the warm assurance many Americans had of their country's technological superiority.

It was in this atmosphere of transition that Dwight D. Eisenhower, on January 5, 1957, gave what became known as the Eisenhower Doctrine address. More than anything, the Eisenhower Doctrine was a regionally specific articulation of the larger policy of "containment." First formulated by George Kennan in his 1946 State Department "Long Telegram" and 1947 "X Article" in *Foreign Affairs,* Kennan's basic premises were (1) that because of internal Russian historical and ideological factors "there [could] be no permanent *modus vivendi*" with the Soviet Union, and therefore (2) the "Soviet pressure against the free institutions of the western world [was] something that [could] be *contained* by the adroit and vigilant application of counterforce" by the United States and its allies (emphasis mine).[1] In other words the immutability of Soviet hostility and the prohibitive cost of overthrowing the Soviet Union combined to make limiting further Communist expansion the most prudent strategic policy option.

The contours of what exactly defined containment, as this strategy came to be called, quickly became the subject of debate amid rapidly deteriorating relations between the United States and the Soviet Union.[2] The highly classified Clifford-Elsey report, which drew heavily from Kennan's "Long Telegram," framed the conflict as largely ideological in nature. It asserted that the Kremlin's

The Eisenhower Doctrine

leaders considered themselves the "defenders of the communist faith." According to the report, this meant that

> the fundamental tenet of the communist philosophy embraced by Soviet leaders is that the peaceful coexistence of communist and capitalist nations is impossible. . . . The key to an understanding of current Soviet foreign policy, in summary, is the realization that Soviet leaders adhere to the Marxian theory of ultimate destruction of capitalist states by communist states, while at the same time they strive to postpone the inevitable conflict in order to strengthen and prepare the Soviet Union for its clash with the western democracies.[3]

This ideological alarmism—belief that the Soviets' Communist worldview made them implacably dedicated to the violent overthrow of the West—reached its apotheosis in National Security Council Report 68, better known as "NSC-68." Developed under the aegis of Paul Nitze and given to President Truman in April 1950, this document stated that the Soviet Union, as the latest of many "aspirants to hegemony," was "animated by a new fanatic faith, antithetical to our own, and [sought] to impose its absolute authority over the rest of the world." Conflict between the United States and Soviet Union was therefore "endemic" and was "waged, on the part of the Soviet Union, by violent or non-violent methods in accordance with the dictates of expediency."[4] Given this analysis it is unsurprising that NSC-68 advocated a massive increase in defense spending to counter what its authors considered the growing Soviet threat. When Truman implemented NSC-68 in December 1950, chiefly due to the outbreak of war in Korea, the 1951 defense budget swelled from a projected $13 billion ceiling to well over $60 billion.

Although he did not disagree with the basic concept of containment, Eisenhower was horrified by these levels of expenditure. In his June 1952 speech announcing his Republican candidacy for the presidency, Ike identified four "threats" to the "American way of life": "disunity, inflation, excessive taxation, and bureaucracy." All four threats were the fault of the

Democrats, and all four were a direct outcome of Truman's bloated defense budget. In concluding his address, Eisenhower restated his desire for a more fiscally lean military: "I believe we can have peace with honor, reasonable security with national solvency."[5] To meet his goal, Eisenhower and his secretary of state, John Foster Dulles, implemented a new version of containment after the 1952 presidential election. The New Look, as their overarching defense strategy came to be called after a speech by Dulles in 1954, was designed to dramatically decrease defense spending.[6] According to John Lewis Gaddis, the New Look had four main components: (1) asymmetric response, or a dependence on full-scale atomic retaliation to deter enemy use of conventional forces; (2) reliance on alliances, especially to buttress limited U.S. manpower; (3) use of what Eisenhower called "psychological warfare," or the utilization of all colors of propaganda and public posture to discredit the Soviet regime; and (4) dramatically expanded covert operations by the CIA. The goal of this iteration of containment was "to achieve the maximum possible deterrence of communism at the minimum possible cost" so that, in Eisenhower's words, "the free world can pick up this burden . . . and do it in a way that we don't have to abandon it" because of the "extravagant" expense.[7] Interestingly, the Eisenhower Doctrine speech more resembled NSC-68's version of containment than the New Look in that it pivoted away from reliance on the United States' allies and promised a conventional, not nuclear, response to future provocation in the Middle East.

On the surface, then, the Eisenhower Doctrine speech can be understood as simply a more specific articulation of the strategy of Soviet containment that had guided American foreign policy for a decade. Just as the United States once shielded Western Europe, Greece, Turkey, and Korea from Soviet ambitions of "communizing" the world, now the United States would take responsibility for thwarting Russia's "long sought" goal of dominating the Middle East. By announcing an intention to prevent Soviet encroachment in the Middle East, Eisenhower was attempting to cordon the region off from additional Communist influence, consistent with the overarching strategy of containment.

To interpret this address as focusing only on containment would be too limited, however, and would belie the complexity of the Eisenhower Doctrine's historical, political, and rhetorical implications. Salim Yaqub identifies one such undercurrent of the Eisenhower Doctrine in his authoritative account *Containing Arab Nationalism: The Eisenhower Doctrine and the Middle East.* Yaqub describes how in addition to Soviet containment, "the Eisenhower Doctrine also sought to contain the radical Arab nationalism of Egyptian president Gamal Abdel Nasser and to discredit his policy of 'positive neutrality' in the Cold War, which held that Arab nations were entitled to profitable relations with both Cold War blocs."[8] Yaqub's work shows how the Eisenhower Doctrine, both as speech and policy, was a debate with the Nasserist movement over the acceptable bounds of Arab nationalism within the larger Cold War conflict.

While Yaqub's study and others ably demonstrate how the Eisenhower Doctrine as a policy was formulated, developed, and implemented—and what these policy choices meant for issues like Arab nationalism or alliance politics—they are not much concerned with how those same policies were communicated to the American people and how that communication functioned rhetorically.[9] That is, these researchers' focus is generally not on explaining the complicated interrelationships among the rhetor, discourse, constraints, exigence, and audience, or the way these texts invited their auditors to perceive themselves and their world in a certain way—the stuff of rhetoric. But just as the Eisenhower Doctrine has special relevance for studies of Arab nationalism, so also this speech bears significance for the study of presidential rhetoric. This address not only provided one of the clearest arguments for containment in Eisenhower's presidency but also publicly testified to the dramatic reconfiguration of America's relationship to the postwar Middle East, a subject largely untouched—at least rhetorically—by presidents before the Eisenhower Doctrine.

The Rhetorical Significance of the Eisenhower Doctrine

According to David Zarefsky, presidential rhetoric "defines political reality."[10] That is to say, the president's rhetorical power stems not from his ability to sway an opinion poll with a single speech but rather from his capacity to set the terms of the debate. The president provides names for the various phenomena that populate the political arena, like the "death tax" or a "surgical strike." By virtue of addressing an issue, the president defines a subject as political and grants it a certain degree of salience. The president frames matters under deliberation and is able to "condense" different concepts and connotations into a coherent symbol, which then possesses emotional resonance such as "America first" or "nation building at home" or "leading from behind."[11] In these ways and others, presidential rhetoric functions to educate the American people and influence political discourse as a whole.

It is important, then, that Eisenhower defined the "reality" of the Middle East in a starkly new way to the American people. The Eisenhower Doctrine speech, in contradistinction to any prior presidential address regarding the Middle East, directly requested permission from Congress "to employ the armed forces of the United States to assist to defend the territorial integrity and the political independence of any nation in the area," in order to combat "Communist armed aggression." Previous presidents addressed different exigences in the Arab world, and did so with differing notions of responsibility to it, but none attempted to directly intervene. In doing so, they predominantly "defined" the Middle East not as an area of concern but as an afterthought.

In fact for most of American history—outside a handful of references to Barbary pirates, the Ottoman Empire, the Egyptian cotton market, or Christian missionary efforts—American presidents virtually ignored the Middle East. Indeed, almost all presidential rhetoric regarding the region before Eisenhower's presidency was uttered by just three executives: Woodrow Wilson, Franklin Roosevelt, and Harry Truman. Their utterances provide the rhetorical context for the Eisenhower Doctrine address.

Under Wilson a new force emerged within presidential discourse that would virtually monopolize presidential rhetoric and policy concerning the Middle East until the Cold War: Zionism. While presidential interest regarding Jewish treatment in the Middle East dated as far back as the Van Buren administration, the rise of modern Zionism, coupled with the dramatic increase of the American Jewish population, gave the "Jewish Question"—whether the Jewish people constituted a nation, and if so, if that meant they were entitled to a homeland—new importance during Wilson's presidency. Motivated by a combination of biblical nostalgia—"To think that I, the son of the manse, should be able to help restore the Holy Land to its people"—and practical politics, namely, supporting Britain, an ally in wartime, Wilson resolved this issue by expressing his agreement with Britain's Balfour Declaration. Issued November 2, 1917, the declaration authorized Jewish immigration and settlement in the newly conquered British mandate of Palestine.[12] In giving his public assent, Wilson enshrined two norms of presidential rhetoric regarding the Middle East that would last until 1945.

First, Wilson recognized Britain's role as the dominant power in the region. By sanctioning the declaration, Wilson acceded to the idea that Britain legally controlled Palestine. Accepting Balfour meant that Wilson effectively conceded hegemony of the region to Whitehall, which already possessed Egypt, indirectly controlled much of Persia and the Hijaz, and would soon legally rule the Transjordan and Iraq, also formerly Ottoman territories.[13] After World War I the British were for practical purposes sovereign over the entire Arab Middle East (except for Syria and Lebanon, which were French mandates), a condition that would endure until the Eisenhower presidency.

Second, by supporting the Balfour Declaration Wilson embraced Zionism's basic premise that a Jewish homeland should be established in Palestine. A year after his endorsement of Balfour, Wilson revisited his decision in a letter to Rabbi Stephen Wise: "I welcome an opportunity to express the satisfaction I have felt in the progress of the Zionist movement in the United States and in the allied countries since the declaration of Mr. Balfour . . . of the establishment in Palestine of a national home for the Jewish people, and his promise that the British Government would use its best endeavors to facilitate the achievement of that object."[14]

The idea that a Jewish national home in Palestine should be established under British supervision was never seriously questioned in presidential discourse in the interwar years.[15] During the same period dissenting or Arab viewpoints were seldom articulated in major American publications and were ignored in presidential discourse.[16] From 1916 to 1945 no president publicly called into question America's backing of British rule in the Middle East or support for a Jewish national home in Palestine.

Near the end of Franklin D. Roosevelt's presidency, however, these norms began to erode. American business investment in Saudi Arabian oil (and the relationships necessary to these endeavors) had quietly skyrocketed since the kingdom's inception in 1932. By the mid-1930s American companies held substantial business interests in the Persian Gulf region. Roosevelt did not bring attention to this development until his return voyage from the 1945 Yalta Conference, when—much to Churchill's chagrin—he met individually with Egypt's King Farouk I, Emperor Haile Selassie of Ethiopia, and Saudi King Abdul Aziz Ibn Saud while aboard the uss *Quincy*. Journalists noticed that Roosevelt enjoyed Ibn Saud's company in particular, and the two "got along famously together."[17] When asked later what he thought of Ibn Saud, Roosevelt replied, "The general feeling is that the Arabs want to be let alone. Do not interfere with the Arabs. Very interesting point of view."[18] By sharing this opinion publicly and describing Ibn Saud as representative of all Arabs, Roosevelt subtly called into question British imperial legitimacy in the Middle East while distancing himself personally from such a critical stance. No matter what Roosevelt said or Churchill wanted, however, American influence was fast rising in the Middle East—regardless of whether the region remained within a formal British sphere of influence or not.[19]

Although Truman's foreign policy and rhetoric were significantly more oriented to internationalism than his predecessors, little of what he said pertained to the Middle East directly. Regarding the establishment of Israel, Truman sought any way possible to avoid U.S. responsibility (and therefore troops) for Palestine, using interviews and speeches to constantly deny that the area had become a "strategic consideration" of the United States.[20] As an outgrowth of this policy, he consistently vocalized his support for whatever solution seemed most viable at the time, be it British rule, UN partition, or Israeli statehood.[21]

The closest Truman came to publicly questioning British hegemony in the Middle East occurred in his Truman Doctrine speech of March 12, 1947. Fearing Communist expansion into Greece and Turkey, Truman went before Congress to ask for increased foreign aid for those countries. Laying out his case, he argued:

> Greece must have assistance if it is to become a self-supporting and self-respecting democracy.
>
> The United States must supply this assistance. We have already extended to Greece certain types of relief and economic aid but these are inadequate.
>
> There is no other country to which democratic Greece can turn.
>
> No other nation is willing and able to provide the necessary support for a democratic Greek government.
>
> The British Government, which has been helping Greece, can give no further financial or economic aid after March 31. Great Britain finds itself under the necessity of reducing or liquidating its commitments in several parts of the world, including Greece.[22]

Notice that Truman's argument for intervention—Greece needs assistance, if Greece does not receive assistance it may cease to be a democracy, and the United States is the only democratic country able and potentially willing to help Greece—is completely dependent on *British* inability to provide such aid. Far from undermining the idea of British hegemony in the region, Truman's speech, like those before it, is presumed on this principle; Truman began with the assumption that it was Britain's military responsibility to secure Greece and by implication the Eastern Mediterranean. Indeed, as Truman framed the issue to the American people, the United States was only reluctantly picking up the slack in Greece so that Whitehall could "liquidate" its "commitment" there, ostensibly to devote its newly freed resources to places from which it was not withdrawing, such as Egypt, Jordan, Palestine, and Iraq.

Truman's presumption of British responsibility for the Middle East became even more obvious as he shifted the discussion to Turkey:

> The British Government has informed us that, owing to its own difficulties, it can no longer extend financial or economic aid to Turkey.
>
> As in the case of Greece, if Turkey is to have the assistance it needs, the United States must supply it. We are the only country able to provide that help.

Here again the president claimed that American aid was "essential to the preservation of order" but framed the extension of aid to Turkey as being done at the behest of London. By characterizing U.S. intervention as limited and done in cooperation with Britain's wishes, Truman reified the belief that the Middle East was primarily a British responsibility and concern.

While he affirmed British hegemony, Truman also acknowledged that London's grasp on the region was fragile—hence the need for American aid. He continued:

> It is necessary only to glance at a map to realize that the survival and integrity of the Greek nation are of grave importance in a much wider situation. If Greece should fall under the control of an armed minority, the effect upon its neighbor, Turkey, would be immediate and serious. Confusion and disorder might well spread throughout the entire Middle East.

The ultimate reason for American intervention in Greece and Turkey, according to Truman, was to prevent "confusion and disorder"—the seedbed of Communism—from spreading. Though he recognized that Britain's control was weakening—after all,

Churchill that same year had decried the "hurried scuttle" and "shameful flight" of the British Empire—Truman's speech did not call for replacing the imperial status quo.[23] Earlier drafts of the speech, evidencing Truman's desire to emphasize London's strength, even sought to downplay Britain's decline by describing how the winter of 1946–47 inflicted tremendous damage to the British economy, a setback from which Britain would theoretically recuperate using Marshall Plan funds.[24] The Truman Doctrine thus publicly reinforced the presumption that the United States would work within the existing British imperial paradigm to contain the Communist threat to the region, *not* that the United States would replace Britain or underwrite the entire region's security itself. This foundational assumption was explicitly reversed in the Eisenhower Doctrine speech, marking a new rhetorical norm in presidential rhetoric regarding the Middle East.

Eisenhower Doctrine: Textual Analysis

Lloyd Bitzer has argued that "rhetorical discourse comes into existence as a response to a situation," and in this instance his insight is apt.[25] In the Eisenhower Doctrine speech, Ike was responding to both the immediate exigence—the risk that Nasser and the Soviets would exploit Britain's post–Suez crisis weakness to gain influence in the Middle East—as well as to the wider exigence of a shift in the regional balance of power in the United States' favor. His response was to propose a joint authorization, called the Middle East Resolution, allowing him to provide increased military and economic aid as well as American troops (upon request) to friendly regimes. Eisenhower's speech can thus be read as addressing both the short-term and the long-term exigences constitutive of the situation. Moreover, this proposal was a clear rhetorical break from previously stated U.S. policy toward the Middle East. Examining how Ike persuasively framed his proposal to his audiences will show how he effectively adapted existing rhetorical discourse surrounding containment to argue for the extension of American influence in the Middle East.

In meeting this multilayered rhetorical challenge, Eisenhower was addressing several audiences. The United States' European allies, who went largely unmentioned in Ike's address, constituted an audience. Soviet leaders were likewise listening, and Eisenhower probably had them in mind when he gave a not-so-veiled threat that if "power-hungry Communists" should attack the Middle East, "that would start a chain of circumstances which would almost surely involve the United States in military action." To listeners in the Middle East, Ike repeatedly emphasized that it was his "profound hope that this authority would never have to be exercised at all," and if it were, it would only be at their request. All these audiences are important and deserving of study; however, for the purpose of this analysis I have chosen to limit my examination to the national scene.

Domestically Eisenhower had two primary audiences: Congress and the American people. To address these audiences, the speech functioned on two levels reflecting the dual exigences of the situation. Eisenhower's persuasive strategy directed toward Congress was designed to address the immediate exigence—the need for the United States to fill the emerging regional power vacuum—and was deliberative in nature. At the same time Eisenhower employed a narrative framework to appeal to the American people. Examining the strategies used for these audiences illuminates how Eisenhower deployed the rhetoric of containment to accomplish his persuasive tasks—and how in doing so he redefined the political reality of the Middle East for the people of the United States.

Congressional Persuasion

In terms of the immediate exigence, Congress was Eisenhower's most important audience; after all, a joint resolution by definition cannot be passed without legislative approval. Getting the votes necessary to pass the resolution was far from a given. Despite Eisenhower's status as a newly reelected president highly skilled in foreign policy and his crushing margin of victory over challenger Adlai Stevenson two months prior, the Republican Party had actually lost two seats in the House of Representatives and failed to increase its numbers in the Senate during the 1956 elections. The electoral verdict, therefore, was hardly an endorsement of Republican leadership as a whole. As a result Ike faced opposition majorities in both congressional chambers eager to capitalize on Democratic gains.

In addition to partisan hostility, the Eisenhower Doctrine also had to overcome the opposition of legislators who believed the resolution would infringe on congressional authority to oversee foreign policy. The sweeping imprecision of Eisenhower's words—"The proposed legislation is *primarily* designed to deal with the *possibility* of Communist aggression, *direct and indirect*" (emphases mine)—could be interpreted in a variety of ways, potentially enabling Eisenhower as commander in chief to circumvent Congress and act however he saw fit in the region. By putting forth the resolution, Ike was claiming for himself not only the right to determine what means should be used to counter Communist aggression but also the freedom to determine whether such aggression was occurring in the first place. Senator J. William Fulbright joined with other Democrats to fully seize on this line of criticism. During congressional deliberation over the Eisenhower Doctrine, Fulbright denounced the resolution, calling it a "blank check for the administration to do as it pleased with our soldiers and with our money."[26] Although they did not all agree with the specific nature of Fulbright's criticism, Senators Mike Mansfield, Wayne Morse, Richard Russell, and Hubert Humphrey all joined him in vociferously combating what a few of them called "the so-called doctrine."[27]

Anticipating (though underestimating) Democratic opposition to the Eisenhower Doctrine, Ike employed three major rhetorical strategies in his address designed to allay congressional concerns. First, he repeatedly characterized the proposed resolution as an accepted foreign-policy strategy with established precedent. Even as he described recent events as constituting "a special situation in the Middle East," he nonetheless argued, "It is nothing new for the President and the Congress to join to recognize that the national integrity of other free nations is directly related to our own security." To support his case, Eisenhower pointed to the ratified United Nations treaty, the Truman Doctrine, the Formosa Straits Resolution, and the "security treaties with 42 other nations" agreed to by the United States as examples of successful joint foreign-policy initiatives.

The clearest precedent in recent memory for the Eisenhower Doctrine was the Formosa Straits Resolution of January 1955, which was passed by Congress at Eisenhower's behest in response to Communist Chinese shelling of Quemoy and Matsu, two Nationalist Chinese–controlled islands off the shore of Fujian Province. The resolution, utilizing strategically ambiguous language, authorized the president "to employ the Armed Forces of the United States as he deem[ed] necessary" to protect Formosa (Taiwan) from attack.[28] By not explicitly defining whether Quemoy and Matsu were "necessary" for the defense of Chiang Kai-shek's government, Congress allowed the Eisenhower administration to threaten reprisals against the Communist Chinese while not tying itself to an untenable defense policy. Similar to that of the Formosa Straits Resolution, the language of the Eisenhower Doctrine also granted the president significant independence from congressional oversight—a point not lost on Fulbright and his supporters.

Critically, Eisenhower claimed continuity not only with the Formosa Straits Resolution but also with the UN Treaty and the Truman Doctrine, both major diplomatic achievements of the previous Democratic administration. In doing so Eisenhower framed his proposed doctrine not as an exercise in executive overreach but as consistent with the actions of the previous Democratic administration. His rhetoric thereby worked to render the resolution's Democratic opposition blatantly partisan and inconsistent for questioning his proposal without having done the same for Truman's undertakings.

Expanding on the theme of continuity, Ike described the Eisenhower Doctrine as a mythic perpetuation of an idealized, bipartisan American foreign-policy tradition: "In those momentous periods of the past, the President and the Congress have united, without partisanship, to serve the vital interests of the United States and of the free world." By characterizing the Eisenhower Doctrine as a natural extension of the United States' transcendent foreign-policy tradition—and one with multiple, recent precedents—Ike sought to undermine congressional objections to the Eisenhower Doctrine, or at least to color any opposition to it as acting in dis-harmony with American tradition. If previous Congresses and presidential administrations could selflessly put aside their differ-ences to serve the nation, why, Eisenhower seemed to ask, could not current senators and representatives do the same? By ask-ing Congress to "manifest again our national unity in support of freedom," Eisenhower placed the burden of breaking that unity on his opponents.

Second, Ike framed the Eisenhower Doctrine as a necessary measure without which disaster, in the form of Communist pen-etration, would befall the Middle East. His persuasive strategy rested on three premises: (1) the Middle East was a region of vital U.S. interest, (2) the Middle Eastern nations were unstable and therefore by definition vulnerable to Communism, and (3) the United States was the only country capable of providing security (and thereby ending instability) in the Middle East.

Although Eisenhower had trumpeted the importance of the Middle East since his 1952 presidential campaign, he seldom spelled out exactly *why* it was a major interest of the United States. After all the country's domestic oil production was enough to meet the nation's needs. The United States had relatively little at stake in terms of investment in the region, and no major threat to national security existed there. However, Eisenhower noted, the Middle East "contains about two thirds of the presently known oil deposits in the world," and the "nations of Europe are pecu-liarly dependent upon this supply." According to the alliance logic of containment, then, American security in Europe was depen-dent on European access to Middle Eastern oil, thus elevating the region to a status of "immense importance." In addition to oil, however, Eisenhower was quick to note, "There are other fac-tors which transcend the material." He emphasized the region's significance to the Abrahamic faiths, declaring that "it would be intolerable if the holy places of the Middle East should be sub-jected to a rule that glorifie[d] atheistic materialism." For rea-sons of faith and economics, then, the Middle East demanded U.S. interest and security investment.

Eisenhower's use of what Phillip Wander calls "prophetic dual-ism" is apparent in these arguments. As Wander describes it, "In its perfected form prophetic dualism divides the world into two camps. Between them there is conflict. One side acts in accord with all that is good, decent, and at one with God's will. The other acts in direct opposition. Conflict between them is resolved only through the total victory of one side over the other. Since no guarantee exists that good will triumph, there is no middle ground. Hence neutrality may be treated as a delusion, compro-mise appeasement, and negotiation a call for surrender."[29]

As Ned O'Gorman has noted, Eisenhower's dualistic bifurca-tion of the region elided the potentially divisive complexities of the Middle East to his American audience.[30] Economically, many countries in the Middle East were bound to Europe by relations forged through colonialism. Iran, for example, possessed virtu-ally zero control over the oil production of the Anglo-Iranian Oil plant at Abadan. The British Foreign Office still maintained pri-mary control over the oil-producing gulf emirates, and Royal Air Force bases still dotted the Middle East landscape. Thus, although Eisenhower claimed disaster would strike if the Soviets took over the region, those nations were in many ways "dominated by alien forces" already. Religiously there existed powerful antagonisms between Muslims and Jews and growing divisions between Chris-tians and Muslims. Yet Eisenhower's dualistic rhetoric, borrowed from containment discourse, worked to flatten these distinctions. By dividing the region between economically free nations and the unfree Communists, between religious peoples and the Soviet atheists, the Middle East Eisenhower presented to Congress was one that shared America's moral orientation and needed its pro-tection. He depicted a region that was in America's camp, at least culturally, and therefore it was in the United States' interest to keep the Middle East on its side. In this way Ike's rhetoric worked to portray the Middle East as a region worthy of major American concern—and therefore military investment.

One of Eisenhower's most consistent rhetorical themes regarding the Middle East was to portray it as a region gripped by insecurity, and this address was no exception. He declared there to be "persistent crosscurrents of distrust and fear" bringing about "a high degree of instability in much of the Mid East." While he blamed this state of affairs mostly on "hostilities involving Western European nations" and "the relatively large attack by Israel in October," Eisenhower made sure to emphasize that the unrest generated by these conflicts made the region susceptible to being "manipulated by International Communism." Indeed, Ike edited the card from which he read the speech to emphasize that the Soviets "soon" hoped to dominate the Middle East, thus adding urgency to the situation.[31] These claims from Eisenhower echoed and built on earlier arguments made by Truman and George Marshall. The Truman Doctrine address described how rule by an "armed minority" (Communists) produced "confusion and disorder," and in his Harvard address unveiling the plan soon to be named after him Marshall declared that, without economic aid, there could be "no political stability" and therefore "no assured peace" in Europe.[32] By invoking the established Cold War topos of equating a nation's instability to its defenselessness before Communism, Eisenhower depicted the Middle East as an insecure region where containment was under threat.

Because no middle ground existed, not providing stabilizing aid to these countries was, according to Eisenhower's dualistic Cold War logic, to invite a Soviet takeover. As Dulles had testified before a closed session of the Senate Committee of Foreign Relations three days prior to Eisenhower's speech, the administration believed that the Arab nations would "almost certainly be taken over by Soviet communism" without an American assurance of security to replace that of the British.[33] To Dulles and Ike it was axiomatic that when the "free world" retreated, "International Communism" advanced. Furthermore, as Ira Chernus notes, stability became an ideal worthy of pursuit in and of itself during the Eisenhower administration.[34] Thus the question to be asked was not *whether* such aid should be provided but *who* would provide it. Glibly ignoring any reference to the discredited British imperial security paradigm that had just collapsed at Suez, Eisenhower explained why the United Nations was not fit to fulfill its role as the "protector of small nations." Referencing the recent Soviet crackdown in Hungary, Eisenhower warned, "The United Nations . . . cannot be a wholly dependable protector of freedom when the ambitions of the Soviet Union are involved." Because the Soviets had shown "callous indifference" to world opinion in Budapest, in accordance with their exposited nature as an atheistic totalitarian regime, the only party capable of protecting the Middle East was the United States, on which "a great responsibility now devolve[d]." Like Truman in 1947, Eisenhower depicted America as the only country capable of providing needed aid to an unstable region. This time, however, the entire Middle East was in play, not just Greece and Turkey.

Eisenhower's third rhetorical strategy to dispel congressional criticism was to emphasize his trustworthiness. As Martin J. Medhurst and others attest, Eisenhower often relied on his formidable ethos when making rhetorical appeals regarding foreign policy. He did so throughout the 1952 and 1956 campaigns, promising to "go to Korea" and reminding voters that he had "kept the peace."[35] He employed this tactic again in the Eisenhower Doctrine speech, repeatedly assuring Congress that he could be trusted with the level of autonomy for which he was asking. Promising he would not abuse his power, Eisenhower stated flatly, "I would of course maintain hour-by-hour contact with the Congress" if a "situation arose which called for the military application of the Eisenhower Doctrine." "And if the Congress were not in session," he continued, "I would, of course, at once call the Congress into special session." Clearly, Eisenhower's repeated reassurances that he would not abuse the Eisenhower Doctrine relied on his reputation as a moral and trustworthy figure. If Ike was honest—and a majority of the American people (including many Democrats) thought he was—then his promise to work closely with Congress functioned rhetorically to negate any accusations of executive overreach. To dispute him on this count would be tantamount to calling him a liar and calling the Americans who had reelected him bad judges of character.[36] Ike, as he often did, selectively and strategically invoked his ethos.

These appeals—framing the Middle East Resolution as consistent with prior U.S. foreign policy, characterizing intervention as necessary, and emphasizing Eisenhower's trustworthy reputation—were structured to support a specific deliberative policy action: passing the Middle East Resolution. As such their primary audience was Congress, and Eisenhower used them to respond to the immediate exigence of preventing an increase of Communist influence in the Middle East. In addition to these appeals, however, Eisenhower also animated his address with persuasive devices designed for the American public, whose support was needed for the long-term viability of the Eisenhower Doctrine.

Public Persuasion: Narrative Construction

Eisenhower's address also sought to influence the American people. While many of the strategies he used for one audience applied to the other as well—after all, legislators must heed their constituents—Ike had much more work to do with the public. Unlike Congress the American people were not privy to closed-door briefings on the Middle East from John Foster Dulles or his brother, CIA director Allen Dulles. Until the Suez crisis the Middle East had not registered as a major concern for most Americans, and media coverage of the region was less extensive than that of Europe or East Asia. Thus Ike's goal in addressing the American public was not to convince his audience to take a specific action—the American public was not a deliberative body anyway—but to explain that the Middle East was now an American responsibility and thereby initiate building the long-term political support necessary for sustained engagement in the region.

To do so Eisenhower relied on the use of narrative. Narrative is a uniquely powerful rhetorical tool thanks to its ability to constitute a comprehensive reality for auditors.[37] According to communication scholar Walter Fisher, "symbols are created and communicated ultimately as stories meant to give order to human experience and to induce others to dwell in them."[38] Eisenhower, by using narrative, imposed order on a complicated situation and invited his audience to embrace his structuring of the "world" of the Middle East. In doing so he drew heavily on the rhetoric of containment to explain why the United States was now obliged to underwrite the region's security.

Ike began his narrative by setting the stage. He described how "since the First World War there ha[d] been a steady evolution toward self-government" in the Middle East, and how the United States "welcomed and encouraged" this development. This simplified story obfuscated the complexities of the McMahon-Hussein correspondence, the Great Arab Revolt, British imperialism, Zionism, nationalism, and Nasserism in shaping the region by instituting a unidimensional reading of the Middle East; in his telling the Middle East was solely a collection of peoples moving toward independent rule. However, as described above, the region was "troubled" by "instability," for freedom opened the path to power for Communists (or Communist sympathizers). Eisenhower depicted a perilous, uncertain state of affairs in the Middle East.

He then highlighted the threat: "Russia's rulers have long sought to dominate the Middle East. . . . Considering her announced purpose of Communizing the world, it is easy to understand her hope of dominating the Middle East." According to Eisenhower's narrative, the Soviet Union's motivation for taking over the Middle East was self-evident; as both Russians and Communists they simply desired to rule the region. Moreover, because they did not need Arab oil or the Suez Canal, their interest was "solely that of power politics." As evidence for this characterization of the Soviets, Eisenhower alluded to three events as examples of their treachery: the forceful incorporation of the Baltic States into the Union of Soviet Socialist Republics, Soviet occupation of the satellite states despite the Yalta agreement, and the "subjugation of Hungary by naked armed force." These events, particularly Yalta, were seen by many Americans as examples of Soviet perfidy. Although

Eisenhower and Dulles never unequivocally denounced the Yalta agreement, many Americans embraced the late Senator Robert Taft's interpretation that Roosevelt and Truman's "wrong-headed policies" led them to accept "all Stalin's promises," which Stalin subsequently violated by occupying Eastern Europe.[39] Eisenhower's narrative alluded to this reading of history, establishing the Soviet Union as not only dangerous but deviously so.

With the threat identified, Eisenhower then posited the problem: "The free nations of the Mid East need, and for the most part want, added strength to assure their continued independence." By using the moniker "free" to describe these countries, Ike defined them as belonging to America's side of the dualistic system; additionally, according to this description these nations already existed in a state of independence, implying that they feely chose to caucus with the West. Eisenhower positioned "International Communism" as therefore seeking to alter the status quo, designating any action taken to assist the Middle East in thwarting this plan as inherently defensive in nature. The average American listening to the address likely heard an equivalency being made—the Middle East was free soil, and just like the free lands of Europe, Korea, and Turkey, it must be kept safe from Communism.

Like the appeal to Congress, the overall narrative of Ike's speech led to a certain conclusion: the Middle East *must* receive help in its resistance of Communism. Again Eisenhower completely ignored the fact that this role had until two months prior been predominantly played by Britain, avoiding uncomfortable questions of whether the United States was playing a game of imperial succession. His narrative posited only the UN Security Council as a possible alternative protector of the region, a body that could not "be a wholly dependable protector of freedom" due to the Soviets' permanent veto power. Thus no one was left to fill this role but the United States. But would America answer the call? Ike left the narrative ending open, likely knowing that any answer in the affirmative required enduring public support.

Eisenhower used three strategies to encourage the American populace to answer his call positively. First, he described the

United States as merely acting in the place of the United Nations in a place where the United Nations could not act. He informed his audience that "the nations of the Middle East [were] aware of the danger that stem[med] from International Communism and welcome[d] closer cooperation with the United States to realize for themselves the United Nations goals of independence, economic well-being, and spiritual growth." The United States was not going into the Middle East for "political or economic domination" of the region. Its presence was a means by which its Middle Eastern friends could realize their own spiritual, political, and economic aims, which simply happened to coincide exactly with the goals of the United Nations. The United States was positioned as a UN surrogate, the friend of small nations. Eisenhower thus rhetorically linked his proposal to Franklin Roosevelt's metaphor of the "good neighbor." This idea, that the American "resolutely respects himself and, because he does so, respects the rights of others," extended the idea of equality to the international stage. Originally coined in reference to FDR's Latin America policy, the "good neighbor" was and is a powerful rhetorical current in U.S. foreign-policy discourse.[40]

Second, Ike also cited numerous precedents of U.S. activity in the region: the 1950 Tripartite Declaration (which was secretly broken by France), presidential declarations given on April 9 and November 29, 1956, and a 1950 presidential assurance to Saudi Arabia. Of note is that all these cited precedents were *rhetorical* in nature—in none of the given instances did the United States act in a significant way. Thus Eisenhower located the Middle East Resolution as a continuation of these prior rhetorical interventions in the Middle East, despite the fact that the resolution explicitly authorized him to mobilize military and economic forces. Indeed, he characterized the Eisenhower Doctrine as a rhetorical solution—providing assurance to Arab allies—to what he effectively characterized as a rhetorical problem, insecurity on the part of the nation's allies.[41] Eisenhower's framing of the conflict as eminently rhetorical in nature was apparent throughout the address (emphases mine):

The Eisenhower Doctrine

"our joint resolve should be so couched as to make it apparent that *if need be* our words will be backed by action."

"It is my profound hope that this authority would never have to be exercised at all."

"Nothing is more necessary . . . than that our policy with respect to the defense of the area be promptly and clearly determined and *declared*. Thus the United Nations and all friendly governments, and indeed governments who are not friendly, *will know where we stand*."

"It is now essential that the United States should *manifest* through joint action . . . *our determination to assist* those nations of the Mid East area, *which desire that assistance*."

"I deem it necessary to seek the cooperation of the Congress. Only with that cooperation can we give the *reassurance* needed to deter aggression."

By classifying his proposal as rhetorical in nature, Ike downplayed the possibility that it might require an actual investment of U.S. blood and treasure; such a framing of the Eisenhower Doctrine was likely essential to gain the support of a public so recently frustrated by the stalemate of the Korean War. It was literally, he claimed, a war of words—and likely nothing more.

Third, Ike concluded his address by asserting that the Eisenhower Doctrine was a step consistent with American belief in freedom and willingness to sacrifice for freedom. He declared that Americans had previously seen "human freedom in jeopardy, and their fortitude and resolution ha[d] been equal to the crisis." He invoked the sacrifices of World War II, "by which great areas of the world ha[d] been preserved to freedom" a prize he insisted "must not be thrown away." And so, Eisenhower finished, "The occasion has come for us to manifest again our national unity in support of freedom and to show our deep respect for the rights and independence of every nation—however great, however small." By vociferously identifying his proposed resolution with the promotion of freedom, Eisenhower appealed to one of the deepest of American ideals, one made all the more salient by the Cold War context.

These three rhetorical strategies, when viewed from the public vantage, were designed less for a deliberative debate than for a project of conversion. Ike sought to instill the belief in the American people that U.S. intervention in the Middle East was consistent with the essence of American identity, that this action was primarily rhetorical, and that Middle Easterners welcomed our arrival as friends. These appeals were designed to create support for a U.S. presence in the Middle East generally, not to pass specific legislation, and were therefore a response to the wider exigence of the regional power vacuum caused by British imperial decline. Moreover, Eisenhower's use of narrative—a narrative laden with Cold War discursive norms—invited the public to enter into and complete the president's story, and by doing so accept his rhetorical construction of the "world" of the Middle East. In short Eisenhower, drawing from existing Cold War rhetoric, created a compelling political reality for his audience, the effective component of which was American responsibility for the Middle East's security.

Effects and Implications of the Eisenhower Doctrine Address

The immediate context should always be considered in discussing the effects of a given text, and judged in this light the Eisenhower Doctrine address must be viewed as a relative success. Although the Middle East Resolution was debated fiercely in Senate committee hearings—resulting in a series of verbal gaffes by Secretary Dulles and an embarrassing delay for the administration—the Eisenhower Doctrine finally cleared the Foreign Relations and Armed Services Committees on February 13, and it was approved by the full Senate on March 5 by a vote of 72–19. An amendment by Senator Mansfield moderated the language used to grant the president authority, changing the phrasing from Ike being "authorized to employ the Armed Forces of the United States" to "the United States is prepared to use armed forces." More significantly, the Mansfield amendment also altered the opening statement of the resolution. The amended statement read, "The United States regards as vital to the national interest and world peace the preservation of the independence and integrity of the nations of the Middle East." This sentence, sweepingly and explicitly, identified the United States' national interest with the Middle East status quo. Ironically, this new sentence alone later provided the justificatory basis for the Eisenhower's administration intervention in Lebanon.[42]

Another effect of the Eisenhower Doctrine speech was its acknowledgment that the United States now possessed a global sphere of influence. Prior to the Eisenhower administration, U.S. defense policy was sometimes understood as consisting of a (gigantic) sphere of influence spanning the Pacific and Atlantic Oceans, a development from prior strategists who conceived of the United States primarily as a naval power. This concept was exemplified by Dean Acheson's infamous "defensive perimeter" statement, in which he implied that South Korea lay outside the American protective sphere, which many Republicans blamed for inviting the North Korean attack in 1950.[43] Regardless of whether this conception of American defense was seriously held in Washington, containment was rhetorically depicted as a kind of fencing in of the Soviet Union, and in this formula the United States was militarily responsible for helping maintain the fence in Europe and East Asia. The Eisenhower Doctrine precluded and overturned this understanding of containment. It favored a globalized conception of American defense that was more consistent with the asymmetric response thinking of the New Look. Breaking from prior presidential rhetoric, it completely eschewed any pretense of British primacy in the Middle East in favor of direct American intervention. Because any war with Communism would be global, American commitment to containment needed to be global as well, a reality that the Eisenhower Doctrine heavily underscored.

Last, perhaps the most significant effect of the Eisenhower Doctrine address was that it, to steal a phrase from Geoffrey Aronson, repositioned the Middle East "from sideshow to center stage" in American foreign-policy discourse. In his work Aronson tracks the growing primacy of Egypt in American foreign-policy formulation after World War II, and he fittingly concludes his account on the eve of the Eisenhower Doctrine address.[44] In this sense the Eisenhower Doctrine can be understood, from a certain ontological vantage, as a case of rhetoric catching up with reality—or at least reality as it existed in the minds of policy makers. Like many other instances of U.S. foreign policy, here rhetoric worked to make public the changed priorities of the government post hoc. For better or worse the Middle East now constituted a major theater of the Cold War and, thanks to Eisenhower, was now openly acknowledged as such. After the Eisenhower Doctrine address, no one could pretend that the Middle East was not a major foreign-policy priority for the United States. This is perhaps the most lasting effect of the Eisenhower Doctrine address because, from the decades of the Cold War to the War on Terror, the Middle East has seldom relinquished its role as a center stage of America's foreign-policy attention.

However, the Eisenhower Doctrine speech is also notable for what it does not say. Important geopolitical issues pertaining to the Middle East simply went unmentioned in the speech, and many of the speech's rhetorical features appear problematic when taken on their own. Some of these features, like Eisenhower's silence regarding the United States' role in helping create and fuel the region's instability, are to be expected. Similarly would one expect Eisenhower to portray his own country's actions as defensive and the Soviet Union's as inherently aggressive. Other issues, however, are more puzzling. Why did Eisenhower hardly mention Europe and fail to discuss Britain or France entirely? Given the dramatic ways in which these nations had shaped the region (not to mention the fact that they had maintained its security arrangement for the previous forty years), it seems odd that Eisenhower would literally cut them out of his speech—especially when doing so broke completely with the precedent of previous presidential rhetoric.[45]

Additionally, Eisenhower made a series of rhetorical leaps that presumed a sympathetic audience if his address was to have any coherence. He repeatedly characterized Russia (*not* the Soviets, so as to maintain continuity with tsarist imperialism) as a foreign actor in the region. He described how Russians operated from behind a "mask" and sought "domination" while asserting that "a greater responsibility now devolve[d] upon the United States," as if it were perfectly natural for the United States to assume charge of a region two oceans away. Indeed, if Russia's interest was "solely that of power politics" because it was a major oil producer and was not dependent on the Suez Canal, then why should America's interest be understood differently, since it met both those criteria as well? Without the enthymematic premise that the United States was an accepted and legitimate actor in the region, Ike's argument that the United States was needed to defend against an *outside* threat made little sense. Furthermore, Eisenhower's discussion of the United Nations also seemed out of place. On its face, would not that body object to a unilateral policy of U.S. intervention? Yet Ike unproblematically presumed that "closer cooperation with the United States" was an obvious means by which the nations of the Middle East could hope "to realize . . . United Nations goals." Other issues, such as Eisenhower's assumption that Arab countries could not defend themselves and his monolithic characterization of Middle Eastern countries despite the rise and leftward turn of Nasserist Egypt, are also perplexing.

The point is not that these omissions amounted to oversights on Eisenhower's part or that they are somehow unanswerable, but that each of these issues indicates the presence of other rhetorical forces at work in this address. When one examines these features of the speech, it becomes apparent that Ike was trading in a rhetorical currency concerning the Middle East established outside this speech alone. The Eisenhower Doctrine speech did not occur in a rhetorical vacuum, and it operated on presumptions established earlier in the Eisenhower presidency. Likewise, it also created certain liabilities—both political and rhetorical—within which Eisenhower would now have to operate.

The project of the remaining chapters of this book is to investigate the ways in which Eisenhower's previous rhetoric worked to establish a set of rhetorical norms regarding the Middle East and how his rhetoric post–Eisenhower Doctrine was similarly influenced and constrained. This investigation shall reveal how certain elements of Ike's rhetorical currency came to be, how the Eisenhower Doctrine was understood in its subsequent application in Lebanon, and how Eisenhower's rhetoric ultimately influenced the speech of future presidents.

In light of previous presidential rhetoric, the Eisenhower Doctrine stands out all the more by discarding any pretense of Middle Eastern security being another nation's responsibility. Eisenhower's claim that "the United States must make more evident its willingness to support the independence of the freedom-loving nations of the area" through direct military support, while a logical extension of containment as expressed by Truman in 1947, nonetheless signified a major rhetorical shift by placing the onus for the security of the entire Middle East exclusively at America's feet. Eisenhower, to frame his case persuasively, adapted elements of containment discourse to structure his speech. The address contained a series of appeals designed to function deliberatively with Congress as well as a narrative that invited the American public to support intervention. These strategies coalesced to offer a rhetorical redefinition of the Middle East for Ike's American audience.

The Eisenhower Doctrine remains a seminal address in U.S. foreign-policy rhetoric. Yet for all its significance, this speech exists not as a singularity but as one (albeit major) step in a rhetorical revolution under Eisenhower that changed how presidents speak about the Middle East. Like many episodes of rhetorical prominence, the Eisenhower Doctrine address was less a standalone moment of oratorical inspiration than a product of unfinished forces in motion. The ensuing chapters seek to capture more snapshots of this metamorphosis and in so doing not only better contextualize the Eisenhower Doctrine but also reveal the dramatic sweep of the Eisenhower era in the Middle East.

2

Operation Ajax

Eisenhower's Rhetoric of Misdirection

The Shah should reign, not rule.

—Mohammed Mossadegh political motto, 1952

It is clear that we are facing an implacable enemy whose avowed
objective is world domination by whatever means and at whatever
cost. There are no rules in such a game. Hitherto acceptable norms of
human conduct do not apply. If the United States is to survive, long-
standing American concepts of "fair play" must be reconsidered. We
must develop effective espionage and counter-espionage services and
must learn to subvert, sabotage, and destroy our enemies by more
clever, more sophisticated, and more effective methods than those used
against us. It may become necessary that the American people be
made acquainted with, understand, and support this
fundamentally repugnant philosophy.

—Doolittle Report to the president, July 26, 1954

Here [Iran] is where they will start trouble if we aren't careful. . . . If we
stand up to them like we did in Greece three years ago, they won't take
any next steps. But if we just stand by, they'll move into Iran and they'll
take over the whole Middle East. There's no telling what they'll
do if we don't put up a fight now.

—Harry Truman, discussion with George Elsey on June 26, 1950,

one day after the start of the Korean War

n the September 20, 2015, edition of CBS's long-running news
show *60 Minutes*, correspondent Steve Kroft interviewed Iranian president Hassan Rouhani regarding his nation's recent
agreement with the United States to allow UN supervision of

Iran's nuclear program. In the course of the interview, Kroft asked Rouhani whether he, like Supreme Ayatollah Ali Khamenei, considered the United States to be "the Great Satan." After being pressed by Kroft for an answer, Rouhani defended Iranians' use of the term on the basis of America's past wrongdoings in his nation. He stated:

> Satan in our religious parlance is used to refer to that power that tricks others and whose words are not clear words, do not match reality. What I can say is that the U.S. has made many mistakes in the past regarding Iran, and must make up for those mistakes. . . . If America puts the enmity aside, if it initiates good will, and if it compensates for the past, the future situation between the United States and Iran will change.[1]

Of the many reasons why the United States must, in Rouhani's view, "compensate for the past," few are as significant as Operation Ajax, the CIA-organized 1953 coup 'd'état against the government of democratically elected Iranian prime minister Mohammed Mossadegh. The "28 Mordad 1332" coup, as the affair is known in Iran, is important for numerous reasons. The event marked the effective end of Iranian democratic constitutionalism, the termination of the Anglo-Iranian Oil Company's monopoly over the Abadan refinery, and the downfall of the Iranian left wing. It inaugurated the increasingly authoritarian rule of Mohammed Reza Shah Pahlavi, thereby sowing the seeds of the 1979 revolution. Most of all the coup established the United States as the dominant foreign economic and political power in Iran, thus setting the stage for the present-day chill in U.S.-Iranian relations following the shah's ultimate demise.

As Rouhani's statement attests, the coup is often interpreted in Iran to this day as historical evidence justifying hostility toward America. The U.S. government, for its part, has only officially acknowledged its covert role in the coup since a speech by Secretary of State Madeline Albright given in March 2000, an admission that Supreme Ayatollah Khamenei condemned as "deceitful" since it "did not even include an apology."[2] In addition to the official diplomatic and intelligence reports, numerous historians, scholars, and journalists have also offered their interpretations of the coup. As historian Hugh Wilford writes in his 2013 account, the story of Mossadegh's fall has been told in countless books, articles, documentaries, and even a graphic novel; he finds this popularity unsurprising "given that, quite apart from its histori- cal importance, the coup had a dramatic, thrilling, almost literary quality that lends itself well to storytelling."[3] Nevertheless, there is still more to say.

My purpose in this chapter is not to resolve historically relevant questions of blame or responsibility for the coup. Neither do I seek to investigate in depth the increasingly important role Iran played in U.S. foreign-policy formulation under Truman and Eisenhower. These issues, as well as the events of Operation Ajax, the decline of British imperialism in the Middle East, and domestic political strife in postwar Iran, have been extensively explored elsewhere. However, with all the attention Operation Ajax has received, no account has concentrated on the Eisenhower administration's rhetorical strategy for dealing with the coup and the interpretive role presidential rhetoric played in presenting the events in Iran to the American people. To accomplish this task Eisenhower and his subordinates adopted a strategy that I have labeled the rhetoric of misdirection.[4] Before delving into an analysis of this approach, a brief sketch of the rhetorical context is necessary.

Context in Iran: Background and Constraints

Postwar Iran possessed a stunning complexity borne from the country's long-held status as a site of tension between Russia and the West. Since the 1828 Treaty of Turkmenchay, Iran had increasingly ceased to operate independently and was instead a pawn in the "Great Game" between Britain and Russia for con- trol of Central Asia. Iran's imperial subjugation culminated in 1941 with "Operation Countenance," the undeclared invasion of the country by Soviet and British forces, whose purposes were to create supply routes for American lend-lease equipment to the eastern front, secure Iran's oil facilities, and end Iran's diplomatic flirtation with Germany. Reza Shah Pahlavi, ruler of Iran and a suspected Nazi sympathizer, was deposed in favor of his twenty-two-year-old son, Mohammed. Soviet troops occupied northern Iran; British (and, after 1942, American) forces controlled the south. The new shah met Churchill, Stalin, and FDR at the 1943 Tehran Conference, where the big three pledged to withdraw from Iran within six months after the conflict's end.[5]

Tensions quickly emerged among the occupying powers. Hoping to weaken the grip of their historic British and Russian enemies, the Iranians requested and received American police, military, and economic advisors. In the fall of 1944, a dispute over an oil concession erupted between the Iranians and the Soviets, who objected to the presence of U.S. oil companies in Iran. Deploying the Tudeh leftist party as a fifth column, the Soviets organized massive countrywide protests against the government. Only after the offending Iranian oil negotiators resigned and the United States explicitly stated its support for the Iranian government to the Kremlin (via a private letter delivered in Moscow by George Kennan to Vyacheslav Molotov) did the Tudeh-organized protests and roadblocks end. The event passed unremarked upon by President Roosevelt, and outside a few back-page news articles, the situation merited little attention in the United States.[6]

However, in a move that would further hasten the onset of the Cold War, Stalin violated his agreement with the Western allies to withdraw all troops from Iran by March 2, 1946. Soviet forces refused to leave Azerbaijan under the official guise of protecting the minorities there from Iranian oppression (and with the unofficial purpose of incorporating these provinces into the Soviet Union). Confronted by a major diplomatic challenge, Truman refused to publicly discuss the Soviet policy. When asked by reporters about Russian escalation in Iran, he repeatedly offered evasive answers, saying, "I only know about that from what I see in the papers, and I have no comment," and "That is a matter that will be handled when it comes up."[7] Nevertheless, the administration strongly backed the United Nations Security Council resolution demanding Soviet withdrawal by May 6. Secretary of State James Byrnes, who argued in favor of the resolution at the United Nations, in a March 16 address also stated, "The United States is committed to the support of the charter of the United Nations. Should the occasion arise, our military strength will be used to support the purpose and principles of the charter."[8] Partially in response to this intimated threat (and partially due to the difficulties they faced in consolidating power in Azerbaijan), the Soviets left Iran within the UN timetable. American aims were again achieved.

Although these two episodes were resolved rather quickly and without major incident, they pertain to Eisenhower's subsequent rhetoric in two ways. First, these episodes established Iran as a site of Cold War conflict and cemented in the minds of American policy makers the notion that the Tudeh Party answered directly to Communist leaders in Moscow—a mistaken idea but one that came to be accepted by Eisenhower and Dulles.[9] Second, in both the 1944 and the 1946 incidents the president did not publicly acknowledge what was at stake for the United States in Iran. By speaking so little on the subject, the president downplayed the importance of Iran in public while working actively to protect U.S. interests through private and diplomatic channels. Indeed, even Secretary Byrnes only framed the 1946 incident as an issue concerning the United States insofar as it validated the legitimacy of the United Nations. While this strategy worked to avoid an unnecessary escalation of tension between the United States and the Soviet Union, it also had the effect of masking the significance of U.S. interest in Iran to the American public.

At the same time, Operation Countenance and the ensuing Allied occupation of Iran also instigated a period of democratic upheaval in the country. Iran's main parliamentary body, the Majlis, had grown progressively more influential since its establishment under the Qajar Dynasty, and it served as the vehicle by which Reza Shah overthrew the Qajar Dynasty and seized power in the early 1920s. Under Reza Shah's increasingly dictatorial rule, the Majlis still held elections and formally held the power of passing the nation's laws.[10] The group convened in secret multiple times to discuss ways to revive its power, and once Reza Shah was removed by the Allies, the Majlis wasted little time in becoming the central power broker of Iranian politics.[11] The deliberative body, however, was less than representative, given to quarreling, and ultimately proved unable to form effective governments. In the decade 1941 to 1951, for example, seventeen cabinets were organized to govern Iran, most of which failed to last longer than a few months. Revolt, chaos, and general misrule prevailed through the years leading to the rise of Mossadegh; in fact, at one point a bounty was even offered on the front pages of a major newspaper for the assassination of a newly elected prime minister.[12]

To put the matter succinctly, the success of Mossadegh's National Front, a loose coalition of democratic constitutionalist nationalists, was fueled by its unyielding drive to eliminate foreign control over Iran's resources and politics. Mossadegh opposed oil concessions and advocated for free elections and a free press in the belief that these reforms would end British imperial domination of Iran, enabling truly democratic rule.[13] This platform was extremely popular. As the shah later wrote, "How could anyone be against Mossadegh? He would enrich everybody, he would fight the foreigner, he would secure our rights. No wonder students, intellectuals, people from all walks of life, flocked to his banner."[14] Thus on May 2, 1951, the same day Mossadegh became prime minister, the Majlis voted to nationalize the British-controlled Anglo-Iranian Oil Company and its plant at Abadan.

The details of the ensuing conflict between the British government, which challenged nationalization using legal, diplomatic, and economic means, and Iran, which was subject to a punitive economic boycott of its oil, are recorded elsewhere. Both sides sought total vindication, and both sides sought American support to that end. As the conflict progressed into the early Eisenhower presidency, however, several major factors emerged that constrained Ike's rhetorical and policy responses to the situation in Iran:

The Rhetoric (or Lack Thereof) of President Truman. While not constraining Eisenhower's range of action in a determinative sense—Ike was elected on a platform of change, after all, including a critique of the Truman administration's "little policy for the Middle East"—in reality Truman's rhetoric regarding Iran functioned to constrain the new president's ability to alter the situation.[15] By creating a discrepancy between Iran's perceived public significance and its significance to American policy makers, Truman bequeathed to Eisenhower a crisis in the making without having warned the American public that a crisis might occur. NSC 136/1, a new Iranian policy directive signed by Truman in late 1952, encapsulated the urgency with which U.S. security officials viewed Iran. It stated:

> It is of critical importance to the United States that Iran remain an independent and sovereign nation, not dominated by the USSR. Because of its key strategic position, its petroleum resources, its vulnerability to intervention or armed attack by the USSR, and its vulnerability to political subversion, Iran must be regarded as a continuing objective of Soviet expansion. . . . Present trends in Iran are unfavorable to the maintenance of control by a non-communist regime for an extended period of time. . . . Any US policy regarding Iran must accordingly take into account the danger that the communists might be enabled to gain the ascendency as a result of such possible developments as a struggle for power within the National Front, more effective communist infiltration of the government than now appears probable, government failure to maintain the security forces and to take effective action against communist activity, or a major crop failure.[16]

In the event of a successful Communist takeover of Iran, one of the goals of NSC 136/1 was "if possible, to bring about the overthrow of the communist regime" and to determine whether such an action constituted a general casus belli with the Soviet Union. Yet despite the magnitude of this policy for the collapse of Iran and the official prediction that such an event was more likely to occur than not, Truman said nothing to the public.

Truman's silence on Iran was emblematic of his Middle East rhetoric as a whole. On one hand the language of the Cold War suggested America's need to combat Communism *everywhere*. Truman articulated the global threat that Communist ideology posed, declaring that America had to be diligent in "helping free and independent nations to maintain their free institutions and their national integrity against aggressive movements that [sought] to impose upon them totalitarian regimes."[17] In Italy, Greece, Turkey, Berlin, Vietnam, and Korea, using guns, advisors, and rhetoric alike, Truman furiously waged the Cold War against the Communists. On the other hand outside of support for Israel and security guarantees for Turkey, this project of rhetorically expanding the United States' global responsibility had done little to undermine the Wilsonian status quo of the Middle East being publicly viewed as a primarily British area of responsibility.

This state of affairs left Eisenhower with difficult rhetorical options upon assuming office. He could inform the American people that Iran was a major priority over which the United States might start a world war—an unpalatable option given the recent stalemate in Korea and Ike's campaign promises to reduce defense spending. He could perpetuate Truman's silence. Or, like he did in the end, he could try to strike a middle path, with mixed results.

Eisenhower and Dulles's Conception of Containment. The Eisenhower administration sought to contain the Soviet Union while reducing defense expenditures. This necessitated relying on the threat of an asymmetrical nuclear response to deter Soviet aggression, meaning that any war with the Soviet Union was likely to be atomic—and therefore to be avoided at all costs. As early as 1948 Dulles declared, "All peoples must end any complacency about war and see it as it really is, namely, something which would engulf all of humanity in utter misery and would make almost impossible the achievement of the ends for which we would profess to be fighting."[18] Likewise, Stephen Ambrose notes that "Eisenhower realized that unlimited war in the nuclear age was unimaginable, and limited war unwinnable. This was the most basic of his strategic insights."[19] Because of the atomic implications of American defense strategy, both men greatly feared a tinderbox war breaking out into a larger conflict as in World War I.[20] Iran, as was little lost on Eisenhower, was a particularly dangerous tinderbox with the potential to ignite World War III, and therefore American strategy in that country had to be coordinated with minute care to avoid provoking a rash response from the Kremlin. Thus in addition to his other concerns, Eisenhower also had to bear in mind that U.S. actions in Iran, if too aggressive, could potentially start a global conflict.

The Need to Maintain Positive Relations with Britain. If forced to choose between Britain and Iran, there was little question that the United States would side with Britain. In addition to the "special relationship" that existed between the two nations, the United States needed the support of the still-considerable British Empire (which composed the world's third largest economy at the time) in order for containment to work in Europe, the Middle East, Africa, and Asia. Although not an enthusiast for British imperialism, America could ill afford to alienate its most important global ally in the Cold War. For this reason Truman chose to pursue a neutral policy with regard to the AIOC-Iran dispute over nationalization. However, the way in which Truman defined neutrality—refusing to grant any economic aid to Iran while the British-organized global embargo on Abadan's oil strangled the Iranian economy—clearly positioned the United States as implicitly on Britain's side. For Eisenhower this meant that any deviation from Truman's rhetorical and policy neutrality, even to prevent the collapse of the Mossadegh regime, would likely alienate London and threaten the allied coordination needed for containment to function (especially under the soon-to-come New Look strategy). U.S. ambassador to Iran Loy Henderson put it neatly in his report to the National Security Council on June 25: "It is impossible for the U.S. to give further aid to Iran at this time because of what it would do to our relations with the British."[21]

The Need to Maintain Positive Relations with Iran and the Third World. As with Britain the United States also needed to maintain the goodwill of the Iranians and the nonaligned nations at large. Ike knew that the Soviets sought to replace the governments of these countries with Communist regimes as they had done with the satellite states of Eastern Europe. However, he also realized they would not risk outright war to achieve this expansionist aim. As he wrote in a private letter, he thought the Russian strategy would be to advance "year by year, month by month, [the] Iron Curtain. . . . The hope of the Soviets [was] to attack each nation separately, beginning with the weaker ones."[22] Because military conflict would be suicidal, Eisenhower knew the Soviets were more likely to rely on subversion, coercion, and persuasion to expand their influence than open attempts at conquest.

Realizing that this meant American security rested on convincing other countries to reject Communism, Ike sought to practice what he called "psychological warfare." He defined this term in a 1952 campaign speech as simply "the struggle for the minds and wills of men."[23] "As a nation," Eisenhower exhorted his audience, "everything we say, everything we do, and everything we fail to say or do, will have its impact in other lands."[24] In other words American security now rested on its ability to win a public relations war with the Soviet Union. As Martin J. Medhurst explains,

> Eisenhower purposed not only to continue the Cold War that he had inherited from the Truman administration; he decided to win it, even though he was under no illusions that victory would come quickly or easily. Eisenhower understood that the nature of that war was essentially rhetorical—that is, that it was a war of words, images, perceptions, attitudes, motives and expectations. It was a war in which the battlefield was in the hearts and minds of people, both in America and throughout the world, especially in those areas ripe for communist exploitation because of poverty, internal turmoil, or political corruption.[25]

Eisenhower's belief that the Cold War was fundamentally psychological in nature—a belief accepted by most Americans by the mid-1950s—became all the more important when knowledge of Stalin's death became public on March 5, 1953. New Soviet leaders Georgi Malenkov and Lavrentiy Beria sought to soften Stalin's antagonistic foreign policy and launched what was deemed a "peace offensive" to win hearts and minds across

Europe, Africa, and Asia.[26] By deemphasizing Soviet military power, scaling back calls for global revolution, and articulating their desire for a permanent European peace settlement, the new Soviet leaders sought to split the Western alliance and frame the United States as a warmongering superpower. The result was, in the words of Walter LaFeber, "a new kind of Cold War."[27] In such a context popular opinion in the resource-rich Third World mattered even more. Because many of these nations were either current or recently freed colonies of Western European powers, there were few quicker ways for the United States to alienate them than by overtly supporting British imperialism. Thus for Eisenhower direct intervention in Iran or open support for the British were also unwise choices, as these decisions would risk undermining containment by driving nonaligned nations into Moscow's arms.

In light of these constraints, it is unsurprising that the Eisenhower administration chose to employ covert action to resolve the issue. Because the status quo was perilous and unsustainable—both NSC 136/1 and the 1952 CIA National Intelligence Estimate for Iran predicted the possibility of an eventual "breakdown of government authority" that would "open the way for at least a gradual assumption of control by [the] Tudeh"—action appeared necessary to preserve Iran's status as a Communist-free government.[28] Indeed, if Mossadegh himself was not perceived as a Communist sympathizer, he was at least seen as someone whose weakness might enable the Tudeh to achieve power. Yet any action undertaken by the United States in Iran could potentially alienate Britain, poison relations with the nonaligned nations, start a war with the Soviet Union, or do all three. Thus Ike's solution was to overthrow Mossadegh to secure Iran's anti-Communist status, but do so covertly to prevent the potential fallout from public knowledge of American intervention.[29]

Operation Ajax and the Rhetoric of Misdirection

The operational details of Ajax, from its birth as British-proposed Operation Boot to its consummation in the sun-drenched streets of Tehran, are recorded extensively in numerous volumes, including the official CIA history authored by Donald Wilber and Kermit Roosevelt's memoir *Countercoup: The Struggle for the Control of Iran*.[30] The main events are recorded in table 1. In terms of rhetoric, however, Eisenhower's decision to employ covert action to remove Mossadegh left him with a straightforward objective: conceal this fact. As Ike's biographers and the National Security Council archives demonstrate, Eisenhower was careful to leave little evidence for posterity that could tie him to the coup, receiving only oral briefings on Iran from CIA director Allen Dulles.[31] His public rhetoric was an extension and enlargement of this strategy as he sought to conceal America's role in Mossadegh's fall from power.

However, because major events were in play—the removal of a democratic government in a friendly, strategically vital, oil-rich country—Eisenhower could hardly expect to replicate Truman's tactic of rhetorically neglecting Iran. Moreover, Ike had attacked the Truman administration's ostensible neglect of the Middle East during the 1952 campaign. Thus rather than employ the prior administration's strategy of rhetorically *misleading* the public, which was a simple matter of devoting more attention to Iran in policy making than was admitted publicly, the Eisenhower administration prosecuted a strategy of rhetorical *misdirection*, which entailed incorporating the concealment of Operation Ajax into the administration's larger rhetorical strategy regarding the Middle East.[32] In effect the Eisenhower administration sought to draw attention to certain aspects of its Middle East policy while diverting suspicion away from its covert actions in Iran. This rhetorical strategy, Michael Martin notes, "contains a fundamental element of deception" in which "language is used simultaneously to reveal and conceal." The result is "an obfuscation of meaning" for the audience, which is invited to embrace the rhetor's professed explanation of reality while he withholds some additional element of significance.[33] For Ike that element was the CIA presence in Iran.

Many critics who study the rhetoric of misdirection have focused on the way this strategy can be used to subvert power hierarchies

Table 1. Events of Operation Ajax

Date	Event
May 2, 1951	Mossadegh sworn in as prime minister and the Iranian oil industry is nationalized
October 6–November 18, 1951	Mossadegh in the United States, visits White House
October 1952	Iran breaks off relations with Britain
November 1952	British officer C. M. Woodhouse proposes the removal of Mossadegh, codenamed Operation Boot
January 20, 1953	Mossadegh sends first telegram to Eisenhower
May 28, 1953	Mossadegh sends second telegram to Eisenhower
June 1953	Operation Ajax approved by high-level committee
July 11, 1953	Eisenhower and Dulles give final approval for Operation Ajax
August 5, 1953	Mossadegh wins plebiscite to rule by decree
August 8, 1953	Soviet Union announces financial aid package for Iran
August 12, 1953	Shah signs decree dismissing Mossadegh
August 15, 1953	First attempt to remove Mossadegh fails
August 17, 1953	Shah flees Iran
August 19, 1953	Second attempt to remove Mossadegh succeeds
August 22, 1953	Shah returns to Iran
September 1953	Iran receives $45 million U.S. aid package, more promised

or "discourse regimes." In addition to Martin's account, which explores Dietrich Bonhoeffer's interactions with his Gestapo interrogators, John Arthos Jr., L. W. Levine, and Michael Hardin investigate racial and colonial dimensions to the rhetoric of misdirection.[34] They and others allude to the "shaman-trickster," a traditional figure in many cultures who uses deception instead of strength to cleverly achieve his goals. Although Eisenhower's rhetoric differs greatly from the examples of misdirection given by these scholars, all these discourses possess commonality in that their rhetors employed the "inventive exploitation of indeterminacy" in pursuit of their objectives. That is, by intentionally introducing an element of ambiguity that is meant *not* to be perceived by the audience, Ike and these other rhetors strove to achieve their aims on the backs of their auditors' ignorance.

Ike's rhetoric similarly bears a functional resemblance to the corporatist rhetoric of misdirection studied by Mike Markel.[35] By seeking to project a certain image (America as an anti-imperial, benevolent good neighbor) while acting in a way contrary to that image, Eisenhower, like a corporation manipulating the nuances of a privacy agreement, used his position of influence to structure the discourse in a way that concealed the true activity taking place. Additionally Mary Stuckey's insight that "presidents both determine and reflect what (and who) is visible as well as what (and who) remains outside their national vision" applies to Eisenhower's Iran rhetoric: by emphasizing the United States' disinterested benevolence toward the Middle East, he rendered invisible that which he did not wish to be seen (Ajax) and directed the public's vision toward that which he did (increased American diplomatic overtures).[36]

Eisenhower's rhetoric of misdirection surrounding Operation Ajax had four component parts: distancing rhetoric, manipulation of the media, use of surrogates, and polyvalence. These elements worked tightly together to create a degree of strategic ambiguity that enabled the Eisenhower administration to assist in the overthrow of Mossadegh while avoiding the detrimental outcomes that overt intervention could have caused.

Distancing Rhetoric

Eisenhower's interaction with Mossadegh began before his assumption of the presidency. On January 7, 1953, he received a cable from the Iranian prime minister congratulating him on his electoral victory and exhorting the president-elect to provide much needed financial aid to Iran. Mossadegh began with an apology: "I dislike taking up with you the problems of my country even before you assume office." He then wrote:

> It is my hope that the new administration which you will head will obtain at the outset a true understanding of the significance of the vital struggle in which the Iranian people have been engaging and assist in removing the obstacles which are preventing them from realizing their aspirations for . . . life as a politically and economically independent nation. . . .
>
> It is not my desire that the relations between the United States and the United Kingdom should be strained because of differences with regard to Iran. I doubt however whether in this day and age a great nation which has such an exalted moral standing in the world can afford to support the internationally immoral policy of a friend and ally merely in order not to disturb good relations with that friend and ally. The Iranian people merely desire to lead their own lives in their own way.[37]

Eisenhower responded to this request noncommittally, stating that he would "study these views with care and with sympathetic concern."[38] From Mossadegh's view it was certainly a positive sign that Eisenhower responded promptly with a hand-drafted reply and assured the prime minister that he had "in no way compromised" his impartiality in the AIOC-Iran dispute.[39] Eisenhower's first inaugural address was likely also encouraging to Mossadegh, as Ike declared, "We Americans know and we observe the difference between world leadership and imperialism," the latter of which Mossadegh incessantly railed against.[40] However, this same speech in which Eisenhower enthusiastically reaffirmed America's spiritual and military commitment to East Asia, Europe, and the Western Hemisphere also conspicuously lacked any reference to Iran or the Middle East. As Mossadegh quickly learned, Eisenhower did not intend to significantly alter Truman's "neutral" policy anytime soon—not least because of

America's own oil interests overseas and the dangerous precedent that would be set by Iran's successful nationalization of a Western oil company's assets.

Although the existence of this original correspondence with Mossadegh became public knowledge in mid-1953, full details of its content were not made known until the publication of Ike's memoir *Mandate for Change* in 1963. In the intervening years, Eisenhower consistently used the language of observation to describe his relation to Mossadegh. In an April 1956 address Ike said, "The Iranian situation . . . only a few short years ago looked so desperate that each morning we thought we would wake up and read in our newspapers that Mossadegh had let them under the Iron Curtain," as if he, the president, were just as unable to change the situation as an ordinary citizen reading the morning paper.[41] Ike expressed similar sentiments as early as 1954, often lumping Iran in with other countries that after a period of uncertainty were "saved" from Communism by domestic actors.[42] The effect of this rhetoric was to distance Eisenhower and the country at large from Mossadegh, and the effort persisted even after the Eisenhower Doctrine speech in 1957. In trying to reinterpret the historical account of what happened—describing himself as simply reading the news about Iran, as if he did not have direct communication with and influence over Mossadegh—Eisenhower continued his rhetorical campaign of misdirection even until the end of his presidency.

This initial exchange of messages is also noteworthy because it established the tone for Ike and Mossadegh's next interaction. As in the first exchange, Mossadegh attempted to communicate directly with Eisenhower in the hope of persuading him to adopt policies friendly to Iran, and Eisenhower responded in a politically reserved statement. The second series of telegrams was initiated by Mossadegh on May 28, 1953, after negotiations continued to fail, little change was made in U.S. policy, and the economic effects of the British-organized boycott were beginning to precipitate a political crisis for the Iranian premier. By this time British and American planning for Operation Ajax was entering its final stages; work on the operation had begun in earnest following Anthony Eden's visit to the White House in March. Following a few introductory niceties and references to the January telegrams, Mossadegh cabled:

> Although it was hoped that during Your Excellency's administration attention of a more sympathetic character would be devoted to the Iranian situation, unfortunately no change seems thus far to have taken place in the position of the American Government. . . .
>
> We are of course grateful for the aid heretofore granted Iran by the Government of the United States. This aid has not, however, been sufficient to solve the problems of Iran and to ensure world peace which is the aim and ideal of the noble people and of the Government of the United States. . . .
>
> In conclusion, I invite Your Excellency's sympathetic and responsive attention to the present dangerous situation of Iran, and I trust that you will ascribe to all the points contained in this message the importance due them.[43]

As other commentators have noted, by characterizing the Iranian political situation as "dangerous" Mossadegh attempted to force Eisenhower's hand. If the situation was such that the government could collapse, then there existed the possibility of a Communist takeover. Thus, the thinking went, Eisenhower should provide aid to prevent such an eventuality. Furthermore, Moscow had begun taking preliminary steps to repair Russo-Iranian relations through the offer of economic aid. As the *New York Times* reported, "[Some believe that] Premier Mossadegh times his appeal for economic assistance to coincide with these Soviet gestures. He had hoped, according to this line of thought, to induce the United States to offer aid as a means of competing with, or forestalling, Soviet aid."[44]

Unfortunately for Mossadegh the Eisenhower administration reacted in the exact opposite of the way he intended. While his letter certainly confirmed suspicions that Iran's government was in danger of collapse or Communist manipulation, Ike's reaction was not to provide aid for Mossadegh but instead to push forward with the covert plan to replace him. Unlike in the first exchange, Eisenhower waited a considerable amount of time before replying, giving the appearance of cool deliberation. When he did respond on July 9, his answer was widely reported in the U.S. media as having "stunned" the Iranian government:[45]

> The Government and people of the United States historically have cherished and still have deep feelings of friendliness for Iran and the Iranian people. . . .
>
> The failure of Iran and of the United Kingdom to reach an agreement with regard to compensation has handicapped the Government of the United States in its efforts to help Iran. . . . It would not be fair to the American taxpayers for the United States Government to extend any considerable amount of economic aid to Iran so long as Iran could have access to funds derived from the sale of its oil and oil products if a reasonable agreement were reached. . . .
>
> I fully understand that the Government of Iran must determine for itself which foreign and domestic policies are likely to be most advantageous to Iran and to the Iranian people. In what I have written, I am not trying to advise the Iranian Government on its best interests. I am merely trying to explain why, in the circumstances, the Government of the United States is not presently in a position to extend more aid to Iran or to purchase Iranian oil.[46]

Eisenhower made two major argumentative moves in his telegram. First, he established that his decision to deny Mossadegh aid was borne not from American animosity toward Iran but instead was due to the failure of Mossadegh to reach an agreement with the British. By blaming Iran for the negotiations' failure—despite the British displaying a sizable amount of intransigence themselves—Ike exonerated Whitehall from any wrongdoing and in so doing created a convenient scapegoat for the worsening crisis. Second, if the failure of negotiations was Iran's fault, then the United States was not obliged to help the country. Such aid would "not be fair" to the American taxpayer and would be "unwise."[47] Thus Eisenhower declared that additional aid would not be forthcoming.

This response can be read through the metaphor of the good neighbor. Unlike the good neighbor, who would respond positively to the request for aid, Ike instead counseled Mossadegh on how his predicament was the inevitable result of his own decisions— and how a strategic failure on Iran's part was not sufficient reason for American economic aid. The enthymematic premise of such a stance is that the United States *really did not* have anything to do with Iran's situation and truly was an observer of, not an actor in, the situation. Regardless of whether one considers America partially responsible for Iran's desperation, Ike's rhetoric worked to promote a conception of the United States as a distinctly neutral party. This positioning of America as an outsider can also be seen in Ike's conclusion: "I note the concern reflected in your letter at the present dangerous situation in Iran and sincerely hope that before it is too late, the Government of Iran will take such steps as are in its power to prevent a further deterioration of that situation."[48] Eisenhower's language was like that of a friend offering guidance at an alcoholic intervention; his letter reflected both amicable earnestness and the firm belief that Iran's present course would lead to destruction. Most of all Ike's language indicated that the onus for solving the present crisis rested not with the United States, or even the United Kingdom, but belonged to Iran.

Throughout his reply to Mossadegh, Eisenhower positioned America as an outside observer completely independent of the situation. As rhetorician Richard Gregg notes of Ike's later rhetoric, Eisenhower used selective presentation of the facts, bracketing of important issues, and an assertion of American innocence to create distance between the United States and himself on one end and a crisis situation on the other.[49] Eisenhower employed distancing rhetoric in a similar fashion here. He presented Tehran's impending economic troubles as predominantly the fault of Iran, declared that American friendship with Iran was a separate issue from providing economic aid, and asserted that the crisis was not the responsibility of the United States. As such Ike's rhetoric preserved the image of America as a benevolently disinterested power in the Middle East, distancing the United States from any culpability in the current state of affairs and rendering U.S. intervention in Iran a farfetched notion.

Manipulation of the Media

In addition to his cable exchanges with Mossadegh, Eisenhower also spoke about Iran during his weekly press conferences. Again Ike gave no impression whatsoever to the American public that the United States was involved in Iran. During the planning phase for Ajax, Ike told reporters, "Our whole Government watches this [Iran situation] with the closest attention. It is a very delicate situation, and since it is an internal one, there is little that any outsider can do, even when they intend to be very helpful." He even went so far as to say, "In any country where a Communist Party is recognized, for them it is an internal situation. . . . it is an internal situation, no matter where the inspiration for the Tudeh Party comes from."[50] Although Eisenhower discussed Iran sparingly throughout the year, his other utterances resemble these; he consistently portrayed America as an outside observer and Iran as a nation at risk.[51]

As presidential scholars Meena Bose and Fred Greenstein note, Eisenhower often used his press conferences to manipulate the American mass media.[52] By avoiding direct answers he created strategic ambiguity and preserved his personal popularity; his dissembling prose, according to *New York Times* columnist Arthur Krock, was one in which "numbers and genders collide, participles hang helplessly and syntax is lost forever."[53] Ike quite simply did not deliver hard truths in question-and-answer format before reporters. In sharp contrast to the logical rigor of his personal communication or the everyman eloquence of his public addresses, Eisenhower's press conferences were often muddled and confusing—which, Bose and Greenstein point out, was precisely the point. When dealing with the media, Eisenhower let slip *exactly* the information he wished to be known, and he often did so in a way that avoided firm policy stances or needless attacks on opponents.

These same practices can be observed in Eisenhower's press conferences dealing with Iran. In a circuitous manner Eisenhower conveyed important information. He defined Iran as meriting "the closest attention" for the United States, making clear that the country was a foreign-policy priority (thus avoiding a potential miscommunication like Dean Acheson's infamous "defensive perimeter" statement regarding Korea). Eisenhower also mentioned that he wished to find a resolution to the conflict, thus implicitly declaring the status quo unacceptable. His language indicated that America was unlikely to get involved directly, since "there [was] little that any outsider [could] do, even when they intend[ed] to be very helpful." Such a statement likely put at ease the American public, which at the time still restively awaited a resolution to the Korean War. Last, Ike let slip that since it was an "internal" matter, America did not consider the possible assumption of power by the Tudeh to be a casus belli. In doing so he downplayed the perceived threat that a Communist Iran would be to U.S. security policy makers and reassured countries that feared a new American imperialism.

Overall, by characterizing the Iranian situation as "internal" and positioning the United States as an "outsider," Eisenhower employed evasive language to *appear* as though he had ruled out American intervention while not categorically rejecting this option. By this action Eisenhower deftly evaded firmly answering the questions of reporters while still communicating salient information to his audiences. This rhetorical maneuvering constituted but one dimension of the Eisenhower administration's manipulation of the media, however, as much was also occurring behind the scene.

When Eisenhower appointed Allen Welsh Dulles (brother of Secretary of State John Foster Dulles) as director of Central Intelligence on February 26, 1953, he ushered in what some have called "the golden years of the CIA's clandestine war against the Soviets."[54] Indeed, during the Eisenhower presidency Allen Dulles would oversee not only Operation Ajax but also covert American interventions in Guatemala, Congo, Egypt, Syria, and many other countries. One of the ways in which Dulles's CIA fought the Cold War's "war of words" was to infiltrate and establish media outlets, publishing houses, radio programs, news stations, and art institutions. By creating voices independent of the United States Information Agency (the official propaganda arm of the U.S. government), the CIA was able to effectively participate in the global campaign of persuasion with the veneer of objectivity. This Kulturkampf was all-encompassing; as Francis Stonor Saunders notes, "Whether they liked it or not, whether they knew it or not, there were few writers, poets, artists, historians, scientists or critics in post-war Europe whose names were not in some way linked to this covert enterprise."[55]

Like Europe Iran was also a major site of psychological warfare. While much of this effort was designed to lay the groundwork for the August coup—namely, a mass propaganda campaign involving religious leaders, media outlets, forged documents, "spontaneous" demonstrations, and false flag terrorist attacks—the Eisenhower administration's propaganda effort also entangled American media outlets in its disinformation campaign.[56] As Kenneth Osgood points out, the State Department worked to inspire the publication of editorials in U.S. media outlets regarding Iran to convey "certain points of view" and for the "benefit" of the American public at large. State Department officials also reworked propaganda materials originally meant for distribution in Iran and gave them to sympathetic journalists in America.[57] In contrast to 1951, in which *Time* named Mossadegh person of the year, many of the articles published by major American media outlets in 1953 used these adapted materials and therefore portrayed the Iranian leader as despotic, eccentric, or sympathetic to Communism.[58] Hence, whether the result of CIA infiltration, State Department suggestion, or reporters acquiescing to the culturally accepted wisdom on the matter, the American media largely fulfilled the Eisenhower administration's wishes regarding their coverage of Iran—the sitting government was shown in a negative light and America was nowhere to be seen. Mossadegh, for example, was routinely referred to as a "dictator" in the pages of the *New York Times*, a title the paper never bestowed on the shah during his twenty-five years of authoritarian rule after Operation Ajax.[59]

In 2000 the *New York Times* released an analysis of the American media's role in the Iran coup, and this study reinforced the conclusions drawn here.[60] First, although none of the reporters at major American newspapers who covered the events of the coup worked directly for the CIA, these same journalists chose to conceal the presence of CIA agents in Iran. While these reporters "filed straightforward, factual dispatches" regarding the August upheaval, they also "prominently mentioned the role of Iran's Communists" in creating street violence and "never reported that some of the unrest had been stage-managed by C.I.A. agents posing as Communists." In other cases reporters simply did not mention their CIA sources. By failing to disclose these facts, the media preserved Eisenhower's depiction of the coup as an internal event in which the United States was not involved.

Second, the report also shows that major U.S. media outlets published CIA-supplied material or used such material in their reporting. In one instance, according to the report, the CIA was able to put on the news wire an article that the CIA itself had written by using its contacts at the Associated Press. In another case a CIA study was placed in *Newsweek* by "using the normal channel of desk officer to journalist," one of "several planted press reports" that U.S. media outlets disseminated. Although the *New York Times* report downplayed the success rate of these attempts, by its own admission the intelligence agencies of the Eisenhower administration were at least somewhat effective in planting news directed at American audiences.

Third, American media sources toned down accurate reports from Iranian and Russian-based news outlets that revealed the American role in Mossadegh's downfall. In the prelude to the coup, Western correspondents in Iran devoted little attention to reports in Iranian newspapers and on Moscow radio claiming that the United States and Britain were secretly arranging the shah's return to power. Little changed following Operation Ajax's completion. While some newspapers did publish articles from Moscow reporting Russian *claims* that America was behind the coup, in the words of the report, "Neither The Times nor other American news organizations appear to have examined such charges seriously." Kennett Love, the *New York Times* reporter based in Tehran during the events of the coup, later wrote in a private letter to that newspaper's foreign editor, "The only instance since I joined The Times in which I have allowed policy to influence a strict news approach was in failing to report the role our own agents played in the overthrow of Mossadegh." By not reporting the CIA presence, Love enabled the Eisenhower administration's manipulation of the media to succeed: the image of America as a benevolently neutral party regarding Iran was maintained, and few in the West suspected American involvement in Mossadegh's demise.

Use of Surrogates

While Eisenhower used distancing rhetoric and manipulated the media to conceal America's involvement in the goings-on in Iran, the active element of his misdirection strategy was executed through the use of surrogates. As counterintelligence specialists Michael Bennett and Edmund Waltz note, "misdirection directs the audience's attention towards the effect and away from the method that produces it."[61] Under this definition Ike's distancing rhetoric and media manipulation worked to draw attention away from the chosen "method" of covert operations. Like all good purveyors of misdirection, however, Eisenhower still needed to focus the audience's attention on something else, and his administration chose to emphasize the renewed diplomatic importance of the Middle East to American Cold War strategy. To accomplish this task, Ike turned to one of his favorite strategies: rhetorical surrogacy.

As others have noted, in both the 1952 and the 1956 presidential elections Ike's rhetorical strategy was to unleash Nixon to make the "hard-hitting partisan speeches" while Eisenhower stayed above the fray.[62] Such tactics were clearly effective, as Eisenhower remained widely popular despite the progressively worsening political climate for the Republican Party throughout his presidential tenure. As Eisenhower's surrogate Nixon absorbed criticism from the press and the public but allowed his boss to remain untainted by partisan politics. This example was typical of Eisenhower's leadership style, in which Ike selectively used publicity to create a genteel public image while relying on mediators to communicate ideas—even within his own cabinet.[63]

In a way similar to his use of Nixon, Eisenhower relied on Secretary of State Dulles to be the face of the administration regarding foreign policy. While Ike certainly delegated to Dulles a large degree of authority, for decades most observers assumed that Dulles was the senior partner in their relationship. Though it *appeared* so to the public, this was not the case. Eisenhower spoke daily with Dulles in person, on the telephone, or via coded cables if either man was abroad. After consultation it was Ike who determined the course of action but Dulles who was the publicly visible executor of American foreign policy. A comparable tactic was used in their press conferences. Dulles met with the press on Tuesdays, introduced new policies, and often went into great detail while dialoguing with reporters. In contrast Eisenhower spoke to the press on Wednesdays, using broad language and commonsense expressions, giving the impression that Dulles was the real foreign-policy expert in the administration. In reality all of Dulles's Tuesday utterances were cleared by Eisenhower beforehand.[64]

In the case of Iran, Eisenhower used Dulles and Ambassador Henderson as his primary surrogates. On May 9, after major planning for Operation Ajax was already under way, Dulles departed on a highly publicized three-week tour of the Middle East. His official purpose for going on the trip was threefold: (1) to promote the concept of a Middle East security arrangement designed to prevent Communist penetration of the region, (2) to meet the leaders of the region in person, and (3) to publicize the new administration's more evenhanded approach toward the Arab states and Israel. Although Dulles returned having concluded few official agreements, his trip helped lay the groundwork for future U.S. policy in the region. The trip also emphasized the Eisenhower administration's break with Truman's foreign policy, which in Dulles's estimation had "gone overboard in favor of Israel."[65]

More importantly, however, Dulles's trip received extensive media attention. Scores of articles in major newspapers, magazines, and radio news programs reported Dulles's meetings, statements, and travels from Cairo to Karachi. In drawing attention to the administration's diplomatic efforts in the Middle East, Dulles focused both the media and the public on the administration's recalibration of policy in the region—and away from any potential suspicion regarding American practices in Iran. He was apparently successful in this regard. The *New York Times* ran an editorial upon his return; it stated, "The American stake in the Middle East is great for the first time in our history. We can even call it vital, when peace, defense, oil and other factors are taken into account."[66] Tellingly, no mention was made of Iran, Mossadegh, or the ongoing crisis in the article. The newspaper also reprinted in its entirety a speech Dulles gave upon his return. Out of the address's fifty-six paragraphs, only two mentioned Iran. His summation was succinct and effectively channeled Ike's tone and message: "It's our policy on the part of the United States to avoid any unwanted interference in the oil dispute, but we can usefully continue technical aid."[67] In other words nothing had changed, but the United States still wished for friendly relations with Britain and Iran.

Although Dulles was the primary surrogate, Henderson, who was considered "one of the outstanding officers of the Foreign Service," also played a role in Ike's rhetoric of misdirection.[68] He and his embassy staff worked to publish articles in *Newsweek*, the *New York Times*, and *Time* magazine (which they could then show their Iranian counterparts) emphasizing the need for Iran to settle the dispute with Britain.[69] Henderson also accompanied Dulles on part of his Middle East tour, and he advised the Eisenhower administration on some technical aspects of Operation Ajax. Most significantly he was the visible face of the United States in Iran following the coup, granting interviews, issuing statements, and negotiating the new aid deal with Iran.[70] Like Dulles Henderson's presence and rhetoric worked to focus the media and public's attention on the diplomatic dimensions of America's relationship with Iran, thereby diverting suspicion away from any covert activity.

Polyvalence

Finally, it is necessary to note that Eisenhower's rhetoric depended on a certain level of strategically ambiguous polyvalence in order to successfully misdirect his audiences. Unlike polysemy—"a condition in which there are more than one denotative readings of a text"—polyvalence can be defined as a situation in which there is a shared understanding as to the denotative meaning of the text but an attitudinal difference with regard to its character.[71] In other words all of Eisenhower's audiences understood that he was not offering additional aid to Iran and that the United States considered Iran important; each of his audiences differed, however, in the ways in which they interpreted the meaning of this information. While the Eisenhower administration clearly articulated that Iran was a foreign-policy priority, did that mean, for example, that Ike and Dulles would potentially start World War III to prevent it from becoming a Communist state? Eisenhower's rhetoric seemed to leave this an open question. The Soviets, based on their prior experiences in Iran with Britain and the United States, probably thought so and ultimately chose not to find out. Many Americans, on the other hand, would have likely considered such an option unthinkable. Eisenhower's strategic use of rhetoric allowed for these polyvalent readings of his statements to play out, as his ambiguity created room for these divergent interpretations.

In short the Eisenhower administration anticipated how its audiences would respond to the rhetoric of misdirection by utilizing intentionally vague language. To take one instance, when Eisenhower stated in his second letter to Mossadegh that he and the American people "sincerely hope[d] that Iran [would] be able to maintain its independence and that the Iranian people [would] be successful in realizing their national aspirations and in developing a contented and free nation," his separate audiences likely understood this message in differing ways. To the American public Eisenhower was merely reaffirming American goodwill toward a Middle Eastern country and articulating a general intention to maintain a friendly relationship, as Dulles had done many times on his trip. Churchill and Eden, with the benefit of knowledge about Operation Ajax, likely focused on the contingency of Ike's words: Americans "hope" Iran could be content and could realize its national ambitions; Eisenhower said nothing about *ensuring* such an outcome. The Soviets, whose interest in Iran was driven by security considerations, were predisposed to hear Eisenhower's emphasis on the language of freedom. Ike expressed the American desire for Iran to be a "free" and "independent" country. Since Iran was neither free from nor independent of Western influence (and to Soviet eyes American involvement in Iran was merely another form of imperialism anyway), Ike's language was likely interpreted as a being directed against any increase of Communist influence in Iran. Thus to the Kremlin this statement could be read as a veiled threat.

The point is not that different audiences interpret a rhetorical performance differently—that much is obvious—but that Eisenhower used rhetoric in such a way as to encourage polyvalent interpretations of his words. By employing strategic ambiguity Eisenhower and his subordinates allowed their audiences' biases and psychological predispositions to create divergent readings of their rhetoric. This use of polyvalence, when considered alongside the Eisenhower administration's distancing rhetoric, manipulation of the media, and use of surrogates, created enough misdirection to enable the successful covert execution of Operation Ajax. Just as Kermit Roosevelt later recounted, the result of this rhetorical strategy could be summarized in one word: "triumph."[72]

After Ajax: A New Status Quo

Taken as a whole Operation Ajax and the Eisenhower administration's rhetoric of misdirection can be seen as having established a new status quo in American policy and rhetoric regarding the Middle East. In an unprecedented step the United States had directly intervened in the affairs of a Middle Eastern nation by facilitating a coup d'état against Mossadegh. Although American policy makers had increasingly taken the Middle East into account since the early Truman administration, the decision to topple Mossadegh clearly marked a new stage in America's relationship to the region in terms of policy. Yet at the same time, Eisenhower's rhetoric of misdirection worked to conceal the dramatic lengths to which the United States would go to maintain its security objectives—as dictated by the Cold War—in the Middle East. Though Dulles's and Ike's rhetoric worked to emphasize the growing importance of America's relationship with the region, their efforts were couched in the language of economic development, technical aid, and diplomatic goodwill, not military intervention. The true nature of the coup was concealed from the American electorate while other dimensions of the Eisenhower administration's Middle East policy were made salient through public discourse. The success of this rhetorical strategy, as I see it, led to two primary effects.

First, the success of Eisenhower's rhetoric of misdirection resulted in a disparity of knowledge surrounding Operation Ajax between the Iranian and American populations. While many Americans did not know about their government's involvement in the 1953 coup until the 1970s (especially following the 1979 revolution), the method of the shah's restoration left a lasting pall over his legitimacy in his own country. As the *Economist* noted in 1973, "Even after 20 years, the ghost of Mossadegh, the politician who laid claim to the mantle of Iranian nationalism and outbid the Arabs in challenging the West, still haunts the Shah."[73] The coup seriously affected many Iranians' view of the United States—and continues to do so, as demonstrated by Hassan Rouhani—yet many Americans even today are not aware of this episode. Their ignorance of Ajax is a testament to the lasting success of the Eisenhower administration's rhetoric of misdirection.

Second, and more pertinent to the interest of this study, the successful execution of rhetorical misdirection by the Eisenhower administration promoted an understanding of containment that was functional within the British imperial paradigm in the Middle East. By maintaining a "neutral" position that effectively supported the British boycott and then providing aid only once the oil concession was restored at Iranian expense (not to mention overthrowing a government after being asked by MI6 for assistance), Eisenhower communicated that the British Empire, for all its unseemliness, was reconcilable with the United States' overarching Cold War objective: containment of the Soviet Union.

Furthermore, although the United States was rapidly assuming the role of senior partner in the region, Ike's preference for covert action and misdirection meant that the public was largely unaware of the extent to which Washington had displaced Whitehall as the dominant power in the Middle East. Eisenhower continued to characterize America's role in the region as that of a neutral arbitrator between the Arab states and Israel—"all of whom," he assured his fellow citizens, "we want as our friends"—without mentioning America's anti-Communist covert activism or questioning British hegemony in the region.[74] In doing so he established a new rhetorical status quo for the region: containment, but containment in concert with the British Empire. This depiction was far from economic or political reality. As the writers of NSC 136/1 announced as early as 1952, "It is clear that the United Kingdom no longer possesses the capability unilaterally to assure stability in the area," and it was in no small part due to American support—as demonstrated by Operation Ajax—that the British were still nominally considered the main global power in the Middle East.[75] This tension between perception and reality, fueled in large part by Eisenhower's rhetoric of misdirection, would continue throughout Ike's first term until its eventual dissolution at Suez.

Operation Ajax and the rhetoric of misdirection born from it were a success: the shah replaced Mossadegh, a showdown with Russia was avoided, the American public was kept in the dark, and a new oil concession was signed (this time with an equal share going to the United Kingdom and the United States). Eisenhower successfully navigated the various constraints presented by the Iranian oil dispute in the shadow of a Cold War that was taking on increasingly psychological dimensions. He and his administration accomplished this task through distancing rhetoric, manipulation of the media, the use of surrogates, and polyvalence. However, this strategy of misdirection also maintained the rhetorical norm of treating the region as a primarily British area of interest and was therefore misleading regarding the nature of American power in the Middle East. As will be shown in the next chapter, Ike's rhetorical misdirection established during Operation Ajax evolved into a repeated pattern of deceptive and surreptitious rhetoric over the course of his first term, with mixed results for American policy aims. In short the new rhetorical status quo not only deceived the American public but also Britain and France, setting the Western powers on a collision course for an eventual showdown at Suez. Before this far more visible—and far more dangerous—test of containment, however, the Eisenhower administration would first learn the difficulties of maintaining containment in a region aflame with Arab nationalism.

3

From Baghdad to Cairo

The Limits of Rhetorical Surreption

In the past we had good relations with the Arab peoples. . . . Today the
Arab peoples are afraid that the United States will back the new state of
Israel in aggressive expansion. They are more fearful of Zionism than
they are of communism and they fear the United States, lest
we become the backer of expansionist Zionism.

—John Foster Dulles, television broadcast to the nation, June 2, 1953

No Englishman living in Iraq can remain unmoved as he sees a
horde of highly paid American experts sweeping into a country
whose traditional ties are with ourselves and hears them denigrating
all that Britain has done here in the past and is attempting to do in
the present. . . . Even though we cannot hope to restore our former
exclusive position in Iraq, there should be a great future for us.
I only trust that we shall be able to work it out in harmony
with our American allies.

—Sir John Troutbeck, British ambassador to Baghdad, December 20, 1954

We know that there is abroad in the world a fierce and growing spirit
of nationalism. Should we try to dam it up completely, it would, like
a mighty river, burst through the barriers and could create havoc. But
again, like a river, if we are intelligent enough to make constructive use
of this force, then the result, far from being disastrous, could redound
greatly to our advantage, particularly in our struggle
against the Kremlin's power.

—Eisenhower, letter to Winston Churchill, July 22, 1954

By the end of his first year in office, Ike could look to many clear accomplishments. Domestically, he had drastically trimmed federal spending on defense, fought off any immediate tax cut, and passed a law increasing immigration quotas from Eastern Europe. In foreign relations Eisenhower and Dulles had successfully negotiated the end of the Korean War and ended Spain's postwar isolation under Franco through the Pact of Madrid, beginning that nation's reintegration with the West. However, as with Operation Ajax each of these decisions was made in consideration of the growing rivalry with the Soviet Union. For example the policy to resettle more refugees, while a humanitarian gesture, also allowed the United States to gain from the skills, labor, and intelligence provided by a quarter million former Communist subjects in addition to providing a propaganda coup.

Likewise the armistice in Korea worked to confirm America's global peaceful intent so eloquently elaborated on three months prior in Eisenhower's "Chance for Peace" speech. As he put it, "Every gun that is made, every warship launched, every rocket fired, signifies, in the final sense, a theft from those who hunger and are not fed, those who are cold and are not clothed."[1] These words, backed up by the United States' signing of the Korean cease-fire, rhetorically functioned to successfully belie Soviet accusations of American warmongering and allow Ike to seize the mantle of peace—U.S. intelligence went so far as to declare it "one of the most effective messages for world-wide impact since World War II."[2] In short the Cold War, including its rhetorical dimensions, only grew in importance to the Eisenhower administration as Ike's first term progressed.

This period of rhetorical escalation of the Cold War coincided with an era of extreme political turmoil in the Middle East: governments fell, heads of state were assassinated, and multiple wars of independence began. However, the basic rhetorical strategy established by the Eisenhower administration during Operation Ajax did not significantly change: Eisenhower continued to downplay American involvement in the Middle East publicly while still attempting to secure U.S. interests in the region through covert or indirect means. By placing Eisenhower's Middle East rhetoric and policy in its Cold War context and analyzing his administration's various attempts to uphold Soviet containment through a myriad of means, I hope in this chapter to show the limitations of this rhetorical approach.

A Rhetorical Cold War

In terms of presidential rhetoric, Eisenhower produced the majority of his most memorable campaigns and speeches in the years 1952–56. From his first inaugural address onward, Eisenhower consistently articulated a Manichaean view of the world. In his first utterance as president, Ike set America and its allies—described as "we who are free"—in contrast to the Soviet Communists, who knew "no god but force, no devotion but its use. . . . Whatever defie[d] them, they torture[d], especially the truth." The tone was set. In this speech and others, Eisenhower employed rhetoric as an instrument of psychological warfare to convince Americans, allies, and nonaligned nations alike "that forces of good and evil [were] massed and armed and opposed as rarely before in history."[3] In doing so he hoped to secure allegiances and alliances across the globe while denying the same to the Soviet Union.

As he had done with the "Chance for Peace" and his first inaugural address, Eisenhower continued to give high-profile speeches about the United States, Communism, peace, and the Cold War as his presidency progressed. These rhetorical performances, as Ira Chernus, Kenneth Osgood, and others note, often inaugurated massive propaganda campaigns by which the United States sought to influence public opinion (both foreign and domestic) in an increasingly globalized, increasingly psychological project of containment.[4] Case in point: Eisenhower's "Atoms for Peace" address given before the UN General Assembly on December 8, 1953, was disseminated and discussed on an incredible scale, in no small part thanks to the global reach of American propaganda. As United States Information Agency (USIA) director Theodore Streibert stated, "Never before in history have the words of the President of the United States been so widely disseminated to all peoples of the earth."[5] The speech was indeed circulated widely. Major newspapers in twenty-five nations reprinted the speech in full, films of the address were dispatched to thirty-five countries, five million reprints of the speech were circulated in the United States in leaflet form, and the USIA distributed sixteen million posters and booklets promoting the speech globally. Other government agencies got in on the act, with the postal service even sponsoring a contest to design a stamp publicizing "Atoms for Peace." Hundreds of private organizations—including Universal Pictures, which developed a documentary dedicated to Ike's proposal and translated it into forty-one languages—and multiple government ministries actively promoted the speech. News organizations across the country voiced their support for Eisenhower, and *Newsweek* bluntly labeled the address "a great psychological victory."[6] "Atoms for Peace" was, in short, a global propaganda offensive of a scope unprecedented in American history.

"Atoms for Peace," while exemplifying Eisenhower's Cold War rhetorical strategy more fully than perhaps any other single address, was hardly the only such endeavor to harness the power of presidential rhetoric for the purposes of shaping global and domestic opinion. Eisenhower and his subordinates continued to wage "psychological warfare" throughout his first administration, their efforts manifested in campaigns such as the "New Look" defense strategy or the "Open Skies" proposal. While varying in scope, scale, subject, and delivery, all of the Eisenhower administration's rhetoric—from major addresses to weekly press conferences—coalesced around a singular purpose: to wage the Cold War. Or as Martin J. Medhurst puts it,

Eisenhower operated from the premise that "The future shall belong to the free." Far from merely announcing this sentiment, Ike set about to make it a reality. Foremost among Eisenhower's weapons in this war was rhetorical discourse—"discourse intentionally designed to achieve a particular goal with one or more specific audience." . . .

For Eisenhower, rhetoric was a weapon with which to wage Cold War. Too often, scholars write about the Cold War as though the crucial component is to be found in the adjective. To Ike, the Cold War was not first and foremost "cold," it was first and foremost "war," though a kind of war requiring special means.[7]

And indeed a rhetorical war it was. Nikita Khrushchev, who by the end of Ike's first term had consolidated control of the Politburo, proved just as adept a propagandist as Eisenhower. He shrewdly supported Ghanaian leader Kwame Nkrumah and the Congo's Patrice Lumumba, both of whom thundered against their nations' former European colonial masters as well as their "American protectors," and he later "discovered" and adopted Fidel Castro's Cuban revolution. Khrushchev consistently branded the United States a "warmongering" superpower intent on dominating the world in the mold of Britain or France.[8] In doing so he positioned the Soviet Union as an anti-imperialist champion, exposed America's alliance with Britain and France as a propaganda Achilles heel, and put the United States on the psychological defensive in the rapidly growing postcolonial world.[9] In sum over the course of Eisenhower's first presidential term, the rhetorical dimensions of the Cold War became increasingly important as the battle for hearts and minds around the world—and the natural resources, diplomatic leverage, and military power they represented—intensified.

The Middle East: Decolonization, Coups, and War

Given that few regions were as much affected by decolonization or were in as much political turmoil as the Middle East during Eisenhower's first term, it is unsurprising that the region quickly became a central—and volatile—front in the Cold War. Along the

Nile an army cabal known as the Free Officers Movement, including the high-ranking General Mohammad Naguib, deposed King Farouk I on July 23, 1952. This group of mostly junior officers' seizure of power not only ridded Egypt of its British-installed monarch but also inspired nationalist movements in neighboring states ruled by Europeans or European-backed monarchs. After winning a power struggle with Naguib, Colonel Gamal Abdel Nasser emerged as Egyptian premier and rose as a swaggering symbol of pan-Arab nationalism across the Middle East. As a political philosophy, by early 1955 Nasser's pan-Arab nationalism came to have four primary emphases: (1) the idea that Arabs were a single people sharing a common destiny, (2) the need for Arab nations to rid themselves of all vestiges of European imperialism and colonialism, (3) the need for domestic social and economic justice, including in Egypt's case land reform and nationalization of certain industries, and (4) nonalignment in the Cold War.[10] While pan-Arabism was ideologically attractive to Middle Easterners for a number of reasons, much of its appeal stemmed from its repudiation of the European presence in the region.

In Jordan and Iraq Hashemite monarchies struggled to contain restive nationalist movements of their own. Many opponents of the British-backed monarchies were inspired by Nasser's "Voice of the Arabs" radio program, which in early 1954 announced, "The Voice of the Arabs speaks for the Arabs, struggles for them and expresses their unity," and Egypt "[is] in the service of the Arab nation and its struggle against Western imperialism and its lackeys in the Arab world."[11] In Jordan especially unrest reigned. Besides the inherent tensions of existence as a British client state, Amman also faced the unique challenge of establishing its rule over the West Bank and East Jerusalem (territory that was supposed to have been part of a Palestinian state after the 1948 Arab-Israeli War). King Abdullah I forcibly annexed this territory, evoking the displeasure of other Arab states, and extended Jordanian citizenship to its Palestinian residents; rather than weaken and eventually eradicate an independent Palestinian national identity, as Abdullah intended, these moves inflamed Palestinian nationalist sentiment. These pressures exploded on July 20, 1951, when a Palestinian dissident assassinated Abdullah while he prayed at the Al-Aqsa mosque in Jerusalem. Adding to the political turmoil, Talal I, Abdullah's son, inherited the crown but abdicated after a year due to a mental condition. As a result the seventeen-year-old son of Talal, Hussein I, assumed the throne as the Eisenhower presidency began, beginning his long struggle to consolidate control over his restive domain.

Meanwhile, bloody raids between Israeli forces and Palestinian fedayeen based in Egypt, Jordan, and Syria became common, with both sides committing atrocities and massacring civilian populations. While their intensity ebbed and flowed, these cross-border attacks continued throughout Ike's first term, reaching a high point in October 1953 with the Israeli annihilation of the West Bank town of Qibya. Making matters worse Israel violated the Tripartite Agreement of 1950 by secretly purchasing weapons from France, all while Britain continued to arm and train the Jordanian military—thus transforming the Levant into a potential powder keg in which Britain and France would be supplying opposite sides.[12]

On the region's periphery Algerian nationalists began a violent war of independence against their French colonial rulers, and tensions threatened to boil over in Yemen between British-controlled Aden and the northern imamate. Eisenhower and Dulles, particularly in North Africa, were forced to walk a very thin line. They wished to maintain good relations with the rebels, whom they were convinced would win, while also not alienating the French or the British. And further afield, of course, the ongoing rivalry between Pakistan and India continually threatened to erupt into war.

With every conflict the potential for the Soviet Union to exploit regional disorder to gain an ally—and thereby overstep containment—grew. In fact the Soviets did not even have to establish a Communist regime in the Middle East in order to seriously damage the West. As Mossadegh had shown, all it took was one unfriendly leader to seriously threaten Western access to Middle East oil, and Middle Eastern oil was vital for the British economy and Western Europe at large. Without the North Sea oilfields or one-hundred-thousand-ton tankers—both developments of the

1960s—the only other feasible energy source for Europe lay behind the Iron Curtain.[13] Consequently, without access to Middle Eastern sources of energy, the European economy would simply collapse.

Because of the Eisenhower administration's New Look emphasis on collective security, a threat to Europe also constituted a threat to America. Thus a scenario in which Western Europe lost access to Middle East oil was considered highly dangerous in the minds of American defense-policy makers. As Ike himself wrote in a letter to Churchill, "The free nations know, for example, that the prosperity and welfare of the entire Western world is inescapably dependent upon Mideast oil and free access thereto. This is particularly true of all Western Europe, and the safety and soundness of that region is indispensable to the rest of us."[14] Oil, however, was not the only threat to American security interests in the Middle East.

Nasser's insistence on forging a pan-Arabism that was not aligned with the United States or the Soviet Union attacked the very core of Eisenhower's depiction of the Cold War as a Manichaean struggle. As Dulles put it, "Neutrality has increasingly become an obsolete conception, and, except under very exceptional circumstances, it is an immoral and shortsighted conception."[15] Nasser clearly thought differently, as he began signing major trade deals with the Soviet Union by early 1954; at the same time, he declared that Egypt stood "in every respect with the West."[16] This position directly contradicted American understanding of the Cold War and, if not addressed, could undermine the West's position in the region. In short the task facing the Eisenhower administration if it was to maintain containment in the Middle East was rather daunting: preserving Western access to Middle East oil and preventing Soviet diplomatic or military penetration of the region, all while navigating the increasingly complex winds of postcolonial politics—not to mention keeping a fragile Arab-Israeli peace.

Rhetorical Surreption

Confronted by the bewildering politics of the region, the Eisenhower administration sought most of all not to create enemies, or in Ike's woolier prose, "Our policies are all directed, in deal-

From Baghdad to Cairo

ing with each of these countries, to promoting friendships in the area."[17] By maintaining positive relationships with all the nations of the Middle East individually, Eisenhower sought to ensure that none of them would turn to the Soviets for economic, military, or diplomatic aid and thereby impair the project of Soviet containment. This in turn required a generally amiable and noncommittal American approach to the region to avoid alienating any particular country by aligning too much with a regional foe or rival. As Dulles also noted, "Our basic problem in this vitally important region is to improve the attitude of the Moslem [sic] States toward the Western democracies, including the United States," and a strategy that veered too much in favor of Britain or Israel, as the Eisenhower administration believed Truman had done, risked provoking an anti-American response.

One way Eisenhower attempted to maintain good relations with all the countries of the Middle East was to treat them all equally. Ike's dedication to impartiality in his approach to the Middle East can be seen in his treatment of Israel and its neighboring Arab states. While not particularly convinced of the need for a Palestinian homeland, Eisenhower nonetheless took Arab grievances against the Jewish state very seriously. This idea of balance in Middle Eastern dealings appears in his diary entry of March 8, 1956:

> Of course, there can be no change in our basic position, which is that we must be friends with both contestants in that region in order that we can bring them closer together. To take sides could do nothing but to destroy our influence in leading toward a peaceful settlement of one of the most explosive situations in the world today.
>
> I cannot help reminiscing just a bit. In 1946 or 1947, I was visited by a couple of young Israelites who were anxious to secure arms for Israel . . . and I was certain they were stirring up a hornets' nest and if they could solve the initial question peacefully and without doing unnecessary violence to the self-respect and interests of the Arabs, they would profit immeasurably in the long run.[18]

For Eisenhower impartiality was critical for fostering positive relations with Israel, Egypt, and the other Arab states, and good relations with these nations were needed to maintain both Soviet containment and European access to Middle East oil.

Rhetorically, the goal of the Eisenhower administration—a foreign-policy posture toward the region of goodwill, reinforced by the president's philosophical dedication to impartiality generally and especially in Arab-Israeli affairs—was implemented by largely staying quiet. As with Operation Ajax Eisenhower rarely gave a direct answer to reporters' questions about the region, and he made no major addresses specifically about the Middle East until the Suez crisis. He often gave meandering answers when asked specific policy questions or generalized about American principles. However, also as with Operation Ajax, the appearance of benign disinterest concealed furious activity beneath the surface. From maintaining oil access to preventing Soviet breakthrough, the United States had very clear interests of the highest importance in the region. The administration still worked to safeguard these interests through security arrangements, peace deals, clandestine intervention, the sending of advisors, and trade agreements; however, it also sought to do so in a way that walked the diplomatic tightrope of sustaining positive relations with Israel, the various Arab factions, and America's European allies alike.

To achieve this aim the Eisenhower administration employed a strategy I have labeled rhetorical surreption. Catherine Egley Waggoner defines surreptitious rhetoric "as intentional concealment that may be used not to deceive but to protect," and she points out that "while enabling participants to succeed within organizational structures, these strategies by virtue of their covert nature also help maintain the dominant organizational structure, thus perhaps constraining their effectiveness."[19] In Eisenhower's case the use of rhetorical surreption—a mode of discourse focused on intentional concealment to covertly achieve aims within a dominant organizational structure—functioned as a strategy to secure American interests within the larger framework of the British Empire in the Middle East. However, as Waggoner notes, this

From Baghdad to Cairo

rhetorical strategy is also limited in its ability to achieve the outcomes desired, and Ike's choice to work within the British imperial paradigm made certain policies and stances impossible for him to pursue.[20]

Rhetorical surreption served two primary purposes for the Eisenhower administration. First, this approach allowed the United States to work in collaboration with Britain (and to a lesser degree, France) in the region. By not overtly denouncing the European imperial presence in Arab lands, Ike and Dulles prevented potential diplomatic fallout that might have threatened the security of Western Europe and the NATO alliance. Because much of the Eisenhower administration's diplomatic energy was focused on deepening European defense integration through measures like the European Defense Community (which ultimately failed), it would make little sense for Ike to publicly criticize Britain or France. Rhetorical surreption, by working within the diplomatic framework of European imperialism, allowed Eisenhower to avoid making such a critique.

Second, rhetorical surreption allowed the Eisenhower administration to work in pursuit of American interests in the Middle East so long as it employed covert action, surrogates, or back channels to achieve its aims. These means enabled Ike and Dulles to avoid having to directly address the American public concerning the United States' shifting role in the region, thereby preserving the fig leaf of British imperial prestige. Thus this approach can be understood as a continuation of the strategy of rhetorical misdirection used during Operation Ajax, in which the Eisenhower administration sought not to offend British sensibilities by downplaying the nature and extent of American activity in the Middle East. Eisenhower still wished to shape outcomes in the region beneficial to American interests; however, it benefited American relations with Britain, the propaganda war with the Soviets, and Ike's ability to manage the American public to do so surreptitiously. Shawn Parry-Giles argues that "we must move beyond the confines of the bully pulpit to the secret strategies and the multifarious messages involved in the performance of the rhetorical presidency" in order to fully understand the way the presidents mobilize their rhetorical power.[21] By examining how the Eisenhower administration prosecuted a rhetorical strategy premised on deception, covert action, backroom politics, and secret missions, I hope to shed light on how this element of the rhetorical presidency was made manifest in the Middle East.

While the Eisenhower administration's responses to the events over the course of its first term varied in each particular case, the overarching strategy of rhetorical surreption held in Ike's treatment of the Middle East. This can be seen in four episodes: the sending of CIA advisors to Egypt, the formation of the Baghdad Pact, Operation Straggle in Syria, and the Project Alpha peace negotiations.

Advisors to Egypt

One of the most clear-cut examples of rhetorical surreption took place in the Eisenhower administration's early dealings with Egypt. As Eisenhower came into office, it was feared that Egyptian anti-British sentiment, stemming in part from the outdated and colonialist defense treaty of 1936, would lead Cairo to bolt the Western camp and ally with the Soviet Union. Following the Free Officers' Coup of 1952, the top priority for the revolutionary Egyptian government was negotiating a new arrangement with the British to end their military presence in Egypt; for the British their preeminent strategic concern was retaining the massive military installation at Suez to ensure Britain's absolute control of the Canal Zone upon which its economy depended.[22] While the negotiations dragged on and tempers flared, a new settlement was eventually agreed upon and signed October 19, 1954.[23]

Throughout the negotiations Eisenhower remained silent concerning the conflict between Egypt and Britain. When asked point-blank whether the United States had "any arrangements [the United States] would like to see established in the Middle East," the president simply responded by saying, "The question is one of the Egyptian Government with the British Government."[24] Dulles likewise limited himself to simple observations of the situation upon returning from his 1953 tour, stating, "The heart of the trouble is not so much the presence of British troops, for both sides now agreed that they should be withdrawn, but the problem is the subsequent authority over and management of this gigantic base, its air strips, and its depots of supplies."[25] Neither official gave any indication that the talks, or the new Egyptian government generally, demanded the particular attention of the Eisenhower administration. After Egypt and Britain negotiated the new Suez Canal Base Agreement, Ike made several statements in press interviews indicating his pleasure that a deal had been signed and that a potential source of international conflict had been addressed. He also took these opportunities to reiterate his administration's limited aims in the region: "I believe that we have been successful in convincing all of the countries of the Mid-East that we are desperately trying to be friends with everybody, trying to make friends between ourselves and each of the nations concerned."[26]

During this same period, however, Eisenhower approved National Security Council directive 155/1. Officially signed into effect on July 14, 1953, NSC 155/1 began by outlining the "critical" importance of the Middle East to American security (thus breaking from the previous NSC 129/1, which described Middle Eastern defense as principally the job of "other nations, particularly the U.K.").[27] The document then charted the growing number of threatening conditions and trends in the region:

> During recent years the prestige and position of the West have declined. The nations of the Near East are determined to assert their independence and are suspicious of outside interest in their affairs. In particular, the influence of the United Kingdom has been weakened, with distrust and hatred replacing the former colonial subservience. France is also disliked and distrusted because of her refusal to free Morocco and Tunisia and because of her former role as a mandate power in Syria and Lebanon. Some of the distrust of the United Kingdom and France has devolved upon the United States, as an ally of both.

Even more important, the Arab nations are incensed by what they believe to be our pro-Israel policy. In addition, acute political and economic instability; military weakness; widespread unrest; Arab-Israel tensions; the UK controversies with Egypt, Iran and Saudi Arabia; the French North African problem; and the Soviet activity are also unfavorable to the West.[28]

In the face of such challenges, the papers' authors concluded, the primary danger in the region was not a direct Soviet military attack but the continuation of trends unfavorable to long-term American interests. And they direly predicted, "Unless these trends are reversed, the Near East may well be lost to the West within the next few years."[29]

The solution to this predicament was given in no uncertain terms: "Efforts to prevent the loss of the Near East will require increasing responsibility, initiative, and leadership by the United States in the area." The paper then listed a series of objectives and ways for American policy makers to prevent the erosion of America's strategic position in the Middle East, including the recommendation that the United States "guide the revolutionary and nationalistic pressures throughout the area into orderly channels not antagonistic to the West, rather than attempt merely to preserve the *status quo*."[30] In the case of Egypt, this policy meant sending numerous CIA advisors to Cairo to instruct Nasser's government on the newest developments in everything from Western political theory to how to run a spy agency. In brief the agents of the Central Intelligence Agency—Miles Copeland and Jim Eichelberger chief among them—set about imparting to Nasser how to build a "constructive" political base to safeguard the legitimacy of his revolutionary government, how to create a first-rate domestic intelligence agency (thereby "coup-proofing" his regime), and how to organize psychological warfare campaigns against domestic and foreign enemies, among many other things.[31]

While the effectiveness of the instruction Nasser received at the hands of the CIA is debated—Egyptian intelligence had extensive connections with West German intelligence at this point, and in his memoirs Copeland concludes that Nasser and his interior minister Abu al-Fadl "built the intelligence and security services with remarkably little outside help"—the blossoming relationship between Nasser's government and the CIA in the years 1953–55 is not.[32] Even Muhammad Heikal, an influential journalist of the era and a friend of Nasser, described the period as a "honeymoon."[33] Far from allowing the British to manage the region while looking on with benign disinterest, representatives from Washington were more integrated into the Egyptian state than those from Whitehall (a fact that led to not insignificant friction between the Foreign Office and the State Department). One Israeli agent even described how American agents got better seats than their British counterparts at an elite sporting club.[34] Just as he did in Iran, Eisenhower actively employed rhetoric to downplay the extent of American involvement in Egypt while CIA agents were busy helping shape the future of a Middle Eastern nation, and this strategy again worked within the formal structure of British imperialism to secure American interests through secret means.

Of course the results of the American efforts in Egypt were mixed. In the hopes of creating an anti-Soviet Egyptian state capable of stamping out any trace of Communist infiltration, the CIA under Eisenhower gave Nasser the knowledge, information-processing techniques, and broadcasting equipment that he would in short order use to become the main supplier of anti-Western and anti-American propaganda in the Arab world (although Nasser's General Intelligence Directorate, which had been trained by the CIA, continued to ruthlessly expunge any domestic traces of Communist influence in Egypt even during his years of outright hostility toward the West). And while the dream that a virulently anti-Communist Egypt, as leader of the Arab world, would set the tone for the region as a whole perished rather quickly, the overall relationship between the United States and Britain was not seriously injured. By employing strategically ambiguous rhetoric in his statements about Egypt, Ike avoided having to justify an increased U.S. presence in Egypt to the American public. By not having to provide a rationale for his CIA advisors' presence, he avoided having to publicly acknowledge British weaknesses in Egypt (the reason for increased American engagement provided in NSC 155/1) and badly damaging British prestige, not to mention Anglo-American relations at a time when this relationship was vital to the larger Cold War. In this case, then, Eisenhower's use of rhetorical surreption worked to limit the damage from a strategic venture—CIA advisors building up the Egyptian state—that to a large degree backfired.

The Baghdad Pact

For over a century the well-trained troops of the Indian Army under the British raj supplied the muscle for British imperial power across Africa and Asia. With the partition of India and Pakistan in August 1947, Whitehall ceased to wield this powerful force, and with the onset of the Cold War Western planners set about trying to prepare for the defense of South Asia and the Middle East against a potential Soviet invasion without these forces. These plans, from the vestigial Allied Middle East Command to the British-led Middle East Defense Organization to the 1951 Four Power Proposal, all failed for various reasons—not least for varying American and British conceptions of regional defense. Consequently, the Truman administration and its British counterparts were ultimately unsuccessful in their attempts to formally organize the collective defense of the greater Middle East against the Soviet Union.[35]

By the time Eisenhower entered office, no regional defense organization or treaty existed for the Middle East. The idea of a group of independent states organized to resist Soviet aggression nevertheless fit nicely with the Eisenhower administration's New Look defense policy of relying on collective security to help uphold Soviet containment; the North Atlantic Treaty Organization (NATO) and soon-to-be-established Southeast Asia Treaty Organization (SEATO) provided a template for this kind of alliance. These arrangements, moreover, bound the signed nations together as opponents of Soviet expansionism, theoretically denying Communism an entrepôt beyond the borders of the Soviet empire and Communist China. Hence, the creation of an anti-Soviet regional defensive pact was an attractive goal for the Eisenhower administration in the Middle East. A regional alliance also appeared to be in line with the interests of the British, who were desperately seeking a new security agreement that would allow them to keep their bases at Habbaniyah and Suez and preserve their rapidly diminishing influence in the region.[36]

Accordingly, Dulles held extended talks during his May 1953 tour of the region with the leaders of each of the nations he visited regarding Middle Eastern security. After an early breakthrough with Egypt faltered—Cairo activated the Arab League Collective Security Pact as a possible avenue for American aid, only for the U.S. director of mutual security Harold Stassen to rule that foreign aid was restricted to countries that agreed to promote an Israeli-Palestinian settlement, thus killing that plan—Dulles reorganized around a "northern tier" approach. Believing that Syria, Lebanon, Iraq, Turkey, Iran, and Pakistan might be amenable to a regional alliance designed to blunt potential Soviet military aggression in the Middle East, Dulles worked to encourage the expansion of a Turkish-proposed bilateral defense agreement with Iraq into a regional alliance. This basic Turkish-Iraqi proposal evolved into the Baghdad Pact, a regional defense agreement that grew to include Pakistan, Iran, and the United Kingdom in early 1955.[37]

While historians differ as to whether Dulles desired that the United States be a part of such an arrangement, in the end the United States did not join the Baghdad Pact. The Eisenhower administration chose this course of action for two main reasons. First, it did not wish to undermine the British position in the Middle East, and by directly joining the Baghdad Pact—a *regional* defense alliance in Britain's supposed sphere of influence—the United States would be visibly sending the message that it had displaced Britain in the Middle East. Such an action would clearly mark the United States as the preeminent Western power in the region and question the British imperial status quo. So unattractive was this idea to the Eisenhower administration that it actually signed a secret treaty of understanding with the British during the 1954 Berlin Conference to assure Whitehall's "political and strategic paramountcy" in Iraq.[38] All this was in keeping with Eisenhower's established rhetorical strategy of working surreptitiously to secure American interests within the framework of British imperialism in the Middle East, not to supplant it.

The second reason the United States did not join the Baghdad Pact was the fear that this action would alienate other countries in the Middle East in direct contradiction of Ike and Dulles's strategy of maintaining friendly relations with all nations of the region. Nasser, for one, viewed the pact as an attempt to establish a new center of Arab politics in Baghdad at his expense (a legitimate concern, considering that Iraqi prime minister Nuri as-Said did appoint himself salesman of the alliance and pitched it unsuccessfully to the entire Arab League).[39] State Department personnel also feared alienating Saudi Arabia, Israel, or India by joining the pact, instead favoring bilateral engagement with each of the countries across the region. These views were reflected in NSC 162/2, which established the basic national security doctrine of the Eisenhower Administration and took effect October 30, 1953. Its writers stated:

> In the Middle East, a strong regional grouping is not now feasible. In order to assure during peace time for the United States and its allies the resources (especially oil) and the strategic positions of the area and their denial to the Soviet bloc, the United States should build on Turkey, Pakistan, and if possible, Iran, and assist in achieving stability in the Middle East by political actions and limited military and economic assistance, and technical assistance, to other countries in the area.[40]

In other words a strong regional alliance was not possible in a Middle East crosscut by so many tensions, from the Israeli-Arab conflict to the Iraqi-Egyptian rivalry, and the United States should instead focus on building up individual allies who could serve as a bulwark against Communist expansion and provide stability for the area. This approach precluded a regional alliance in the form of NATO in favor of strengthening the United States' bilateral ties with the countries of the Middle East through the sending of aid and advisors.

In short the Eisenhower administration feared, with good cause, the psychological impression that America's joining the Baghdad Pact would have on British prestige. It also doubted the strategic efficacy of such an alliance, given Iraqi pretensions to Arab leadership and the administration's wariness of alienating Israel, India, Saudi Arabia, and, most of all, Egypt. As such the administration steadfastly refused to blatantly assert American power in the region and confined itself to working through less overt means: aid packages, arms deals, back-channel diplomacy, and the sending of advisors. And rhetorically the president very rarely spoke of the Baghdad Pact (or the Middle East in general); when he did, he obfuscated the level of American involvement in these matters as best he could. He generalized, referring to the Baghdad Pact as "major gain" for the collective security of the free world; he denied outright conversing with Anthony Eden about the Baghdad Pact during a moment of tension; and he was strategically ambiguous, more than once stating that the United States simply wished "to retain friendships with both sides" in regional conflicts and that he and his subordinates "never [gave] up trying to bring every peaceful influence [they could] into settling these quarrels around the world."[41]

Taken as a whole the Eisenhower administration's handling of the Baghdad Pact was consistent with its overall strategy of rhetorical surreption. Joining the alliance would have required making a clear and controversial policy stance, one that powerfully communicated American assertiveness in the Middle East and risked alienating a number of neutral nations in the region. By not joining the Eisenhower administration maintained the diplomatic illusion of neutrality and a policy of benign friendliness in the region. Far from describing an active and deeply involved American presence in the Middle East, newspaper discussions of the Baghdad Pact described the United States as "reluctant" to participate in regional defense arrangements with "powers tarred as 'colonial'"; the Eisenhower administration was simply bowing to "the realities of the situation" in its limited cooperation with the British.[42] By employing a strategy of rhetorical surreption, Ike, in theory, got the best of both worlds: his administration's appearance of friendly impartiality to Middle Eastern nations was preserved, and to go along with it a regional defense pact was organized along the "northern tier" of the Middle East, joining with NATO and SEATO to complete Communist geographical containment.[43]

Syria: Operation Straggle

One nation where the Eisenhower administration's diplomatic friendship offensive utterly failed to take root was Syria. Partly as a result of the corrosive attempts by the French to maintain colonial control following World War II, Syria suffered from acute political instability; a succession of military coups and countercoups saw power change hands between leftward-leaning nationalists and conservatives three times in the year 1949 alone.[44] Syria, moreover, was the only state in the area to reject all forms of American economic and military assistance. The U.S. Mutual Security Act of 1955 stipulated that nations receiving American aid agree to contribute to "the defensive strength of the free world," an activity that clearly did not interest the leftist government of Shukri al-Quwatli.[45] Even worse in the Eisenhower administration's eyes, al-Quwatli's Ba'athist government welcomed a visit from the Soviet foreign minister in June 1956 and recognized Communist China shortly thereafter. These actions appeared to reinforce earlier estimations by the National Security Council concerning Syria, which warned, "Of all the Arab states Syria is at the present time the most wholeheartedly devoted to a neutralist policy with strong anti-Western overtones," and "if the present trend continues there is a strong possibility that a Communist-dominated Syria will result, threatening the peace and stability of the area and endangering the achievement of our objective in the Near East."[46]

It is perhaps unsurprising, then, that the Eisenhower administration conspired to overthrow the government of Syria in a CIA-organized coup as it did in Iran. Archie Roosevelt, the cousin of Kermit Roosevelt, was designated the point man for Operation

Straggle, as the Syrian coup attempt was code-named. Recalling the moment he was given his orders, he recorded his conversation with John Foster Dulles: "As you know, Archie, we're much concerned about what's going on in Syria—especially the way the Communists and nationalists appear to be ganging up for some kind of action there. . . . I'd like you to fly out to Damascus right away, talk to our ambassador, and see . . . what can be done about it."[47] The actual mechanics of the coup were fairly straightforward. Guided by Syria-based fellow CIA agent Bill Eveland, Roosevelt was to make contact with Mikhail Ilyan, a powerful conservative politician and wealthy Christian landowner from Aleppo. Ilyan was then to bribe the proper politicians, secure the allegiance of the necessary senior military officers, and purchase the cooperation of the appropriate media organs using American-furnished money. All this could be done for half a million Syrian pounds ($167,000), which Ilyan asked for and received. After several delays the date for the coup was set for October 25, 1956.

However, Ilyan had one additional request: to ensure the participation of the other Syrian plotters, a guarantee had to come from the highest levels of the U.S. government that the Eisenhower administration would immediately recognize the new Syrian regime. This assurance could be communicated, Ilyan explained, by the president repeating an earlier statement he had made in April to the effect that the United States would oppose aggression in the Middle East but not without congressional approval. Shortly thereafter, on October 16, Secretary Dulles held a press conference condemning recent Israeli raids against Jordan as contributing to the "deterioration of the situation" in the Middle East. Then, Dulles declared, "I believe the President's statement—there was a statement the President made from I think Augusta last April in which he said that within Constitutional means we would assist and that we would give aid to any victims of aggression. That holds." In publicly referencing Ike's April 9 statement, Dulles fulfilled Ilyan's request for confirmation of American support for the coup from the top levels of the Eisenhower administration.[48]

As it turns out, Operation Straggle was never set in motion, and the effort to remove the Ba'thist government of al-Quwatli failed. After another delay at the request of Colonel Kabbani, who informed Ilyan that his people were not ready, the date was set for October 30—the same day Israel invaded Egypt, triggering the Suez Canal crisis. Ilyan, pointing out the impossibility of over-throwing the government at the exact moment Israel started a war with an Arab state, fled to Beirut. This left the feared chief of Syr-ian security, Abd al-Hamid Sarraj, to capture the remaining con-spirators and mop up what was left of the attempted coup.[49] At the direction of CIA chief Allen Dulles, another coup was attempted against the Syrian government following the Suez crisis, this time code-named Operation Wappen. After Sarraj easily unraveled that plot and expelled the CIA agents responsible, the Syrian govern-ment went public with its criticism of the American intelligence agency. A minor diplomatic crisis ensued, with the United States recalling its ambassador to Syria and expelling the Syrian ambas-sador in Washington (the first time the chief of a foreign mission to America had been expelled since 1915). Cementing its anti-American position, Syria joined Nasser's United Arab Republic (UAR) not long thereafter.[50]

In terms of presidential rhetoric, Operation Straggle demon-strated not only the Eisenhower administration's affinity for using clandestine means to remove uncooperative governments—hardly the stuff of impartial neutrality—but also its willingness to employ public rhetoric as a method of supporting such plots. Dulles con-sciously crafted his press conference statements to send a secret message to the Syrian conspirators. In doing so he strategically employed the rhetorical concept of polysemy (multiple mean-ings being present in a text), embedding within his ostensibly plainspoken answer to a reporter's question a secondary, hidden meaning intended for a second audience, the Syrian plotters. In this regard Dulles's words shared a certain resemblance to strat-egies of "passing," in which public texts contain covert messages concealed within them; as Peter Rabinowitz notes, this complex rhetorical strategy "requires a speaker and *two* audiences: one audience that's ignorant and another that knows the truth *and remains silent about it.*" This kind of text contains "hidden meanings beneath the surface," discernible only to an audience armed with foreknowledge of how to correctly interpret the polysemous nature of the text. In the case of Dulles, the Syrian conspirators were able to interpret the veiled, true meaning of his speech while the American people were, obviously, ignorant of the fact that a secret message was being broadcast through their radios.[51] Significantly, this strategy reflected a skillful and willing use of rhetoric for deceptive purposes by the secretary of state, a clear instance of surreptitious rhetoric in action.

Beyond Dulles the Eisenhower administration's handling of the Operation Straggle failure as a whole also demonstrated commitment to rhetorical surreption. Ike himself, as might be expected, said nothing publicly of Syria, Straggle, or American fears of Communist infiltration of the Levant throughout the entire affair. In fact Eisenhower did not even utter the word "Syria" or its derivatives in a public statement as president until August 21, 1957, well after Operations Straggle and Wappen had concluded.[52] Unsurprisingly, then, after the Syrian government went forward with its public criticism of the United States, the *New York Times* reported on the "numerous theories about why the Syrians struck at the United States," preferring, just as with Operation Ajax and Iran, to speculate on the motivations of Damascus rather than take the Syrian accusations seriously. As a result the Eisenhower administration's covert action in Syria remained so. The use of surreptitious rhetoric effectively concealed the attempted coup from the American public, and even though Operation Straggle was a failure, the administration paid no real cost in terms of domestic blowback. Its only losses were a few hundred thousand dollars, CIA assets, and any remaining goodwill of the Syrian people.

Project Alpha: The Quest for Arab-Israeli Peace

Besides the fear of Communist penetration, nothing concerned the Eisenhower administration more about the Middle East than the ongoing Arab-Israeli conflict. Its general view was that American support for Israel, especially strong during the Truman administration, hurt the United States' standing among Arab states, which in turn hindered anti-Communist ventures in the region. In an interview after his May 1953 tour of the region, Dulles referred to Britain, France, and Israel as "millstones around our necks," their unpopularity sinking efforts to convince Arab and Muslim states to align with the free world.[53] Although Ike was much less vocal publicly about his concern, privately he lamented the repercussions of the conflict:

> The oil of the Arab world has grown increasingly important to all of Europe. The economy of European countries would collapse if these oil supplies were cut off. If the economy of Europe would collapse, the United States would be in a situation of which the difficulty could scarcely be exaggerated. On the other hand, Israel, a tiny nation, surrounded by enemies, is nevertheless one that we have recognized—and on top of this, that has a very strong position in the heart and emotions of the Western world because of the tragic suffering of the Jews throughout twenty-five hundred years of history.[54]

While the Arab-Israeli conflict was important in its own right, Eisenhower's primary concern, consistent with his dualistic view of foreign policy, was how the dispute hurt the larger effort against Communism. His administration therefore tended to view Israel as an impediment to peace while offering various sorts of assets to woo Arab countries.

The United States and Britain participated in five major UN-coordinated efforts to resolve the Arab-Israeli conflict between the years 1948 to 1954, all of which failed.[55] By the autumn of 1954, with fears of Communist penetration high and Israeli border skirmishes occurring at an alarming rate in the aftermath of the Qibya massacre, the Eisenhower administration and the conservative-led British government set out to independently bring about an Arab-Israeli peace through coercive diplomacy. The plan, originally stemming from an April 1954 meeting in which Eden raised the idea to Dulles of their nations working together to achieve "effective frontier control," was premised on both powers applying pressure simultaneously on the Arabs and the Israelis to bring about a reasonable peace (understood as requiring Israeli concession of territory to Arabs and Arab peaceful recognition of Israel as a Jewish state).[56] The timing for a peace deal was also seen as propitious, as Nasser had finished consolidating control of Egypt by early 1955 and was the first Arab leader in some time who had the regional standing to bear the weight of a negotiated settlement with Israel. Ike and Dulles also feared that American Zionist organizations such as the American Israel Public Affairs Committee (AIPAC) might alter public opinion in the United States, so they wished to act quickly while they had public support and political capital (or as Dulles put it in an ALPHA planning meeting in January 1955, "the Israeli position was now weaker than it ever had been, but by 1956 it was likely to gain new strength").[57] Speed, as well as secrecy, was of the essence.

To that end top-secret negotiators were appointed to shuttle between Tel Aviv and Cairo to ascertain what conditions would be necessary for Ben Gurion and Nasser to arrive at a peaceful settlement of the issue. The Eisenhower administration had previously used this tactic—dispatching low-profile surrogates to directly represent Eisenhower so as to avoid scrutiny—in its dealings with the Middle East. In 1953, for example, Ike dispatched businessman Eric Johnston as his personal ambassador to the Middle East. Johnston's mission was, in Eisenhower's intentionally vague words, to "explore with the governments of the countries of that region certain steps which might be expected to contribute to an improvement of the general situation in the region."[58] In reality Johnston was specifically tasked with arriving at a regional settlement regarding the use of water resources—a charge he successfully accomplished after two years of arduous mediation—and with feeling out the contours of a potential peace deal.

This time around the Foreign Office's Evelyn Shuckburgh and the State Department's Francis Russell led the effort. Knowledge of their mission, code-named Project Alpha, was initially limited to those at the absolute highest levels of government. Neither the Arabs nor the Israelis were given full information about the other's peace conditions, as both American and British officials were wary that the Israelis, who in their estimation were "given to devious ways of achieving their ends," would release information about the talks to damage Nasser.[59] Stated otherwise the original plan was *not* for the Egyptians and Israelis to come to an agreement on their own with Western help but for the conditions of a minimally acceptable agreement to be covertly ascertained by the Americans and the British, who would then impose those terms through the various means at their disposal (withholding or granting of aid, sanctions, a UN resolution, etc.). Throughout this feeling-out period Western diplomats offered all sorts of inducements and attacked perceived deal breakers with a creative ferocity. Confronted, for instance, by the seemingly impossible task of granting a contiguous Israel access to the Red Sea and establishing a land border between Egypt and Jordan (to allow the Arab nations to continuously stretch from the Atlantic to the Persian Gulf), the diplomats devised a system of "kissing triangles," land with overpasses arched above their points of contact, allowing one to drive without stopping in either direction—a marvel Dulles likened to "the judgment of Solomon."[60]

In the end the attempts to negotiate peace never even got past the precondition phase. In a last-ditch effort to make progress toward a peace treaty, Dulles publicized the Project Alpha talks in speech given August 26, 1955. During his talk, in which he made sure to mention that he spoke "in this matter with the authority of President Eisenhower," Dulles proposed U.S.-funded resettling of refugees, a massive economic aid and development package for Israel, and the United States' entry into formal treaty arrangements with both Arab nations and Israel to guarantee their security.[61] It was, in short, the indication of a major policy shift in regard to American investment in the region.

However, the American media's main reaction to the speech was to praise Dulles for demonstrating "good will" and "characteristic courage" rather than seriously reevaluating America's deepening commitment to the Middle East. According to the *Providence Journal*, the United States had done "a fine and inspiring" thing; the *New York News*, in another case, wrote, "We don't doubt Mr. Dulles' sincerity. . . . But it seems to us that the U.S. is once again finding out how rocky the road usually is for a nation that tries to be everybody's well-heeled sweetheart."[62] By emphasizing the idealistic naïveté of America's effort to reach an Arab-Israeli settlement—in a speech in which Dulles explicitly admitted that Ike desired that "the United States join in formal treaty engagements" for regional "collective security" purposes—these media outlets reinforced the narrative that America was not the emerging regional hegemon or even a significantly involved foreign power in the region.[63] Thus the Eisenhower administration's strategy of publicly downplaying its role in the Middle East remained largely intact, even in this instance.[64]

Furthermore, the Eisenhower administration was not finished with secret peace missions, even after Dulles's gambit of going public failed. In January 1956 Eisenhower protégé Robert Anderson was also dispatched to the region to mediate a peace agreement between Ben Gurion and Nasser. In Anderson's words Eisenhower "just about gave me carte blanche" to offer virtually any inducement to achieve a settlement. Yet after dozens of flights, conflict points, negotiations, and clandestine meetings, Anderson failed too.

What to make of Project Alpha? In terms of rhetoric the Eisenhower administration, rather than engage publicly in an attempt to bring about an Arab-Israeli peace, largely dealt in an economy of secrecy: it sent surrogates on covert missions and plotted with the British to force a settlement on (at least) two sovereign nations. In this case rhetorical surreption functioned as a strategy to avoid inflaming domestic opinion, and it also enabled the Eisenhower administration to conceal its full intent from the nations that the settlement concerned. Unlike the public image of America's dealings with the Middle East that his administration cultivated, Eisenhower oversaw a program of fundamentally aggressive action in the region; after all, impartial nations do not, of their own initiative, secretly negotiate and impose peace settlements on others. Although ultimately ineffective these missions and their covert natures underscored not only the deepening U.S. commitment to the Middle East but also the way in which this commitment remained largely hidden from the public eye beyond announcements of economic aid packages and diplomatic platitudes of friendship. And of course Eisenhower himself said very little about the Arab-Israeli peace process, continually returning to the theme of friendship to describe American interests in the region. Nothing he said challenged British imperialism in the region as the status quo or suggested that America's relationship to the region was in the process of dramatically changing.

The Limits of Rhetorical Surreption

In each of these instances and throughout Ike's first term, he and his cabinet never publicly advanced the claim that the Middle East was an area of direct American security responsibility, even as their actions and defense doctrine operated on exactly that assumption. Whether in Egypt, regarding the Baghdad Pact, Syria, or Project Alpha, the Eisenhower administration aggressively pursued actions that it believed would be in the interests of the United States against the Soviet Union. However, Eisenhower and Dulles also understood the fundamentally rhetorical nature of the Cold War, so they employed surreptitious methods to achieve their aims. In doing so they used rhetoric to help conceal their actions while working within the larger diplomatic framework of European imperialism, a strategy I have labeled rhetorical surreption.

But was this method effective? While this strategy helped the Eisenhower administration maintain more positive relations with some nations and a better public image than it would have otherwise, Ike hardly accomplished all he wished to in the region. The proliferation of CIA advisors did not prevent Nasser from turning to the Communists for arms or stop him from producing massive amounts of anti-American propaganda, even at one point denouncing Iraqi prime minister Nuri as-Said as "an American stooge."[65] An unfriendly regime still ruled in Damascus. Israel and the Arabs were as antagonistic as ever, no matter the Project Alpha peace talks. And even though the Baghdad Pact was formed, it was an alliance largely without teeth and with few prospects for expansion.

Thus it seems fair to conclude that rhetorical surreption, as a strategy of engagement with the Middle East, was not conducive to achieving American aims proportionate to the expressed importance of the region to American security. If power can be defined, as political scientist Joseph Nye says, as "the ability to affect others to get the outcomes one wants," then the Eisenhower administration's approach to the Middle East in the years 1953–56 can be understood as, more often than not, a failure to translate American advantages into desirable outcomes.[66] While the use of surreptitious rhetoric likely mitigated the adverse effects of many of the policy failures the Eisenhower administration experienced—the domestic blowback regarding Operation Straggle, for example, would have been far greater had the operation not been essentially kept under wraps—it also contributed to these failures. As with Operation Ajax a disconnect existed between the president's words and his administration's actions, constraining Eisenhower's freedom of action politically and therefore contributing to his policy failures in the region. In addition to this flaw, the strategy of rhetorical surreption had three other major shortcomings.

First, it was antidemocratic. Because he concealed the depth and extent of American activity, Ike did not have to explain his administration's activity to the U.S. population or make a persuasive case to the American people that the region and specific countries in it demanded the investment of American blood and treasure. While all governments (democratic or not) keep certain information hidden from their citizens, Ike and his subordinates, including Allen Dulles and the CIA, went to extraordinary lengths to covertly combat what they perceived to be Communist infiltration of the Middle East. By engaging in rhetorical surreption, the Eisenhower administration circumvented public opinion's check on presidential initiative and avoided accountability for its actions.

Second, the Eisenhower administration's approach to the region enabled Middle Eastern nations to take advantage of it. Because

Ike's method of rhetorical surreption often worked through less overt means to build influence—trade deals, advisors, aid packages, arms, and the like—target nations were able to manipulate the Eisenhower administration into supporting their local agenda. Nuri as-Said, for example, was accused by Nasser and others of promoting the Baghdad Pact simply as a way for Iraq to receive more arms from the United States and Britain. Pakistan, in another example, was more than happy to go along with American plans for a "northern tier" alliance, as this would result in a stronger Pakistani army, which would then be more capable of fighting India. In brief, by dealing surreptitiously across the region, the Eisenhower administration allowed itself to be taken advantage of by nations willing to verbally adhere to an anti-Communist agenda. This was an inefficient and ultimately ineffective mode of containment.

Third, and most important, this rhetorical approach to the Middle East created space for the British and the French to dangerously misinterpret American interests and intentions in the region. Surreptitious strategies always work subversively within a larger system. In this case Eisenhower's rhetoric worked to reaffirm the viability of a vestigial European imperial presence in the Middle East while using concealed methods to covertly promote American interests, at times with British awareness and at times without. Yet European imperialism was exactly the driving force behind Arab resistance to Western overtures. Nasser railed endlessly against the "imperialist yoke" of the West and complained to Dulles of the "psychological battle" it would be to convince Arabs that the Communists were the real menace.[67] Unless it could bridge the gulf between pan-Arabism and anti-Communism, the Eisenhower administration faced an uphill battle to create any sort of regional balance favorable to American interests. As Ike's first term ended, these tensions began to expose themselves.

Khrushchev's propaganda offensive made sure to highlight the incongruity of American claims of promoting freedom while allying with European colonialist powers. By masking the American presence in the Middle East and allowing Britain (and to a lesser degree France) to remain the face of containment in the region, Eisenhower played into the Soviet critique that the United States was a supporter of imperialism. While not a new line of criticism, the salience of this argument increased throughout Ike's first term. Not only in the Middle East but across the world, access to resources residing in (post)colonial lands was being determined more and more by the formerly colonized people, not their colonizers. Eisenhower's public stances of impartiality belied his conviction that America must not lose the Cold War by estranging these new nations. As Ike wrote in a private letter, "Among all the powerful nations of the world the United States is the only one with a tradition of anti-colonialism. . . . The standing of the United States as the most powerful of the anti-colonial powers is an asset of incalculable value to the Free World."[68] He would not risk losing this advantage, even if it meant going against his old allies and overturning decades of American policy and rhetoric. Of this fact Britain and France were unaware, setting the stage for the Suez crisis.

Overall the Eisenhower administration's rhetorical approach to the Middle East, by ultimately working within an imperialist framework, prioritized American relations with the European powers over those of Middle Eastern countries. While flawed in many respects, this surreptitious strategy worked to prevent the Eisenhower administration's relationship with its allies from deteriorating too far and enabled Ike to keep his administration's actions in the Middle East out of the public eye. However, this mixed bag of successes and failures also papered over larger issues that remained unaddressed. Britain, already unable to police the Middle East on its own, emerged from Ike's first term weaker than before, and the United States was rapidly assuming the role of senior partner in the region. Thus, although he rhetorically positioned the Middle East as an important theater of the Cold War and was willing to act to preserve U.S. interests, Eisenhower's public rhetoric did not reflect the reality of America's growing interventionist policy in the region. He continued to characterize the United States' role in the region as that of neutral arbitrator between the Arab states and Israel, "all of whom" America wanted as "friends," much less make mention of America's anti-Communist Middle East activism.

Even so, as Ike's first term neared its end, the rumblings of change could be heard. As Henry Byroade, the assistant secretary of state for Near Eastern, South Asian, and African affairs, put it,

> Our position in the Middle East has changed simply because our world position has changed and because the world in which we live has changed, changed to where there is in the East-West situation for the first time an ever present and continuous threat to the security of our own country. The day when we could look at a few large countries and say "these—and what happens there—are important to us" is unfortunately gone. Today one can scarcely think of an area and say it is safe and secure and we need not concern ourselves. Least of all can we say that about the Middle East.[69]

Whatever else he said, Byroade got one thing right: the days in which the United States would allow its interests—especially fighting Communism—to take the back seat in any region of the world were over. This was a lesson the world would soon learn at Suez.

4

Lion's Last Roar, Eagle's First Flight
Eisenhower at Suez

When the crisis was over, when the abscess had burst, the world was
a different place. But, of all the nations involved, Great Britain was
affected most immediately, most dramatically. For although Britain's
economic and military strength had long been trickling away, Anthony
Eden's Suez policy and its mortifying aftermath made it apparent
to everyone there and to most people everywhere that Britain could
no longer exercise power on a global scale. Sixty years after Queen
Victoria's Jubilee, the lion roared for the last time.

—Chester Cooper, *The Lion's Last Roar: Suez, 1956*

All my life I have been a man of peace, working for peace, striving for
peace, negotiating for peace. I have been a League of Nations man
and a United Nations man and I'm still the same man, with the same
convictions. I couldn't be other, even if I wished.

—Sir Anthony Eden, BBC Address to the Nation, November 3, 1956

We have given our whole thought to Hungary and the Middle East. I
don't give a damn how the election goes.

—Dwight Eisenhower, telephone call with Anthony Eden, November 1, 1956

So significant was the Suez crisis for the political life of
Anthony Eden, the British prime minister from 1955 to 1957,
that he dedicated fully one-third of his 654-page memoir to
the episode.[1] As historian D. R. Thorpe notes, the event was so
central to Eden's legacy that scholars and journalists have tended
to judge his entire thirty-three-year political career through the
lens of Suez. Unfortunately for Eden most of these assessments
are "unremittingly hostile" in their treatment of him, often view-

ing the choices he made at Suez as incriminating evidence of "devious recklessness" and "anachronistic colonialism."[2] Regardless of whether one embraces this view of Eden or not, it is nevertheless impossible to discuss the man without also addressing the crisis he caused.

As with Eden, so with presidential rhetoric: the Suez crisis, among its manifold implications, marked a clear end to the indirect rhetorical approach to the Middle East practiced by presidents since Woodrow Wilson, for better or for worse. Occurring at the literal conclusion of Eisenhower's first term, the events of Suez—the nationalization and blocking of the canal, the Israeli army's invasion of Egypt followed shortly by the armies of Britain and France, Nikolai Bulganin's threat to rain rockets on Paris and London, and the American decision to wage economic and diplomatic war on its allies to end the crisis—affected the various nations involved in differing ways.[3] For students of presidential rhetoric, however, the words by which Eisenhower addressed the situation are as significant as the events of Suez themselves, for it was in Ike's Suez crisis speech that the president first argued for a uniquely American responsibility to solve the problems of the Middle East. In doing so Ike initiated the rhetorical transformation of America's relationship to the Middle East that would be consummated in the Eisenhower Doctrine.

Context: Eisenhower's First Administration

Eisenhower's first term was eventful, to say the least. The Cold War with the Soviets grew frostier still, with both superpowers in possession of hydrogen bombs and little progress made toward disarmament or peace beyond the nebulous "spirit" of the Geneva Conference. In addition to Operations Ajax and Straggle, the CIA had covertly intervened in Guatemala, began a full-scale propaganda war against Communism in Europe, and sent advisors to countries far and wide. West Germany was integrated as a full NATO member after the European Defense Community failed to form, to which the Soviets responded by organizing their European satellite states into the Warsaw Pact. In Asia Ike and Dulles successfully negotiated the end of the Korean War and avoided a military conflagration with Communist China over Taiwan, and a tentative ceasefire was reached in Vietnam after the French defeat at Dien Bien Phu. Though Eisenhower could honestly tell American voters that he had "kept us at peace" as they went to the polls in 1956, after a decade of cold war the world remained a tinderbox.[4]

Not all was going well for the Western powers in the Middle East. The British position continued to weaken, as seen most evidently in the unceremonious expulsion of John Glubb, the longtime commander of the Arab Legion, from Jordan in March 1956.[5] The Baghdad Pact, furthermore, was not shaping up to be the anti-Communist bulwark of which Western policymakers originally dreamed. After rapidly expanding to include Turkey, Iraq, Iran, Pakistan, and Britain, its prospects for further growth ground to a halt due to Iraqi prime minister Nuri as-Said's inability to persuade any other Arab nations to go against Nasser's wishes and join.[6] The pact also alienated the Soviet Union (for obvious reasons), France (because it was not invited to join), and Israel (due to anxiety regarding Arab ability to threaten its national security). Seeking a patron Israel aligned with a spurned France, and the two quickly struck a secret arms deal in circumvention of the Tripartite Agreement of 1950; although the CIA knew about this secret agreement, Eisenhower chose not to confront either side about the treaty violation in keeping with his overall strategy of maintaining a public posture of benign nonintervention in the region's politics. Dulles, for one, maintained confidence that this action would serve American interests by allowing Israel to feel secure while not requiring the United States to provide arms to Tel Aviv. As he remarked in a cable to Eisenhower, "Nothing had yet happened that leads us to feel that we had to abandon our basic policies of friendship for both Jews and Arabs, avoidance of an arms race and aggression by each side. . . . We do not want to lose Arab good will unless the Arabs themselves in conspiracy with the Soviets force this result upon us. I am not without hope that the situation will work out."[7]

Unfortunately for Dulles his hopes were soon shattered. When Nasser asked the United States for weapons to defend against Israeli commando raids, he was declined by Eisenhower and Dulles, who feared sparking a regional arms race. So Nasser went to the Communists, and he announced the $200 million Egyptian-Czech arms deal in July 1955.[8] With Egypt seemingly aligned with the Soviet Union, London's grip on its colonial assets slipping, Israel clandestinely supported by France, and both the United States and Britain concerned about Nasser, the region was ripe for a crisis.

Meanwhile, Nikita Khrushchev had fully assumed power in Moscow, and he began moving beyond Stalin's hard belief in the "inevitability of global war." Convinced (like his Western counterparts) that thermonuclear weapons rendered World War III a political impossibility, Khrushchev developed a new theoretical basis for waging Cold War premised on cultivating sources of soft power that would counter the "dark forces" of capitalism in the West.[9] In its practical application, this strategy resulted in Khrushchev launching a series of "peace offensives," in the Eisenhower administration's parlance, designed to make the foundations of Western security—NATO and access to postcolonial markets and resources, in particular—politically untenable. By demonstrating that the Soviet Union was dedicated to peace, friendly to small countries, supportive of postcolonial peoples, and eager to settle disputes with its opponents, Khrushchev hoped to end European polarization and with it the Soviet Union's diplomatic isolation from the West. As Khrushchev told Danish prime minister Hans-Christian Hansen in March 1956, "[The Soviets] convincingly proved our peacemaking nature, and we will continue to prove it. Thereby we will shake NATO loose. We will continue to reduce armed forces unilaterally," the result of which will be that "you [the West] will find it hard to justify NATO before public opinion." In this way Khrushchev's assumption of power intensified the psychological dimensions of the Cold War even as the Soviet leadership reduced its military footprint and downplayed the possibility of war.[10]

In the Middle East, an area in which Communism had made very little ideological headway, Soviet propaganda tended to exploit the

Lion's Last Roar, Eagle's First Flight

implicit tensions present in Western policy. Khrushchev pointed out that while the United States advocated peace, it encouraged military alliances like the Baghdad Pact. While the Eisenhower administration claimed to be an impartial promoter of freedom, it maintained alliances with the colonial overlords of the region. And of course American support for Israel, regardless of Ike's attempts to be balanced in his treatment of Middle Eastern countries, served as a continual reminder of the United States' perfidy toward Arab nations. In short Soviet rhetorical appeals worked to expose the contradiction at the heart of American Middle East policy: British and French support was necessary for global containment to work, therefore it was U.S. policy to support them (at least rhetorically), but support for the European allies was driving resistance to policies and relationships crucial for containment to succeed in the Middle East. For example the Soviet declaration concerning the Baghdad Pact stated:

> Plans to create aggressive blocs in the Near and Middle East have nothing in common with the preservation of peace and security or with the basic national interests of the countries of that region. Those plans reveal once again that the policy of Western Powers vis-à-vis the countries of the Near and Middle East is directed, as in the past, to political and economic subordination of those countries to imperialist Powers endeavoring to superimpose the yoke of colonial oppression and exploitation on the peoples of those countries. . . .
>
> As in the past attempts are being made to conceal the aggressive nature of the plans of the United States and England in the Near and Middle East by fictitious fabrications of 'Soviet danger' to the countries of that region. Those kinds of fantasies have nothing in common with the reality since the basis of the foreign policy of the Soviet Union, as it is known, is the unswerving desire to preserve peace among nations on the basis of the preservation of the principles of equality, noninterference in domestic affairs, respect for national independence and state sovereignty.[11]

Appeals such as these worked on several levels. They functioned to (1) emphasize the peacefulness of Soviet foreign policy, thereby neutering Ike's and Dulles's warnings of Communist expansionism; (2) decry Western dedication to regional security as attempts to uphold an outdated status quo, thus positioning the Soviet Union as a natural ally for postcolonial nations and revolutionary movements—Nasserist pan-Arabism in particular; and (3) implicate the United States as an imperialist power through its association with Britain and France, consequently discrediting American claims to promote freedom, equality, or justice. Eisenhower and Dulles, therefore, keenly sought to counteract Soviet propaganda by demonstrating how the United States was not a neocolonialist power in the mold of Britain and France and that the Eisenhower administration stood by Ike's declaration that the United States believed in "a society of equals, both nationally and internationally."[12] In the Suez crisis Ike was forced to choose—and he chose to uphold American dedication to the rule of law in international affairs over partiality to Britain, Israel, or France.

Richard Gregg's illuminating study of Eisenhower's Suez crisis address speaks to this tension present in Ike's speech.[13] Gregg's work shows how Eisenhower's rhetoric was shaped by the desire not to offend the postcolonial world and how he sought to distance the United States from the actions of its allies. Using a situational analysis of the speech, Gregg shows how Eisenhower "employed idealistic rhetoric" to "distance two areas of conflict in the world [Eastern Europe and Suez] from the shores of this country and thus from the immediate concerns of the American public."[14] He also explains how Eisenhower's speech attempted to navigate the complex diplomatic dance of balancing America's need to reassure its allies of its continuing commitment to them with the need to appeal to their virulently anticolonial former subjects. However, as Gregg also states, the complexity of the Suez crisis dictated that "Eisenhower's speech must be explicated on several different levels."[15] To answer the question of how he negotiated the multifaceted demands confronting him, a closer analysis of how Eisenhower addressed the problem of Cold War–era imperialism in the Middle East is required. It is my contention that Ike not only sought to *distance* America from its allies, but that he used this speech and the crisis it addressed to make an argument for why America should *displace* them. In other words Ike's speech marked the first time an American president made a comprehensive case for a uniquely American responsibility to maintain order and safeguard the Middle East independently of other powers, and therefore it marked a dramatic (though understated) shift in presidential rhetoric that directly prepared the way for the Eisenhower Doctrine.

Setting the Stage: Nationalization and Crisis

Colonel Nasser came to power in Egypt following the Free Officers' coup at the ripe age of thirty-six. He despised the continuing presence of British troops at Suez even after the 1954 settlement, and he became even further alienated from the West by the Baghdad Pact, which he saw as strengthening Iraq at Egypt's expense.[16] Frustrated by successful Israeli military incursions in the Sinai (made possible by French weapons), he eventually circumvented the Tripartite Agreement himself and agreed to a $200 million arms deal with the Soviets. These actions and others—particularly Nasser's recognition of Communist China—caused America and Britain to cancel their offer to finance the construction of the Aswan Dam.[17] In retaliation Nasser nationalized the Suez Canal on July 26, 1956, infuriating not only British prime minister Eden but also French premier Guy Mollet, who opposed Nasser for his pan-Arabist support for the Algerian rebels.[18]

Eisenhower, wishing to avoid an invasion of Egypt by its former colonial masters and the inevitable international backlash such an action would bring, sought to adjudicate the situation through a series of conferences overseen by Secretary of State Dulles. The British and the French, however, secretly began plans to collaborate with Israel to bring down Nasser through military force. In a Foreign Office cable, Undersecretary Sir Ivone Kirkpatrick described Whitehall's thinking, revealing the disparity in American and British Cold War strategy:

I wish the President were right. But I am convinced that he is wrong. . . . If we sit back while Nasser consolidates his position and gradually acquires control of the oil-bearing countries, he can, and is, according to our information, resolved to wreck us. If Middle East oil is denied to us for a year or two our gold reserves will disappear. If our gold reserves disappear the sterling area disintegrates. If the sterling area disintegrates and we have no reserves we shall not be able to maintain a force in Germany or, indeed, anywhere else. I doubt whether we shall be able to pay for the bare minimum necessary for our defence. And a country that cannot provide for its defence is finished.[19]

As Kirkpatrick's quote indicates, British policy makers viewed the situation in the Middle East primarily as an issue of national security, as did Eisenhower and Dulles. However, Ike viewed virtually all security issues within the larger framework of containment; in this instance the strategy of containment necessitated not fueling Khrushchev's anti-imperialist propaganda machine. British planners such as Kirkpatrick, on the other hand, conceived of national security in terms of access to resources and preserving British prestige; they thus chose to attack Nasser. These responses were in diametric opposition to each other. Yet because the British apparently did not realize that they were acting against the wishes of their strongest ally—a condition made possible by Eisenhower's surreptitious rhetorical style—neither the United States nor Britain was aware of the fact that they were on a collision course.

It bears noting that Ike and Dulles were not entirely clear in their private communication with the British. They indulged Eden in his characterization of Nasser as a would-be Hitler, with Dulles describing him as "an extremely dangerous fanatic," and Ike stating, "We do not intend to stand by helplessly and let this one man get away with what he is trying to do." At the same time Dulles warned the British and the French that they "had not yet made their case" and cautioned them about doing anything rash.[20] Also complicating the communication between Ike and Eden was the fact that the messages were being delivered by Dulles, who was

Lion's Last Roar, Eagle's First Flight

personally quite stridently anti-Nasser. In any case Bose and Green-stein's judgment of how Ike responded to the spurious "missile gap" controversy would also seem to apply to this situation: "An Eisenhower who did more to be publicly articulate might have prevented that outcome."[21] But he was not more articulate, and serious misunderstanding soon gave way to grave blunder on the part of America's allies.

Eden, Mollet, and Ben-Gurion's plan to overthrow Nasser was fairly straightforward. Israel would attack Egypt in the Sinai, claim-ing that it was responding to fedayeen attacks. Britain and France would next "intervene" to prevent further bloodshed; the Royal Air Force would destroy Egyptian military installations and demor-alize the civilian populace. Delivering the coup de grâce, eighty thousand European troops would then land in the Canal Zone, destroy whatever Arab resistance was offered, and depose Nasser if his own people had not already done so. The secret plot was aptly code-named Operation Musketeer.[22]

The plan went into effect October 29. Complicating matters, on October 22 popular protests erupted in Budapest against the Rus-sian occupation of Hungary, much as had happened in Poland ear-lier that year.[23] Though at first it appeared as though the protests might be successful, by October 31 Soviet troops had poured into Budapest and crushed the uprising, initiating a weeklong blood-bath starting just a few hours after Eisenhower's Suez speech.[24] These bewildering events took place, no less, during the final stretch of the 1956 presidential campaign between Ike and chal-lenger Adlai Stevenson. And so yet a mere six days from the elec-tion, with bombs falling on Cairo and Soviet soldiers rounding up Hungarian dissidents, Eisenhower went before the American public and addressed the nation.

Analysis of the Address

Medhurst, writing about how the "Cold War weapons" of "words, images, [and] symbolic actions" were deployed, describes how the primary aim of Cold War rhetors such as Eisenhower was to improve their nation's strategic position "without sacrificing the concomitant goal of avoiding world conflagration."[25] It is in consideration of this strategic use of rhetoric, within the frameworks of presidential discourse on the Middle East, the Cold War, and the president's capacity as the chief symbol-creator and sense-maker in American political discourse, that I analyze the Eisenhower's address of October 31.

The speech was brief. Excluding the salutation and closing, it consisted of forty-eight paragraphs, thirty-two of which were one or two sentences long. Eisenhower opened with, "My fellow Americans: Tonight I report to you as your President," clearly identifying the American public as his primary audience, although his words bore significance for multiple listeners: Congress, unsure of whether military action would be taken or requested; Eden, Ben-Gurion, and Mollet; America's other allies around the globe; Nasser and the Egyptian people; the Communist bloc, which mistrusted America's intent in Hungary and Suez; and the nonaligned nations.[26] Though his words carried obvious weight for the many parties involved, Ike continued to treat the American public as his primary audience by assuming the guise of a reporter giving only "a report of essential facts." He did his utmost to remove himself from the text; he continued to speak positioned as a third party, disconnected from the events that were taking place. The pronoun "I" was employed only eleven times in the body of the speech. In its stead Ike referred to the actions of "your government" and used the plural pronoun "we" thirty-five times. Throughout the speech Ike's tone was firm, straightforwardly informing the nation about the "swiftly changing world scene." Yet by removing himself from the text, Ike maintained that the words he spoke were an accurate, *objective* interpretation of the world, thereby rendering competing explanations by definition subjective—the realm of mere opinion. Commenting on the factual and inexpressive nature of the address, rhetorician James Pratt notes, "The speech could have been read by [news anchor] Chet Huntley."[27] Clearly Eisenhower wished to insert himself sparingly in this speech, and in examining the domestic political setting we are given reason why.

As many have noted, especially Fred Greenstein, Eisenhower was supremely adept at propagating an image of noble statesmanship, even at times accused of inattention, all while astutely navigating the nation's political winds. This strategy insulated Ike from volatile issues like McCarthyism, civil rights legislation, and intraparty power struggles. He was perceived to be "confident but modest, cheerful but able to be appropriately stern, direct and candid in speech, paternalistically caring and honest."[28] Given Ike's stature and success, many 1956 GOP candidates relied heavily on Eisenhower's popularity in their bid to retake Congress, hoping to achieve reelection on the back of the "man of peace."[29] The Republican Party's electoral chances, not to mention Ike's reputation, were thrown in doubt with the eruption of conflict in Hungary and Egypt. Democratic challenger Adlai Stevenson had repeatedly and thus far unsuccessfully attempted to criticize Eisenhower's foreign-policy track record, and the twin crises, conveniently arriving at the race's conclusion, presented evidence that Stevenson could be right about the president's foreign-policy flaws.

However, by creating rhetorical distance with phrases like "your government" and using the protreptic "we," Eisenhower depoliticized the events taking place across the world, his rhetoric functioning to refute Stevenson without acknowledging Stevenson's critique.[30] He acknowledged that "the full and free debate of a political campaign" surrounded him and his audience yet then immediately asserted, "But the events and issues I wish to place before you this evening have no connection whatsoever with matters of partisanship. They are concerns of every American."[31] By defining the topic he was about to address as outside the bounds of the current presidential campaign, Eisenhower delegitimized any response the opposition could give. In doing so he also claimed the epistemological high ground. As president his perspective was not that of a mere candidate running for office but the lofty view of one who possessed all the available information, speaking not from opinion but from fact. Here Eisenhower's ethos, moreover, worked to establish for his audience both the facts of the events *and* the perspective from which to view them. Since he was discussing foreign-policy happenings of a military nature, Ike's perceived authority on the matter was virtually unassailable.

Having identified himself and his audience, Eisenhower did not then relinquish his reporter guise but rather employed its authority to define the situation: "In Eastern Europe there is the dawning of a new day. It has not been short or easy in coming." Eisenhower next traced the reason why such a day had been long in arriving, explaining, "After World War II, the Soviet Union used military force to impose on the nations of Eastern Europe, governments of Soviet choice—servants of Moscow." Thus did Ike, consistent with his prior Cold War rhetoric, effectively characterize the Soviet Union as a military oppressor occupying half of Europe.[32] After all for what reason did "the people of Poland—with their proud and deathless devotion to freedom" desire a new government that would "strive genuinely to serve the Polish people," and why had the Hungarians "offered their very lives for independence from foreign masters" if not because of Soviet occupation?[33] Eisenhower's language classified the actions of the Poles and the Hungarians as freedom loving—even going so far as to reference the role emigrants from those nations played in the American Revolution—enabling him to play on the established dualism of his prior depictions of the Soviet Union as a threat to liberty without explicitly saying such a thing.

Consistent with Eisenhower's desire not to exacerbate the Cold War, he also did not blatantly vilify the Soviets.[34] In this speech he sought to remove any "false fears" Soviet leaders might have that America "would look upon new governments in these Eastern European countries as potential military allies," insisting, "We have no such ulterior purpose." The last thing the president wanted was to precipitate a war. Yet the distinction he made in the speech was clear. By suppressing the Eastern Europeans, the Soviets were an unabashed threat to democracy, rightful independence, and freedom. Indeed, given the American political climate at the time, having lived through six years of Senator McCarthy, it is likely that any additional Soviet demonization or saber-rattling on Eisenhower's part would have led to needlessly dangerous alarm—after all, Nikolai Bulganin had just threatened to attack London and Paris.[35]

In reality Soviet soldiers had already begun cracking down on Hungarian protestors by the time Eisenhower gave his address. This disconnect highlighted even further the differences between America and its Communist rival. Whereas the Soviets were forcibly imposing their will on subjugated populaces, Eisenhower declared, "We see these people as friends, and we wish simply that they be friends who are free." According to Ike the United States sought not to dominate smaller nations. Instead, Americans "help[ed] to keep alive the hope of these peoples for freedom" while they suffered under Communist oppression. Ike repeatedly contrasted the Soviet Union, which refused to grant true independence and employed brute military might to overpower "Poland, Hungary, and Rumania [sic]," with America, whose only wish was for these people to experience the same liberty it enjoyed. Unlike that of the oppressive Russians, America's interest in Hungary was innocently impartial and benign.[36]

Robert Ivie identifies this force-versus-freedom contrasting technique as a common topos, or place of rhetorical invention, employed by American presidents to characterize enemies of the nation.[37] Metaphors of aggressive savagery often function as vehicles of decivilization, creating the image of an implacably evil and hostile foe.[38] Describing how Communist enemies were represented during the Cold War, Ivie writes,

> Critics are likely to encounter a number of recurring motives in Cold War rhetoric. The metaphor of savagery, for instance, and its support cast of decivilizing vehicles play a central role in constructing the image of a hostile and threatening enemy. Various terms characterize the enemy as irrational, coercive, and aggressive. . . . They speak of Soviets as if they were snakes, wolves, and other kinds of dangerous predators, and as if they were primitives, brutes, barbarians, mindless machines, criminals, lunatics, fanatics, and the enemies of God.[39]

Such a rendering allowed the Communists to "symbolize the perfect enemy of freedom."[40] While Eisenhower stopped somewhat short of such a dramatic exposition of the Soviet Union in this speech, the theme of force versus freedom was clearly present. With such a powerful enemy opposed to the liberty of humankind running globally amok, a necessary counterweight needed to emerge to ensure the rule of law and enable democratic values to flourish—the United States.[41] Playing upon the Manichaean, dualistic nature of his Cold War rhetoric, Ike used a negative depiction of the Soviet Union to implicitly characterize the United States as a virtuous, genuinely good-willed friend to small nations such as Hungary and Poland. Thus Eisenhower, employing the contrasting topos of force versus freedom, firmly established American virtue (particularly dedication to freedom) before advancing to his description of Suez.

At this critical juncture the president shifted his focus to "that other part of the world where, at [that] moment, the situation [was] somber." Before addressing the developing situation in Suez, he first situated the political context of the crisis for his listeners:

> I speak of course, of the Middle East. This ancient crossroads of the world was, as we all know, an area long subject to colonial rule. This rule ended after World War II, when all countries there won full independence. Out of the Palestinian mandated territory was born the new State of Israel.
>
> These historic changes could not, however, instantly banish animosities born of the ages. Israel and her Arab neighbors soon found themselves at war with one another. And the Arab nations showed continuing anger toward their former colonial rulers, notably France and Great Britain.[42]

Eisenhower's account portrayed Arabs in several desensitizing ways. First, he described the Middle East as existing in a different chronological reality than the United States. It remained an "ancient" land "long subject" to colonial powers, ruled by "animosities born of the ages"—an oft-iterated romantic trope used to describe the region by Westerners. In fact this language was toned down from an earlier draft that read, "These antagonisms are lost in legend."[43] Speaking to this phenomenon, in his seminal work *Orientalism* Edward Said identifies the ways in which time and space have rhetorical imaginative functions; they acquire poetic dimensions, says Said, through which "anonymous reaches of distances are converted into meaning for us here."[44] In other words the way in which time is linguistically depicted carries rhetorical force.

Said notes that Western European characterizations of the "Orient" seemingly always associate it with being "not quite ignorant, not quite informed," a portrayal he claims goes as far back as Classical Greece.[45] For the British and the French, this view of the Middle East often took a literary or poetic turn. However, Orientalism in its American iteration, Said argues, is concerned not with romantic reconstructions but rather with facts—such as the "fact" that Arab and Jews, in Ike's explication, simply possessed an entropic tendency to violence. Said writes, "The net effect of this remarkable omission in modern American awareness of the Arab or Islamic Orient is to keep the region and its people conceptually emasculated, reduced to 'attitudes,' 'trends,' statistics: in short, dehumanized."[46] By placing them in a different chronological reality and expositing them as being ruled by passion, Eisenhower denied the Arab Egyptians full, rational personhood. They were not real people, only trends; they served the role of static stock characters in his rhetorical drama replete with Orientalist assumptions.

By characterizing the Egyptians in this way, Eisenhower's rhetoric drew heavily from the American Orientalist frame.[47] Very palpable causes and motivations existed for Egyptian behavior regarding the British occupation. The Arab-Israeli conflict was a relatively recent phenomenon beginning with the original Zionist settlement of the second decade of the twentieth century, and the failure of Project Alpha in addition to American and British refusal to sell Egypt arms or fund the Aswan Dam exacerbated Nasser's conflict with the West.[48] Yet Eisenhower ignored this history. He instead chose to characterize the Middle East as a capricious territory ruled by ahistorical forces, often violent and full of vengeance. He ascribed Egyptian violence not to its immediate sources but to vague cultural forces and attitudes timelessly at work. In articulating an inert Middle East, Ike perpetuated an errant Orientalist understanding of the region to the American public.[49]

Second, having constituted in the minds of his listeners a Middle East chronologically outside modernity and riddled with blood feuds, Eisenhower then allocated blame for the conflict's genesis. As he had with Iran, Eisenhower depicted Egypt as at fault for the conflict. Showing "continual anger" toward the colonial powers, Egypt exercised "misguided policy" and "aggravated" tensions in the region by rearming via Soviet weapons and then "seizing" the Suez Canal. Ike's description of a young nation-state prone to unwise and emotional decisions reinforced aspects of this Orientalist narrative and contrasted Egyptian behavior with that of the prudential United States. America did not turn to force after the canal's seizure but rather "insistently urged" its allies not to act out of violence. The president, emphasizing the rationality of the United States, remarked how America desired the path of negotiation and sought the involvement of the United Nations. Furthermore, his characterization of Egypt's actions as an understandable yet excessive response to colonialism allowed a comparison to be drawn to America's own postcolonial experience, during which it restored diplomatic relations relatively quickly after independence and became a major trading partner with Britain.[50] Through synchronic and diachronic contrast, Eisenhower set up an unwise Arab Egypt as the foil to the sensibly reasonable United States.

Third, Eisenhower described the intense regional conflict resulting in Israeli nationhood (and Palestinian lack of statehood) in passive, selectively factual language that obfuscated America's role in the creation of the modern Middle East. While independence had come to the region in a technical sense, in reality the British were still deeply embedded as a colonial power at the time of the address. Israel, moreover, was widely viewed by Arabs as an extension of Western hegemony and had received extensive backing (much of it private) from France and the United States. Thus by declaring that "all nations there won full independence" and that the Israelis and Arabs simply "found themselves at war with one another," Eisenhower reified an Orientalist explanation of the past decade's violence—warfare is simply a regular occurrence in this region resulting from antediluvian animosities—and concealed the much more tangible factors leading to conflict, such as the creation of Israel or the ongoing British military presence. In doing so he censored his audience's knowledge of prior American forays into the Middle East undertaken in the decade leading up to the crisis, such as Truman's support for Israel, secret peace negotiations, and the CIA activities across the region.

Again Eisenhower argued that the Egyptians existed atemporally, behaved out of irrational aggression, and reacted to colonial actions in which America was uninvolved. Thus, according to the speech's logic, Nasser, as the embodiment of Arab Egypt and the region's most powerful leader, could not be relied on to resolve the situation. However, as Eisenhower next pointed out, neither could Israel, Britain, or France be trusted because they acted outside the prudent leadership of the United States. While Eisenhower sympathetically painted all three nations as acting out of "anxiety" and "fear" for their interests, he elaborated most fully on America's relationship with Israel: "We have considered it a basic matter of United States policy to support the new state of Israel and—at the same time—to strengthen our bonds with both Israel and with the Arab countries. But, unfortunately through all these years, passion in the area threatened to prevail over peaceful purposes, and in one form or another, there has been almost continuous fighting."[51]

Israel was paradoxically viewed by the Eisenhower administration as both a Cold War asset—Israel shared American democratic values and was staunchly anti-Communist—and a hindrance—American support for Israel contaminated its attempts to attract Muslim states as allies. In addition to its perceived strategic value, Israel also elicited widespread emotional sympathy in America. The electoral influence of American Jews was strong in states such as New York and California, and their importance would not have been lost on the president with an election taking place in six days.[52] Despite this factor Eisenhower condemned the attack on Egypt. He resisted American Zionist pressure to inflexibly support Israel and remained dedicated to a policy of impartiality between Arab and Jewish concerns. As a result of Israeli aggression, then, the president determined that American allies had unacceptably violated the 1950 Tripartite Agreement. Unlike the United States and its president, which "since the close of World War II" had "labored tirelessly to bring peace and stability to this area," Britain, France, and Israel unceremoniously exposed themselves as enthusiasts of war—and therefore as deserving of America's wrathful response.

Having completely misread Eisenhower, Eden, Mollet, and Ben-Gurion subsequently found themselves in the position they least expected and for which they had not prepared: in opposition to the United States.[53] Not only would America decline to support them, but it was stridently opposed to the actions of its allies. Eisenhower, transitioning to the last phase of the speech, announced his policy: "As it is the manifest right of any of these nations to take such decisions and actions, it is likewise our right—if our judgment so dictates—to dissent. We believe these actions to have been taken in error. For we do not accept the use of force as a wise or proper instrument for the settlement of international disputes."[54]

Eisenhower, aware of the magnitude of his announcement and the weight it would hold for global diplomacy, restated America's desire to maintain friendships with Israel, Britain, and France, and he affirmed that he understood their anxieties. Indeed, he sought to accomplish a difficult rhetorical task, namely, to dissociate his nation from the actions of its allies while remaining a part of the group.[55] Yet his position was clear: "The action taken can scarcely be reconciled with the principles and purposes of the United Nations to which we have all subscribed. . . . *There will be no United States involvement in these present hostilities*" (emphasis mine). As Gregg and others note, one of Ike's and Dulles's major concerns was that the Soviets would successfully submit a resolution at the UN General Assembly calling for a cease-fire, thus forcing America to effectively choose between supporting the Soviet resolution or its allies. This decision was made all the more frustrating by Soviet control in Eastern Europe seemingly beginning to break down in Hungary.[56] By quickly coming to a decision *against* his allies (and submitting a UN resolution before the Soviets), Eisenhower avoided a Soviet propaganda coup and demonstrated that a new day had dawned in American Middle East policy.

This was a transition a long time in the making. Ike had publicly lamented the effect of the Europeans' imperialist tendencies in the Arab world since the 1952 campaign, during which he framed America's challenge in the region as a relational problem between the Western world and the predominantly Muslim Middle East. In a press conference given June 22, 1952, for example, Eisenhower directly stated, "I believe there is no possibility this moment of establishing the kind of connection between the Middle East and the Western European powers which you are apparently seeking to do for the simple reason you have a very great hatred, you have a deep-seated prejudice. It is going to take long and patient work . . . to win the friendship of those nations." At another point Ike stated, "In the Mid East you have a question of just cold hatred of us over a number of instances of the past, and there we have got to win friends. . . . All the way through the Moslem world."[57] Eisenhower, since before he became president, had bemoaned the state of affairs between the Middle East and the "free world." What he did not do, during the 1952 campaign or during the first four years of his presidency, was blame America's allies and outright state that this animosity was in large part the fault of Britain's and France's imperialistic policies. Here, in Eisenhower's Suez crisis address, the decisive turn was finally made. While understated Ike's rebuke was impossible to miss: the Europeans had at last gone too far, and the United States would not support their aggressive use of force. America finally broke, rhetorically, with Britain and France.

To review: Eisenhower opened his address in the guise of president-as-reporter, and as Timothy Cole states, effective "foreign policy rhetoric . . . must also account for the behavior and motives of foreign policy actors."[58] Thus, like a good reporter, Ike then extended his "objective" lens to define the actors on stage and their motivations. First, he identified the Communist Soviet Union, a villain who knows no language but aggression and no reason but force. Next, Ike exposed Nasser's Egypt as an oriental entity that was yet to mature to enlightened statehood, the generator of the conflict, and an analogue for the Arabs at large. Finally, he advanced to the Israelis, the British, and the French—friends all, but friends who could not be trusted with looking after the region due to their foolish military retaliation to the canal nationalization. Thus Eisenhower's rhetorical narrative still required an answer to the questions: What is the solution? How will America respond to this threat? How will this crisis be resolved (implicitly, who is responsible for the Middle East)? Here the president broke with the Truman Doctrine—and every other presidential precedent for articulating America's stake in the Middle East—by not reaffirming a commitment to the imperialist status quo, with minor adjustments. Eisenhower, having disqualified all other contenders, found that only America remained to answer the call of duty. A close reading of the text shows that, having discarding the idea of British responsibility, Ike proposed a new premise for U.S. engagement in the Middle East: that it was America's job.

Announcing the nation's willingness to assume the leadership mantle in the Middle East, Eisenhower proclaimed, "It is—and it will remain—the dedicated purpose of your government to do all in its power to localize the fighting and end the conflict." Despite its unwillingness to fight militarily, Eisenhower's America still devoted itself to resolving the conflict. Far from accepting the Middle East as a British area of concern, Eisenhower announced that the United States had already and would continue to work toward responsibly ending the fight via "the processes of the United Nations."[59] Here the president carefully described the United Nations as supporting *America's* policy, not vice versa; the United Nations was thus positioned as a means for achieving the end of the United States: peace. Moreover, invoking the United Nations allowed Eisenhower to avoid direct American insertion into the conflict. He asserted, "In the past the United Nations has proved able to find a way to end bloodshed. We believe it can and that it will do so again" (despite the organization's complete failure in the region's most intractable conflict, Palestine).[60] Thus Eisenhower's speech provided a complete narrative of threat, conflict, need for solution, and entrance of the United States as the solution—in this case presenting America as the guarantor of liberty against imperialism.[61] That Eisenhower was able to soften the impact of this narrative arc and concomitant redefinition of America's stake in the Middle East by excluding a call to U.S. military intervention in favor of UN mediation did not change the speech's logic. The president had now publicly affirmed the Middle East as a whole as an American interest, and the foundational premise justifying American engagement there had been permanently altered.

This shift in thinking is made evident by a comparison to the Truman Doctrine address of 1947.[62] In that speech President Truman argued for increased aid allotments for Greece and Turkey, claiming, "Greece must have assistance if it is to become a self-supporting and self-respecting democracy," and "if Turkey is to have the assistance it needs, the United States must supply it." As noted earlier, however, Truman couched his argument by framing the additional investiture of American aid as necessary because of London's economic inability, not its moral failings: "The British Government, which has been helping Greece, can give no further financial or economic aid after March 31. . . . [London] has informed us that, owing to its own difficulties, it can no longer extend financial or economic aid to Turkey."[63] According to Truman's framing of the issue, America was providing aid to Greece and Turkey only because Britain was incapable of doing so—not because Britain was unworthy or unfit for the task. The underlying rationale for the Truman Doctrine was financial in nature and had little to do with a dispute over principle.

By contrast Eisenhower characterized the failings of Britain, France, and Israel at Suez as *moral* in nature. They acted in opposition to "the principles and purposes" of peaceful coexistence enshrined at the United Nations and "determined that, in their judgment, there could be no protection of their vital interests without resort to force."[64] Whereas Truman described an exhausted

Britain in need of fresh American strength to uphold regional order, Ike depicted America's allies as doubly capricious and foolhardy, reminding his audience that the United States was "forced to doubt that resort to force and war [would] for long serve the permanent interest of the attacking nations." In his framing America's obligation to the Middle East stemmed not from its economic might, as the Truman Doctrine argued, but from its prudential and moral exemplarity, as evidenced by its consistent pursuit of peace. The United States was thus dissociated from its allies on a moral plane while still bonded with them in friendship. Moreover, America was now authorized to intervene in the region on the basis of its moral superiority.

Having redefined America's role in the region, Eisenhower then justified this shift by using idealistic, almost supernatural language to diagnose the world's ideological needs. Ned O'Gorman goes so far as to describe this aspect of Eisenhower's rhetoric as "priestly," in that he mediated between the ultimate reality of "America's spiritual greatness and the mundane material world," loftily interpreting events in a way that gave meaning to America's Cold War experience.[65] In concluding his address Eisenhower divined the deeper, spiritual meaning of these events and his chosen course of action for the American people. As he proceeded to wax philosophic, Ike invoked within his report transcendent themes such as equality, justice, and humankind's quest for peace, all of which he formulated in vague enough terms to be universally appealing. By so doing he also provided the moral basis for an increased American presence in the Middle East:

> There can be no peace—without law. And there can be no law—if we were to invoke one code of international conduct for those who oppose us—and another for our friends.
>
> The society of nations has been slow in developing means to apply this truth.
>
> But the passionate longing for peace—on the part of all peoples of the earth—compels us to speed our search for new and more effective instruments of justice.

The peace we seek and need means much more than mere absence of war. It means the acceptance of law, and the fostering of justice, in all the world.

To our principles guiding us in this quest we must stand fast. In so doing we can honor the hopes of all men for a world in which peace will truly and justly reign.[66]

Eisenhower, having already announced his policy decisions, left his listeners with a simple argument. Without law there is no peace. There presently is no law. Therefore, there is no peace—at Suez and in the Middle East generally.

However, as Eisenhower claimed, all peoples of the earth desire peace, providing a moral basis for American regional engagement as the nation of peace (with, conveniently, the "man of peace" at the helm). Again, regardless of the literal actions proposed, this language amounted to a *rhetorical* transformation of American Middle East policy because it was now the United States' solemn duty to "stand fast" and bring about a "world in which peace [would] truly and justly reign." This was a task for America, not compromised Britain. It was now America's job, perhaps via the "instrument" of the United Nations or perhaps independently (as the subsequent Eisenhower Doctrine made clear), to maintain peace in the Middle East—a peace that meant far more than mere lack of conflict, but the adoption and flourishing of justice and law. Such Wilsonian, American-value-spreading rhetoric underscored the fact that an interventionist shift in policy had actually already occurred—Ike's America had very much sought to enact major change in the region, just covertly.

Eisenhower's speech also contained a narratival frame often used to justify intervention in American foreign-policy discourse, that of rescue and salvation.[67] If other nations had been "slow in developing means to apply this truth," then the responsibility again fell on the United States to promote a world in which "peace [would] truly and justly reign." Only America could do this in the Middle East, as already established in the speech via respective contrast with the other countries. Where the Soviets sought domination, America wanted freedom; where Egypt acted out of indignant immaturity, America prudently suggested negotiation; while Israel, Britain, and France wielded power irresponsibly, America pursued the interests of the entire world. According to Eisenhower's narrative the United States of America was the only nation with the requisite virtue and prudence to vouchsafe such a vision of global prosperity, which would "honor the hopes of all men."

Postcrisis Postscript: The Suez Crisis and the Eisenhower Doctrine

Eisenhower's speech, by providing a new American raison d'être in the Middle East, rhetorically paved the way for a much more assertive Middle East presence. Therefore, the Suez crisis represents not only a major shift in American Middle East policy, as numerous historians, political scientists, and former diplomats have attested, but equally marks a rhetorical evolution in the presidential speech authorizing this change. Several major effects of Ike's rhetoric stand out when one considers the significance of this address.

As with all political discourse, Eisenhower's speech must first be understood within its immediate contextual frame. The president determined that America should control the situation, and he communicated his intent to oppose Britain, France, and Israel clearly, despite the amicable language used. This decision was supported with the threat and limited application of military, political, and economic force.[68] In bringing the former imperial masters of the Middle East to the brink of economic disaster, Eisenhower left no doubt that America was in charge and would remain so.[69] Ike's rhetoric functioned within this strategy to frame the United States' new approach to the Middle East in as persuasive terms as possible, articulating an interventionist ethic borne not from imperialist ambition but from the necessary dictates of the Cold War. For the sake of containment—not grandeur—America assumed its new responsibility to protect the Middle East from unwarranted outside aggression. This step, while ultimately directed against Russia, also necessitated that the United States protect the neutrality of Nasser's Egypt. And indeed Eisenhower's speech was celebrated throughout the Middle East as just that, a defense of the rights of Arab nations against the rapacious Europeans and Israelis. In that sense the Suez crisis speech stands out as a hallmark pronouncement of American support for the sanctity of international law.

More broadly Ike's Suez crisis speech can be understood as constructing the underlying rhetorical foundation of the Eisenhower Doctrine announced sixty-six days later. The address did this in three primary ways. First, and most importantly, Ike's speech positioned the United States as an *inside* actor in the Middle East standing in opposition to the *outside* forces that sought to subjugate the region. When confronted by the crisis, Ike could have adopted a policy of "neutrality" and stated that, though he regretted the actions of U.S. allies, the problems of the Middle East were in the end not America's concern. Instead, by announcing that the United States would do "all in its power" to resolve the conflict, Eisenhower implicitly asserted that America had a right to act as the region's protector. America was therefore not an outside party seeking to impose its will on the Middle East but a friend of the region defending it from such aggressors. In framing the issue as he did, Ike created an unspoken discrepancy between the actions of the United States, which were assumed to be legitimate, and those of other powers, which were by nature hostile.

While in this instance Ike applied his rubric to Britain, France, and Israel, in the Eisenhower Doctrine speech he would articulate this principle in far more robust terms as it pertained to "Communist aggression, both direct and indirect."[70] Indeed, Eisenhower went so far as to state that the simple declaration of his eponymous doctrine would "serve to halt any contemplated aggression." In essence Ike argued that America's policy of being ready to intervene militarily anywhere in the Middle East to prevent the spread of Communism meant that these nations would "not feel that they [stood] alone, under the menace of a great power." The only way in which such an overtly assertive U.S. policy was *not* the menace of a great power in this context was if America's actions were inherently legitimate—the actions of an accepted defender, not those of an external aggressor. In the Suez crisis speech, Eisenhower's rhetoric worked to establish the United States as exactly that, an internal actor acting in defense of the Middle East.

Second, the Suez crisis address functioned to categorize the United States as a suitable stand-in for the United Nations in the Middle East. In Eisenhower's parlance the United Nations and America were virtually indistinguishable in terms of ideals: both abhorred the use of violence and preferred negotiations, both were motivated by the desire to protect smaller nations, and both were wholly dedicated to the cause of peace. In terms of action Ike characterized America and the United Nations as consubstantial in deed as well as word; though Britain and France vetoed the UN Security Council proposal, temporarily thwarting "justice under international law," America would unilaterally enforce justice via economic sanctions.[71] Where the United Nations could not go, America was willing to act—in presumably similar fashion, toward similar ends. Eisenhower's rhetoric also functioned to characterize the United Nations as the vehicle by which America's regional objectives would be realized, thus blurring the boundaries between the two organizations' purposes in the Middle East.

This haziness would be directly addressed in the Eisenhower Doctrine speech, in which Ike explicitly laid out the argument for why the United Nations was incapable of adequately serving as the sole "protector of small nations." As he stated, "when the ambitions of the Soviet Union [were] involved," that nation's Security Council veto prevented UN resolutions from succeeding—yet the United States, undeterred by the Communists, was willing to fulfill the United Nation's role as a "dependable protector of freedom." In Ike's formulation the United States was clearly identified with the United Nations vis-à-vis the security of Middle Eastern countries, thus authorizing American intervention in the name of regional self-defense. By describing American and UN aims as virtually interchangeable, Eisenhower's rhetoric in the Suez crisis speech began the process of identifying the United States with the mission of the United Nations in the region.

Third, the Suez crisis speech worked to disqualify Britain and

France from the mantle of leadership in the Middle East and thus explains their notable absence in the Eisenhower Doctrine address. As this analysis demonstrates, Eisenhower made the case that Britain and France opted to use an "instrument of injustice—war" instead of employing peaceful means to remedy the "wrongs" done to them. The brazen choice to use force, which Ike labeled not "a wise or proper instrument for the settlement of international disputes," could "scarcely be reconciled with the principles and purposes of the United Nations to which [the nations involved] have all subscribed." In short Britain and France violated their word through their naked use of power. This offense thus precluded any claim to authority in the Middle East that either of those countries might have possessed, opening the way for the United States to assume their mantle as the preeminent Western power in the region. In the Suez crisis address, Eisenhower rhetorically revoked the European decades-old mandates to rule the region.

With the Western European powers out of the picture, Ike could then argue in the Eisenhower Doctrine speech that the United States needed to fill "any lack of power in the area" should Communist aggression surface—a power vacuum supposedly caused by the collapse of the European imperial order imposed on the Middle East after World War I. The prior work of delegitimizing Britain and France performed in the Suez crisis speech provided an answer for why America could not simply reinforce its allies' position in the region, as the backing of such unsavory imperialists would be counterproductive to the larger strategy of containment. This rendering of Britain and France as unfit for authority appears to function as an enthymeme in the Eisenhower Doctrine speech; that is, Ike never argued explicitly for why the European imperial system was no longer suitable for the Middle East and was not in keeping with America's interest, yet this idea was necessary for the speech's logic to work. In syllogistic form Ike's argument went something like this: the Europeans underwrote the Middle East's security for decades (stated premise), Britain and France were no longer capable of fulfilling this function (unstated premise), and therefore the United States needed to fulfill this role if Communism was to be contained (conclusion). Without the Suez crisis address, the argumentative heart of the Eisenhower Doctrine speech did not make sense. The former should therefore be understood as preparing the way for the latter.

In the first chapter, I noted several features of the Eisenhower Doctrine speech that could not be easily explained by examining that address alone. As I have shown, the Suez crisis speech worked to lay the groundwork for Ike's pronouncement of the Middle East Resolution by establishing certain *assumptions*: positioning the United States as an insider in the Middle East, by classifying the United States as an appropriate substitute for the United Nations, and by removing Britain and France from the pool of appropriate leaders of the region. Taken together these elements reappeared in the Eisenhower Doctrine address in a formulation meant to prevent the expansion of Communism in the Middle East. In the next chapter I investigate how the Eisenhower Doctrine was applied to justify the landing of American troops in Lebanon— and how this event produced a rhetorical template for Middle Eastern intervention that endures to this day.

The meaning of Suez differed for the various parties involved. For Britain and France, which before the crisis appeared as weakened but still functional colonial powers, Suez provided an exclamation point on their increasing global impotence, economic fragility, and dependence on the United States to protect Western interests. For Egypt and other Arab states, the crisis served as an affirmation of Gamal Abdul Nasser's pan-Arab nationalism and led to regime changes and uprisings in response to his message. For Israel Suez increased hostilities with Egypt, resulted in access to the Red Sea, and revealed the need to develop closer ties with the United States, thus setting the stage for the 1967 war. And for the superpowers the Suez Canal crisis introduced full-scale Cold War to the lands of Ramses, Muhammad, and Moses.

Rhetorically the speech reversed much of the Eisenhower administration's prior language regarding the Middle East. Far from being a disinterested neutral party, America was now an insider, defending the region from outside interference. Eisenhower's characterization of the crisis's events and actors enabled him to provide a new basis for U.S. engagement in the Middle East—the role of guardian and guarantor of liberty—that broke from previously articulated rationales for American activity in the region premised on neutrality and deference to European sensibilities. By envisioning America as an independent agent for peace, Eisenhower prepared the United States to be thrust into the role that previous presidents had insisted belonged to Britain—that of regional hegemon. Ike's America, as exposited in this speech, was the only nation worthy of protecting the Middle East from Communism, and in the Eisenhower Doctrine address Ike would claim that it must. As made evident by the Eisenhower administration's intervention in Lebanon a year later, the twilight of British suzerainty in the Middle East had faded into an American dawn. After the lion's last roar, the eagle took flight.

5

The Doctrine Applied

Intervention in Lebanon and the Rhetoric of Justification

Of course, everybody is always scared of war. But, as I say, you have to
face up to it.—it's a possibility every once in a while—if you're going to
be effective in this business of maintaining the peace

—Eisenhower, oral interview, 1967

This was one meeting in which my mind was practically made up . . .
even before we met. The time was rapidly approaching, I believed,
when we had to move into the Middle East, and specifically into
Lebanon, to stop the trend toward chaos.

—Eisenhower, on the special NSC meeting of July 14, 1958

The genius of you Americans is that you never make clear-cut stupid
moves, only complicated stupid moves which makes us wonder at the
possibility that there may be something to them we are missing.

—Gamal Abdul Nasser to CIA agent Miles Copeland, 1957

Nasser thrives on drama.

—Eisenhower, letter to Eden, August 31, 1956

I f, as I have argued, the Eisenhower presidency changed the way
in which the Middle East is configured in presidential discourse,
then one might expect these changes to manifest themselves
in policy. In this chapter I contend that this exact scenario played
out in the Eisenhower administration's decision to deploy American troops to Lebanon in the summer of 1958. Viewed thusly
Ike's rhetoric regarding the Middle East, which had helped shape
policy options over the course of his two administrations, found
its apogee in this event. The addresses justifying Ike's choice to

send the marines to Beirut drew heavily from his previous rhetoric regarding the region, and in canvassing these familiar arguments to build the case for yet another step of U.S. engagement in
the Middle East—the landing of American soldiers—Eisenhower
laid the rhetorical foundation for American regional hegemony
on which future presidents would build.

Context: Eisenhower Doctrine

A year and half after its declaration, the Eisenhower Doctrine was
in retreat. Few Arab leaders had publicly aligned themselves with
the new policy, fearful that openly supporting American aims in
the region would incite revolt among populations still wary of
Western imperialism and incensed at U.S. popular support for
Israel. The handful of leaders who did embrace Eisenhower's
entreaty to denounce Communism were not important enough
to sway regional opinion in any significant direction. Nasser was
still ascendant. Worse, he remained on friendly terms with the
Soviet Union, going so far as to visit Moscow for a personal meeting with Khrushchev. Even American-Israeli relations were cool at
best. After Israel defied a U.S.-supported UN resolution demanding that the Jewish state withdraw from all the Egyptian lands captured during the Suez crisis, Eisenhower retaliated: he publicly
denounced the occupation, considered imposing trade sanctions,
and threatened to cut off private American assistance to Israel.[1]
By late March 1957 all Israeli forces had left the Sinai—but not
before laying waste to every form of infrastructure in their path,
in a clear display of contempt for Eisenhower and the United
Nations ruling. And so it went. Though "International Communism" had not exactly invaded the Middle East, at every turn the
Eisenhower administration met nothing but foreign-policy failure in the region.

Indeed, events over the eighteen months following the declaration of the Eisenhower Doctrine seemingly conspired to wreck
U.S. ambitions for the region. The new strategy, far from strengthening America's allies, worked to weaken them. In Jordan, for
example, the doctrine worked to exacerbate internal political divi-

sions regarding Amman's relationship to the West to the point of crisis, with King Hussein preserving his throne only through a series of high-risk political maneuvers.[2] The Eisenhower Doctrine also failed to prevent leftward political drift. Syria was feared by U.S. officials to be in the midst of becoming a "Soviet tool and base of Communist operations" in the Middle East, leading to Operation Wappen, another botched coup attempt by the Central Intelligence Agency, leading to yet more anti-American sentiment in the Levant.[3] Sensationalist reports of the coup attempt drove millions of Arabs across the Middle East even further from the U.S. camp. Perhaps the most alarming development for U.S. defense planners, Nasser's pan-Arab message directly led to the incorporation of Egypt and Syria into the United Arab Republic in February 1958. This amalgamation created the popular expectation that more nations would shortly follow. This move, while actually more the result of instability in Damascus than a master plan executed from Cairo, was nonetheless a major propaganda coup for Nasser; Egypt and Syria's union fired the imaginations of Middle Easterners from Algeria to Iraq with visions of pan-Arab unity. It also struck dread into the hearts of America's conservative Arab allies, who knew the populations they ruled were among those inspired.

Thus as a policy the Eisenhower Doctrine mostly flopped. The doctrine's ostensive function—promising an American security guarantee to any Middle Eastern government that overtly opposed Communism—worked to too closely identify supportive Arab regimes with the unpopular United States, thereby weakening U.S. regional allies in the face of Nasser's Arab nationalism. If, as I have argued, Ike framed the Eisenhower Doctrine as a rhetorical solution to what was effectively a rhetorical problem, then the ideological triumph of Nasser's pan-Arabism, fueled as it was by Cairo Radio and Egyptian popular culture, can be read as one rhetorical appeal trumping another. By the summer of 1958, the Eisenhower administration had grasped this reality and begun deemphasizing the confrontational Eisenhower Doctrine, seeking other means of protecting U.S. interests in the region. However, just as Ike and his subordinates were seeking to move away from the Middle East Resolution, the unexpected intervened—and the United States of America, invoking the Eisenhower Doctrine, occupied Lebanon.

As numerous commentators have observed, Eisenhower's decision to send marines to the beaches of Beirut in the afternoon hours of July 15, 1958, was, on the face of it, "puzzling at best, senseless at worst."[4] It was the only time during his presidency that Ike deployed American military personnel in a potential combat operation, and his ostensive justification for doing so—the Eisenhower Doctrine—seemed utterly inapplicable to the situation at hand. Civil war had erupted in Lebanon over President Camille Chamoun's refusal to rule out an unconstitutional second consecutive term, a situation that turned explosive after the assassination of a prominent journalist on May 8. Hence, Beirut was under threat not from the "Communist aggression" stipulated in the Eisenhower Doctrine address but rather from Arab nationalists who wished to unite their country with the United Arab Republic.[5] The Soviet Union had little to do with Beirut's upheaval.

Furthermore, the Eisenhower administration had allowed the political crisis to fester for weeks before intervening. Concerns regarding Lebanon's stability were raised as early as the March 14 meeting of the National Security Council, and Chamoun—who argued that Nasser was supplying his opponents with weapons via Syria and that this act constituted a provocation worthy of invoking the Eisenhower Doctrine—formally requested military aid from Eisenhower on May 13.[6] It is thus necessary to ask why Eisenhower chose to ignore Chamoun for two months before dispatching the marines, and why Ike felt it necessary after such a delay to send American troops at all. On the surface Eisenhower's actions appeared, to put it nicely, erratic.

The answer to these questions can be found in a combination of Ike's dedication to waging the Cold War and the diplomatic constraints created by his prior rhetoric regarding the Middle East. By investigating Eisenhower's reasons for sending troops to

Lebanon, I hope to illuminate the complex political task that confronted the president and shed light on how he used rhetoric to navigate the exigences and constraints presented by this particular situation. In doing so I investigate (1) the rhetorical strategies employed by Eisenhower to justify this military intervention, (2) how these rhetorical choices were influenced by Eisenhower's prior rhetoric regarding the Middle East, and (3) the importance of his rhetoric for future presidential discourse. Eisenhower's psychological conception of containment, in addition to the prominent rhetorical stance regarding the Middle East's defense taken in the Eisenhower Doctrine address, led to him ordering the American military to stabilize Lebanon. This decision, in turn, required a rhetorical justification, which Ike found by employing various elements of his prior presidential rhetoric regarding the Middle East and by reinterpreting the Eisenhower Doctrine and the UN Charter. In doing so Ike created a site of rhetorical invention or topos—an argument field—for intervention in the Middle East (and elsewhere) on which future presidents would build.

Containment, Commitment, and Chamoun

Although American security concerns in the Middle East had multiplied following the proclamation of the Eisenhower Doctrine, the tensions in Lebanon did not catch the Eisenhower administration unaware. CIA director Allen Dulles gave periodic reports on the country's conditions in NSC meetings throughout the spring and summer of 1958, and although he argued that there was "continued clear evidence of UAR financial and other resources to the rebel forces," the costs of intervening in Lebanon appeared to outweigh the benefits (in a later exchange with Senator Fulbright, Ike made clear that while the United Arab Republic was not Soviet-controlled, "whatever Nasser [might] think he [was] doing, the Soviets ha[d] a tremendous interest in this").[7] Deploying troops to Lebanon, Ike and his advisors feared, would not only provide the Soviets with a major propaganda victory and "create a wave of anti-Western feeling in the Arab world" but also risk incurring the ire of UN secretary-general Dag Hammarskjöld, who made sure that Ike knew he was "opposed to the intervention of foreign troops in Lebanon, whether UN forces or other forces."[8]

Furthermore, there was doubt that American intervention would even be effective. NSC members believed that General Chehab, head of the Lebanese military and eventual successor to Chamoun, "could break the back of the rebel resistance if he would move vigorously," the exact course of action he declined to do in order to avoid politically alienating Chamoun's Maronite Christian base or its Arab nationalist opposition.[9] In abstaining from decisively ending the conflict in Lebanon, Chehab sought merely to mitigate the violence and thereby preserve his viability as a national, not factional, leader. In a June 15 meeting reviewing the Sixth Fleet's provisional plan for deploying troops to Beirut, Eisenhower expressed his own ambivalence regarding the use of U.S. soldiers to prop up Chamoun's divisive regime. He remarked that in the face of such political machinations he had "little, if any, enthusiasm for . . . intervening at this time." Bewildered by Chamoun and Chehab's intransigence, at one point Ike even vented: "How do you save a country from its own leaders?"[10] The case for inaction was, to put it mildly, strong.

Yet despite its initial unwillingness to contemplate intervention, the Eisenhower administration still sought to preserve all possible options. In his May 20 press conference, for example, Secretary of State Dulles reminded reporters that although Lebanon was unlikely to be subject to "an armed attack . . . from a country which [the administration] would consider under the control of international communism," that the Eisenhower Doctrine still provided a "mandate" for expanding U.S. aid to Lebanon that could potentially include military personnel; these troops would among other things ensure the "protection of American life and property."[11] And indeed Eisenhower and his subordinates acknowledged that inaction also had a price. Allowing the United Arab Republic to foment unrest in Lebanon "would add to Nasser's prestige," warned Dulles in a June 9 cable, "and seriously discourage Iraq and the other pro-Western elements in the area." In similar fashion Ike felt that refraining from action would communicate that America was now "Nasser's lackey" in the Middle East.[12] Both men also believed that failure to come to an ally's aid, even one as self-aggrandizing as Chamoun, could have dire consequences for American security guarantees elsewhere.

After the landings had occurred, Dulles retroactively explained his and Eisenhower's thinking on the matter to his fellow cabinet members in a July 18 meeting. The following quote encapsulates the two men's interventionist logic:

> We were faced with the question of what to do—to respond or not to respond. . . . We have no illusions that this response will solve the problems of that area—in fact it may make them worse. It is not a popular action and in fact it is pregnant with difficulties. . . .
>
> These moves will not, in our opinion, quickly or easily or perhaps at all solve the problems of that immediate area. But failure to act would have shaken the foundations of the free world—from Morrocco [sic] to the Western Pacific. In that arc, every free government would have felt that it was faced with a threat which it could not handle by itself—and would have noticed that when the need came, the United States looked the other way. Morroco [sic], Tunis, Sudan, Ethiopia, Turkey, Iran, Pakistan, Burma, Thailand, Laos, Cambodia, S. Vietnam, Formosa, Phillippines [sic], Japan and Korea—all would have felt that the forces organized against them were so powerful that they could not resist—and that when the crisis came, we would not respond.
>
> We responded—not because this response showed the way to clear and easy solutions—it rather opens the way to more problems—to some very dangerous problems—but to have done otherwise would have destroyed in one blow the faith and confidence which scores of nations have in the United States— that we are strong and loyal to our friends in their hour of need in cases of indirect aggression.[13]

As Dulles argued, if the United States allowed Chamoun and his "free" government to fall in Lebanon, then nations around the world would question America's commitment to them—thus leading to defections away from the Western camp, inviting Soviet adventurism among the nonaligned nations, and ultimately weakening containment. Because Ike and Dulles conceived of the Cold War as total, it was both psychological and global.[14] Psychological containment meant that perceived setbacks (such as if Chamoun was overthrown) were just as damaging as actual defeats. Containment was also global, which meant that a loss of American prestige anywhere harmed U.S. security—which under the New Look relied heavily on allied strength—everywhere. Therefore, in Eisenhower's eyes the spectacle of Chamoun going down in ignominious defeat while America passively watched was unacceptable, as this could potentially threaten the entire project of containment.

In short I agree with Douglass Little's assessment of this episode: Eisenhower ultimately chose to intervene in Lebanon "for the same reason that Lyndon Johnson would plunge into the Vietnamese quagmire after 1964: credibility."[15] The possible cost, both psychological and military, of sending troops to Lebanon was prohibitive so long as its purpose was only to end Chamoun's self-inflicted stalemate. If the alternative was to watch an American ally lose power in a way that would seriously damage U.S. credibility, however, then intervention became an imperfect but palatable option. Indeed, Ike believed that losing Lebanon could trigger a series of crises across the Middle East resulting in a loss of access to needed oil resources, and *that* disaster, in his words, "would be far worse than the loss in China" suffered by the previous administration.[16] As Ike's fellow Republicans loved to say, Truman lost China; Eisenhower, fearful of the domino effect and convinced of the psychological and global nature of the Cold War, refused to lose Lebanon.

Critically, then, it was not the loss of Lebanon per se that troubled Eisenhower but rather what the loss of Lebanon might communicate to other U.S. allies: American prestige was at stake in preserving, if not Chamoun, at least friendly semidemocratic rule in Beirut.[17] And the Eisenhower Doctrine, by ostentatiously promising American support to the United States' Middle Eastern allies, now worked to constrain Ike; the same lofty rhetorical performance that announced benevolent American hegemony over the region—in which Eisenhower proclaimed the United States' "national unity in support of freedom and to show [America's] deep respect for the rights and independence of every nation—however great, however small"—now tied America's reputation to Chamoun, who more than any other Middle Eastern head of state vocally and proudly supported the Eisenhower Doctrine. Thus Ike's prior rhetoric, more than any military or economic considerations, constrained the field of allowable outcomes in Lebanon.

In effect this situation can be read as the opposite of Operation Ajax in Iran. Unlike Ajax, whose underlying rationales were in nature military (the Soviets would gain strategic territory) and economic (the Abadan refinery was critical to the European economy), Ike's reasons for intervention in Lebanon were almost completely rhetorical (the United States could not appear to abandon an ally, lest other allies' confidence falter). Unsurprisingly, then, Eisenhower's highly visible, even theatrical method of intervention—a beachhead landing by marines midafternoon—was also the inverse of the secretive Operation Ajax. Operation Blue Bat, as the Lebanon landing was code-named, was meant to communicate one thing: that America could be counted on to defend its allies. By initiating Operation Blue Bat, Eisenhower implemented a strategy that was openly acknowledged as a likely policy failure, one that could lead, in Dulles's parlance, to "very dangerous problems," almost entirely for reasons of appearance.[18]

Yet for two months Eisenhower chose to disregard Chamoun's request for aid and not initiate Operation Blue Bat, and in fact by early July it appeared as though Lebanon's turmoil might be resolved without outside interference. Ike's strategy of nonintervention appeared to be working. Events of July 14, 1958, however, completely changed his thinking. In the early morning hours several Iraqi military officials, who styled themselves after the Egyptian Free Officers Movement, implemented a violent takeover of Baghdad and the central government by brutally executing the royal family and the prime minister. The Iraqi Hashemite monarchy, a stalwart ally of the West for over a generation, was eliminated in a few short hours. Stunned officials in Washington believed that Cairo was behind the coup and therefore registered the event as belonging to a long series of successes enjoyed by Nasser and pan-Arabism following the Suez crisis. Ike's strategic calculus immediately changed. If this violent upheaval could occur in Iraq, which had been considered at least as stable as Lebanon and Jordan, then anything was possible. In the fog of war, it looked as though the first domino might be falling—which meant that free government in Beirut, and by extension American prestige, was under terrific threat. As Eisenhower resolved at the special NSC meeting shortly after 11:00 a.m. Eastern Standard Time, "This is our last chance to make a move. We cannot ignore this one."[19] Despite the risks, despite the cost, Ike unleashed the American military. Operation Blue Bat, under executive order, was set in motion.

Presidential rhetoric can serve many purposes. Rhetoric is, after all, intrinsic to the presidential office; in the words of Medhurst, "the American presidency has always been a place of rhetorical leadership."[20] In this volume alone I have examined how presidents can use rhetoric to misdirect their audiences, redefine relationships between the American people and other regions of the world, and navigate high-stakes crisis situations. Presidential rhetoric can be administered anywhere from the bully pulpit to the witness stand, and its functionality as a means of political innovation is limited only by the opportunity, creativity, and skill of the commander in chief. But while presidential rhetoric can be used for such grandiose purposes as rallying the nation to war or declaring the "universal brotherhood of man," in this instance Eisenhower's overriding purpose was to accomplish a much more focused task: damage control.[21]

The Rhetorical Task

In terms of rhetoric, there was no audience that Ike *had* to convince. Because of the Middle East Resolution embedded in the

Eisenhower Doctrine, Ike was free to act without congressional (much less public) approval. Because American troops were being deployed unilaterally and suddenly—the U.S. military did not even inform the Lebanese government that troops were coming until mere hours beforehand—there was no international actor whose persuasion was absolutely imperative for Operation Blue Bat's success (although Eisenhower did use private communication channels to closely coordinate U.S. actions with Prime Minister Harold Macmillan, who was concurrently sending British troops to Jordan).[22] However, for the reasons enumerated above, the all-important cause of containment could still be damaged by the intervention in the long run if Eisenhower did not effectively frame U.S. actions in a compelling way. Internationally, Ike's use of what has been derisively termed "gunboat diplomacy" could still be marshaled as propaganda evidence of a renewed American imperialism by Nasser in the Arab world and Khrushchev worldwide.[23] Domestically, criticism of American actions in Lebanon could undermine the resolve of either Congress or the public to wage the Cold War; indeed, the sending of American soldiers via executive order to a faraway shore for reasons not fully understood invited a powerful comparison to the recent—and in the public mind, costly—Korean War. Nothing less than Ike's ethos as a "man of peace" was at stake.

Therefore, Eisenhower's rhetorical task was to *justify* American military actions, both in terms of legitimacy and necessity, in what was effectively an attempt to limit the damage that the landing was expected to cause. His audiences included a wary Third World, a skeptical Congress, and an uncertain American populace. As one letter to the White House remarking on the "explosive situation in the Middle East" stated, "for all anyone knows, U.S. intervention might mean the beginning of total war."[24] The situation demanded that Ike address the concern of this citizen and the millions like her around the world who were unsure what the presence of American troops in Lebanon meant for the larger Cold War. To perform this task Eisenhower needed to find a compelling argumentative warrant for the U.S.

landing. Assuming the mantle of textual critic-in-chief, he did so in part by seizing on a suggestion originally floated by Secretary Dulles on May 13: invoking the Mansfield Amendment, which the secretary argued "stated that the preservation of the independence and integrity of the nations of the Middle East was vital to the national interests and world peace."[25] In addition to employing the Eisenhower Doctrine, Ike adapted and expanded on the themes established in his prior Middle East rhetoric to build the justificatory case for Operation Blue Bat, thereby reassuring his audiences of the legitimacy and necessity of America's actions.

Textual Analysis

From the moment he learned of the Iraqi coup, Eisenhower acted swiftly and decisively, and he crafted the rhetorical element of his response to the situation in the Middle East accordingly. At 9:00 a.m. (Washington time) on the morning of July 15, an advance battalion of marines was scheduled to land near Beirut with several thousand troops following shortly; by midafternoon the president sent a message to Congress, and at 5:00 p.m. Eisenhower went before the television cameras to announce the landings to the American public (a pretaped radio message was released at the same time). Though the Eisenhower administration produced a host of ancillary texts regarding the Lebanon intervention, my analysis will primarily focus on these two major addresses as they most fully encapsulate the administration's arguments surrounding the deployment.[26]

As with all of Ike's Middle East rhetoric, his utterances justifying the American landings in Lebanon were salient for multiple audiences. In discussing the relationship between justificatory presidential rhetoric and audience, Richard Cherwitz and Kenneth Zagacki argue that, "in justificatory rhetoric, the American public and instigators of crises are the two major audiences for presidential addresses."[27] While their concept of justificatory rhetoric (which they define in strictly confrontational terms) has lim-

Table 2. Events of Operation Blue Bat

Date	Event
January 5, 1957	Eisenhower Doctrine Address
April 1957	Anti-monarchy elements in Jordan defeated by King Hussein and loyal military officers
August 13, 1957	Operation Wappen publicly exposed by Syrian officials
October 25, 1957	Plans for joint Anglo-American intervention in Jordan or Lebanon first discussed at Bermuda conference
February 1, 1958	Egypt and Syria unite as the United Arab Republic (UAR)
May 8, 1958	Lebanese Maronite journalist Nasib al-Matni assassinated, sparking civil war
May 22, 1958	President Chamoun submits complaint against UAR interference to the UN Security Council
June 16, 1958	UN observer group dispatched to Lebanon
July 14–15, 1958	Iraqi government overthrown by Free Officers Movement; Nuri as-Said and royal family executed
July 14, 1958	Eisenhower approves Operation Blue Bat; he and Secretary Dulles meet privately with legislators
July 15, 1958	U.S. soldiers land peacefully and occupy Lebanon
July 15, 1958	Eisenhower gives congressional message and TV address to the nation
July 16, 1958	King Hussein requests outside intervention
July 17, 1958	British troops arrive in Jordan
July 19, 1958	Eisenhower gives message to U.S. troops in Lebanon
October 25, 1958	Final U.S. forces withdraw from Lebanon

ited applicability to Eisenhower's rhetoric of July 15, 1958, their basic insight is apposite: Ike's rhetoric was primarily addressed to the international community and the American public, not Congress.[28] Congress, although crucial in its own way, was not among Ike's main audiences because it was more or less deferential to his leadership, was well informed about U.S. policy, and could do little to prevent Operation Blue Bat anyway. This reasoning appears to have been shared by the Eisenhower administration, which in an internal memo described the address to Congress as given "mainly for purpose of record," not persuasive intent (whereas the address to the public was, in the same document, described as done to communicate "to people on necessity of action").[29] Although the task of unpacking the nuance of Ike's rhetoric for the Soviets, Nasser, the nonaligned nations, and American allies around the globe is certainly worthwhile, in the interests of space and maintaining analytical continuity with the previous chapters I will focus on Ike's address from the vantage of his domestic audience, namely, the American public.

Eisenhower's rhetoric in this situation, as an example of a president seeking to justify the use of military force, is hardly singular. As Jason A. Edwards, Joseph M. Valenzano III, and Karla Stevenson argue, "U.S. presidents have ordered the use of military force for a variety of reasons. However, no matter what the reason, they first had to rhetorically ready U.S.'s citizens for these interventions."[30] Because of the extreme secrecy surrounding Operation Blue Bat pre-landing, however, Eisenhower did *not* have an opportunity to prepare the American people for the landing before it occurred. Moreover, the administration believed that "the people show[ed] no awareness of the seriousness of the Mid East crisis," meaning that the gravity of the situation—and therefore the duty of the United States to act—also needed to be made clear to the public if a backlash was to be avoided.[31] Thus Ike's rhetoric was compressed; in addition to the need to "characterize the circumstances of compelling action," something that typically happens before the troops land, he also needed to justify an intervention that was already under way.[32] Hence, Ike's rhetoric of justification simultaneously sought to set the stage for intervention, demonstrate the necessity of intervention, and justify U.S. intervention as legitimate legally and morally. He accomplished this task through four rhetorical maneuvers, each of which is identifiable in both his television address to the public and the more succinct congressional message.

Justificatory Rhetoric: Executive Authority

First, Eisenhower's rhetoric worked to establish the president as the appropriate authority to authorize American intervention in Lebanon. In the special message to Congress, Ike attempted to accomplish this task without direct reference to the Eisenhower Doctrine. The third paragraph of the text, presumably meant to elucidate the reasons for American intervention, reads as follows: "United States forces are being sent to Lebanon to protect American lives and by their presence to assist the Government of Lebanon in the preservation of Lebanon's territorial integrity and independence, which have been deemed vital to United States national interests and world peace."[33]

Eisenhower's adoption of the passive voice in this paragraph worked to elide the question of who exactly "deemed" the weighty issues of "national interests and world peace" to be at stake in Beirut and "sent" U.S. forces there. By using such evasive language, Ike asserted his authority to deploy forces to Lebanon absent congressional approval without explicitly stating such a thing. In fact evidence that the landings were purely the prerogative of the Eisenhower administration can be found only in the message's ninth paragraph (out of twelve). Here Eisenhower used the first person three times to communicate that every aspect of Operation Blue Bat was, in fact, completely his decision: "After the most detailed consideration, I have concluded that, given the developments in Iraq, the measures thus far taken by the United Nations Security Council are not sufficient to preserve the independence and integrity of Lebanon. I have considered, furthermore, the question of our responsibility. . . . I repeat that we wish to withdraw our forces as soon as the United Nations has taken further effective steps designed to safeguard Lebanese independence."[34]

By using the first person, Eisenhower deployed his formidable military ethos in his description of the decision-making process surrounding the intervention. If Ike *personally* determined that the situation necessitated the services of the U.S. military, then any congressperson who questioned this stance was inexorably drawn into a comparison with Eisenhower—a comparison that person would assuredly lose. By phrasing his decision to dispatch troops in the first person, Eisenhower grounded his authority in his unparalleled military expertise. In so doing he avoided having to make an overt reference to the Eisenhower Doctrine in the congressional message, sidestepping a potentially troublesome argument with the legislature over the bounds of executive authority.

Ike was more willing to rely on the Eisenhower Doctrine to substantiate his authority in his address to the public. Near the two-thirds mark of the address, he cited the Middle East Resolution as the reason for intervention, stating: "Last year, the Congress of the United States joined with the President to declare that 'the United States regards as vital to the national interests and world peace the preservation of the independence and integrity of the nations of the Middle East.'"[35] Interestingly, Ike chose to depict the Eisenhower Doctrine as the equal creation of Congress and his administration. While technically true in that the Eisenhower Doctrine was a joint declaration, by framing the Middle East Resolution in this way Eisenhower's rhetoric appears to have been designed to share culpability for the intervention with Congress. Such a depiction could have proved politically useful if the landings had gone poorly, and it also worked to erase the memory of the prolonged debate over the doctrine that took place on the Senate floor. To the public Eisenhower presented a united governmental front.

To be sure Eisenhower's interpretive understanding of the Eisenhower Doctrine—on which he based the U.S. government's legal authority to intervene—was far from widely accepted. Because evidence for the presence of "International Communism" in Lebanon was speculative at best, Eisenhower relied on Dulles's suggestion and cited the Mansfield Amendment of the Middle East Resolution, which his administration, ironically, had opposed when it was first introduced.[36] Senator Mansfield himself, in fact, did not believe his amendment should be interpreted as justifying intervention in this instance. He argued that the Lebanon crisis appeared to be the result of internal disturbances, not Communism or foreign intrigue.[37] Nevertheless, Ike quoted the amendment.

Although Eisenhower used the Middle East Resolution as the basis for Operation Blue Bat's legitimacy, he by no means neglected the opportunity to employ his reputation as a five-star general in the address to the public. Rather than use his ethos to provide evidence that he was the appropriate person to authorize the intervention, Ike instead used the first person to reassure the public that the chosen course of action would be effective and was indeed necessary. Immediately following his reference to the Eisenhower Doctrine, Eisenhower shifted to the first-person singular for just the second time in the address.[38] In a clear change in tone, Eisenhower stated, "I believe that the presence of the United States forces now being sent to Lebanon will have a stabilizing effect," an estimate whose plausibility relied directly on Ike's ability to diagnose a military operation's chances of success. A few paragraphs later he continued: "I am well aware of the fact that landing of United States troops in Lebanon could have some serious consequences. . . . I have, however, come to the sober and clear conclusion that the action taken was essential to the welfare of the United States."[39] Acknowledging that the marine landing could have "serious consequences," Eisenhower nevertheless reassured the American populace that this action was, in his "sober and clear" estimation, necessary.

While this language might be expected of a president attempting to justify the use of American forces in a foreign intervention, it is worth noting that Eisenhower avoided the word "I" throughout the rest of the address. By strategically using the first-person singular only in this section, Ike obliquely inserted his ethos as a military commander into the speech; the intent of this strategy appears to have been to reassure Americans across the nation that he *personally* sanctioned the intervention, and therefore all would be well. Thus by establishing himself as the appropriate authority to authorize Operation Blue Bat, Eisenhower's rhetoric worked to persuade his audience that the effort was necessary, legitimate, and would be effective.

Justificatory Rhetoric: Threat Conflation

In both speeches Eisenhower's rhetoric worked to conflate the Soviet Union with the threat posed to Lebanon by Nasser's pan-Arabism movement. In his address to the public, for example, Ike began his speech by immediately enumerating the recent events that had destabilized the region—but he did so without articulating *why* they were performed. He described how "in Iraq a highly organized military blow [had] struck down the duly constituted government . . . with great brutality," while "at about the same time there was discovered a highly organized plot to overthrow the lawful government of Jordan."[40] To emphasize the ruthlessness of these actors, Ike explained in detail how many Iraqi leaders were "beaten to death or hanged and their bodies dragged through the streets." Ike did not, however, specify exactly *who* was behind the attempted coup in Amman or for what purposes the Iraqi military officers executed their bloody takeover of Baghdad. Yet by describing both efforts as "highly organized" and in vividly violent terms, Eisenhower played on the Cold War tendency to depict America's enemies—typically Communists—in mindless, mechanistic, and inhumanly violent terms.

Robert Ivie and Oscar Giner point out that such a characterization is typical of presidential war rhetoric, with its "threatening picture of the enemy's evil savagery" working to rally the population to action.[41] Uniformity—an implicit characteristic of a group that is "highly organized"—is also identified by Ivie as a trait often imputed to the Communist enemy in Cold War presidential discourse.[42] Eisenhower, by using descriptive language usually linked to America's Communist adversaries and by avoiding a discussion of motivation, subtly conflated the nameless villains of Jordan and Iraq with the Soviet foe.

Less subtly Ike also represented propaganda from the Soviet Union and the United Arab Republic as equally responsible for inspiring the strife in Lebanon. Chamoun's "little country," in Eisenhower's words, had "for about two months been subjected to civil strife. This has been actively fomented by Soviet and Cairo broadcasts and abetted and aided by substantial amounts of arms, money and personnel infiltrated into Lebanon across the Syrian border. . . . Chamoun stated that without an immediate show of United States support, the Government of Lebanon would be unable to survive against the forces which had been set loose in the area."[43] Again Eisenhower employed intentionally imprecise language in his description of the threat facing Lebanon: vague "forces" were at work, and they had been given "arms, money and personnel" of indeterminate origin to accomplish their destructive task. Because the American public had been conditioned to correlate subversive and nefarious forces with Communism for years, it is not implausible to assume that many of Ike's listeners made such an associative leap here. The corollary of this inference was that the United States must oppose such dark powers, thus morally justifying the dispatching of marines to Lebanon.

The claim that Soviet and United Arab Republic radio broadcasts provoked the uprisings also advanced the thesis that American intervention was justified in another way: such an action demonstrated that external actors were already involved in the conflict in Beirut. Ike's rhetoric, by designating the unrest as instigated unequivocally by outside forces, portrayed Chamoun's request for American aid as a natural response to a foreign threat and not an escalation of the conflict. In this telling radio broadcasts from *both* Moscow and Cairo helped spark the civil strife. Thus no matter what the degree of Nasser's influence in Beirut, the Lebanese rebels could now be labeled as Soviet-inspired—and therefore unquestionably enemies of the United States.

Similarly, in the message to Congress Eisenhower explained how "a violent insurrection broke out in Lebanon. . . . The revolt was encouraged and strongly backed by the official Cairo, Damascus, and Soviet radios which broadcast into Lebanon in the Arabic language."[44] Here again Ike used sequential language to equate the Soviet efforts with those of the United Arab Republic. While his claims were technically true—the Soviets did broadcast propaganda in Arabic into Lebanon—there is little doubt that pan-Arabism, not Communism, was the predominant ideology (to the extent there was an ideology) motivating the uprisings. Eisenhower's use of language worked to obfuscate this reality and elevate the Soviet threat.

In both the public address and congressional messages, then, Eisenhower's rhetoric worked to complicate the relationships among the Lebanese rebels, the Soviet Union, and Nasser's United Arab Republic. By obscuring exactly which parties were behind the uprisings, Ike was able to frame the intervention in Lebanon as an exercise in limiting Communist expansion. By invoking the Soviet threat, Eisenhower reduced the complicated situation in Lebanon into a simple—and easily understood—binary between the unfree Communist world and the free West; in this way he attempted to "camouflage the facts of international politics under the colors of domestic politics."[45] Ike allowed the paradigm of "prophetic dualism" to provide the reasons for "why the United States should engage in certain kinds of action abroad."[46] In this case dualism worked to provide the justificatory logic for why America needed to intervene in Lebanon: because the Soviets had already done so. Containment must be maintained.

Justificatory Rhetoric: Independence and Intervention

Because the civil strife in Lebanon was the result of foreign intrigue, Ike depicted Lebanon's request for outside support as an apt response to the situation and the United States as the appropriate party to respond to this request. Eisenhower's argument rested on two premises, namely, that Lebanon had a right to independence under the charter of the United Nations and that it was the role of the United States to ensure that this right was not infringed upon.

Eisenhower argued these points clearly and succinctly in the congressional message. After describing the situation in Beirut, Ike offered his diagnosis. Because UN efforts were "not sufficient" to protect Lebanon, he announced that the United States would step in: "I have concluded that, given the developments in Iraq, the measures thus far taken by the United Nations Security Council are not sufficient to preserve the independence and integrity of Lebanon. . . . Pending the taking of adequate measures by the United Nations, the United States will be acting pursuant to what the United Nations Charter recognizes is an inherent right—the right of all nations to work together and to seek help when necessary to preserve their independence."[47] As he did during the Suez crisis, Eisenhower presented the United States not as replacing the United Nations or intervening independent of its authority but rather as acting in the UN Security Council's stead. The United States was doing what the United Nations would do if it were free from the Soviet veto; America's deployment of troops was "pursuant" to the United Nation's goals, not in circumvention of them. As if to underscore his point, Eisenhower followed the statement quoted above by reminding his audience that the administration wished to withdraw U.S. forces "as soon as the United Nations [took] further effective steps designed to safeguard Lebanese independence." Thus not only was the United States under Eisenhower fulfilling the mission of the United Nations by intervening in Lebanon, but it also established itself as the arbiter of whether the UN steps taken were "effective"—and if not, then the U.S. troops would simply stay. In describing the situation in this way, Eisenhower—as in his Suez crisis and Eisenhower Doctrine speeches—insisted that the United States paradoxically acted in the Middle East both in the place of the United Nations (as the body ultimately responsible for settling conflict) and in perfect accord with the United Nations (by affirming that the United Nations' forces would simply take the place of their American counterparts, Ike depicted the missions of the two groups as perfectly identical).

In the address to the public, more explicitly premised on the Eisenhower Doctrine as it was, the argument that Lebanese independence was assured by the United Nations was dispersed throughout the speech. The effect of the speech's saturation with references to the United Nations was to again create the impression that American and UN purposes in Lebanon were indistinguishable. To cite several examples: (1) Eisenhower declared that the "primary responsibility" of the United Nations was to "maintain international peace and security," which was the reason given for Operation Blue Bat. (2) He referenced the UN "Peace through Deeds" resolution of 1950, which "called upon every nation to refrain from 'fomenting civil strife'" in other countries; by sending the marines, Ike sought to counteract Soviet and Nasserist efforts to do exactly that—at least according to his representation of the situation. (3) Offering his analysis as interpreter-in-chief, Eisenhower insisted that the "basic pledge" of the UN Charter was "the preservation of the independence of every state." As with the Mansfield Amendment, Eisenhower argued that American commitment to the UN Charter thus required a reinforcement of the Lebanese status quo ante. (4) He contended that Lebanon was tacitly granted "measures of collective security for self-defense" as an "inherent right," since the UN Charter guaranteed the right to independence, and that the United States military was simply helping the Lebanese exercise their UN-recognized right.

Finally, near the conclusion of the address, Eisenhower drew a parallel between the League of Nations failures in the 1930s and the current crisis. He reminded his audience that "the League of Nations became indifferent to direct and indirect aggression. . . . The result was to strengthen and stimulate aggressive forces that made World War II inevitable," and asserted, "The United States is determined that that history shall not now be repeated." This tightly packed statement invoked multiple Cold War topoi and allusions: Ike explicitly stated that he wished to avoid encouraging "aggressive forces," a kind of antithesis to Acheson's infamous "defensive perimeter" statement regarding Korea; by indirectly referencing the Munich agreement, Ike analogized Soviet aggression to German aggression, with the implication being that a show of force now would prevent total war later; in using the phrase "direct and indirect aggression," Ike made an explicit reference to the policy of containment articulated in the Eisenhower Doctrine and thus the strategic rationale behind America's commitment to aid Lebanon. Perhaps most powerfully, this appeal was made following the references to the United Nations. If the League of Nations failed because of the indifference of member states, Ike seemed to be saying, then the United Nations could fail for the same reason. Thus by intervening in Lebanon, the United States preserved not only Chamoun but the United Nations and the entire postwar international diplomatic system.

The effect of all these references to the United Nations was to more fully develop the argument Eisenhower made in the Suez crisis address and in the Eisenhower Doctrine speech, namely, that because the United Nations was incapable of securing peace and stability in the Middle East due to the "ambitions of the Soviet Union," the United States would assume the mantle of responsibility for the region and act in the United Nations' place.[48] This mission was depicted as being done not to the exclusion of the United Nations from the region but rather as a means of fulfilling that organization's goals for the Middle East. However, this portrayal of the United States as acting in the place of the United Nations required a reinterpretation of UN aims in American terms, thus relegating the United Nations to little more than a rhetorical rubber stamp for U.S. actions in the region.

The nation's capacity to serve in this role—as a UN proxy—can be understood as a redefinition of American exceptionalism. If, as Kundai Chirindo and Ryan Neville-Shepard argue, "the rhetoric of exceptionalism" is used "to both defend and rally support for America's peculiar mission on the world's stage," then by declaring America's role to be the peacekeeper of the Middle East, Eisenhower defined the nation's global responsibility in a new way. While Ike had made this argument about the United Nations since the Suez crisis address, the Lebanon intervention was the instance in which Ike applied this new understanding of America's role as regional hegemon to material effect. In short Ike's rhetoric worked to create a new way "by which Americans understand their nation's orientation to the world," and this new orientation authorized the American military to come ashore and occupy Lebanon.[49] As the first deployment of American combat troops on Arab soil since the end of the Barbary Wars in 1815, Operation Blue Bat was momentous—if not militarily, then in terms of precedent—indeed.

Justificatory Rhetoric: Situational Transcendence

Eisenhower's rhetoric worked to situate Operation Blue Bat as a stand not only for a minor American ally but also on behalf of transcendent, universal ideals. Ike argued near the end of his address to the public that in defending the independence of Lebanon, the United States was "striving for an ideal which [was] close to the heart of every American and for which in the past many Americans [had] laid down their lives." The purpose was not simply to secure Chamoun's hold on Beirut but to create "a world in which nations, be they great or be they small, [could] preserve their independence."[50] Eisenhower elevated this loosely defined value of respecting other nations' independence to transcendent status by linking it to other moral principles. "To serve these ideals," Ike suggested to the public, "is also to serve the cause of peace, security and well-being, not only for us, but for all men everywhere."[51] Echoing the universalist rhetoric of the Suez crisis address and the Eisenhower Doctrine, Ike claimed that the U.S. intervention in Lebanon was done in the service of aims few would dispute. Indeed, in safeguarding these values not only for America or Lebanon but (in a very Wilsonian turn of phrase) for "all men everywhere," Ike reinforced his claim that the United States' efforts in the Middle East effectively took the place of the United Nations. Though not explicitly stated, by working for the welfare of all nations the United States rendered any additional UN effort redundant.

While less strongly put, the same sentiment was present in Eisenhower's congressional message. Tying American intervention to the norms of diplomatic conduct, Ike informed Congress that "despite the risks involved this action [was] required to support the principles of justice and international law upon which peace and a stable international order depend."[52] In this formulation failure to initiate Operation Blue Bat would have weakened the postwar global order and therefore increased the risk that a larger conflict might erupt. By exhibiting "an admirable characteristic of the American people"—in Ike's words, the "readiness to help a friend in need"—the United States was not only rescuing Lebanon from its "grave peril" but also "acting to reaffirm and strengthen principles upon which the safety and security of the United States depend."[53] Here Ike described the transcendent values that America was defending as essential to American security; by following the virtuous path of the good neighbor the nation could thereby preserve its own safety. Ironically, it was this perceived need to enforce peace that led Eisenhower to deploy the military, thus increasing the risk that a global conflict might erupt. As Ira Chernus notes, such a contradiction was intrinsic to Ike's strategic thinking and discourse, in which "a single-minded pursuit of national security consistently undermined the nation's sense of security."[54]

Nevertheless, by framing the intervention in Lebanon as a defense of transcendent ideals, Eisenhower's rhetoric functioned to justify Operation Blue Bat as necessary and legitimate. It was necessary because a peaceful global order depended on the enumerated ideals, and it was legitimate because America claimed the moral high ground in defending such transcendent principles. Moreover, Ike continued to prosecute this argument—that the American troops in Lebanon were not merely protecting an allied regime but were serving a higher purpose—in the days and weeks following July 15. On July 19, for example, Eisenhower issued a message to "the officers and men of our forces—Marines, Sailors, Soldiers and Airmen—who are now in Lebanon, on the Mediterranean Sea, or in the skies over that area."[55] Ike's message, which sought to more clearly explain to the troops the reason for their presence, was saturated with references to freedom and the right of the Lebanese to be free. The troops were there to defend Chamoun's "democratic government" that was "based upon free popular elections." He expounded on the mission of the soldiers in idealistic terms: they were to safeguard the "cherished independence" of the Lebanese people, who "want[ed] only to live in peace and in freedom." As Eisenhower bluntly directed, "You are helping the Lebanese people to remain free. You are there at their invitation—as friends—to preserve for them the same freedoms that we have here at home." By infusing his message to the troops with references to freedom—to the point of even equating the level of freedom enjoyed in Lebanon to that of America—Eisenhower justified their mission on the basis of a transcendent ideal (perhaps *the* ideal in American Cold War discourse). The threat to Beirut, which Ike described as coming largely "from outside forces," was rhetorically escalated to a battle for freedom itself. Intervention was thereby elevated to the cosmic ground on which the Cold War was fought—as a rhetorical war between ideals.

In addition to the message to the troops, Eisenhower also made his case in a series of letters he exchanged with Khrushchev that were published in newspapers nationwide.[56] Throughout these letters Eisenhower consistently situated "peace" as the heart of his appeal. Khrushchev's basic argument, contained in letters dispatched July 19 and July 23, was that the United States and Britain were acting belligerently by deploying troops to the Middle East and that the "bayonets of U.S. and British troops" swept aside the United Nations and heightened the risk of war.[57]

In his responses, issued July 22 and July 25, Ike declared that "the establishment and maintenance of a just peace was the dominant influence in American policy," and that the deployment of American troops in Lebanon was a result of "the instability of peace and security . . . due to the jeopardy in which small nations [were] placed."[58] The United States, inveighed Eisenhower, was on the side of peace—a "real peace," a "just peace," not merely

The Doctrine Applied

the absence of conflict, and that stance required supporting small nations like Lebanon. Hence, it was America that sought to "genuinely promote the cause of peace and justice," and the Soviets were the ones truly endangering the world with their calls for revolution. "The real danger of war would come if one small nation after another were to be engulfed by expansionist and aggressive forces supported by the Soviet Union," Ike wrote in his letter, stressing that "such processes cannot be reconciled with a peaceful world or with the ideals of the United Nations."[59] Again Ike presented America as working in concert with the United Nations to accomplish the work of peace—a peace defined in American terms. Stated otherwise, the transcendent value of a "just" peace, first invoked in reference to the Middle East by Eisenhower in his Suez crisis address, now provided a warrant for American intervention in Lebanon. This peace/aggression binary, like the other ideals expressed in Manichaean terms in Ike's rhetoric, worked to situate the conflict in Lebanon on a transcendent plane that justified Operation Blue Bat.

An Enduring Legacy: Effects and Implications of Operation Blue Bat

In sum Eisenhower's rhetoric was intended to justify the American intervention in Lebanon in terms of both legitimacy and necessity so as to limit the political damage Operation Blue Bat was expected to cause. In response to this situation Ike's rhetoric of July 15, 1958, exhibited four powerful strategies designed to convince his audience that there was a need for American troops and that the United States was morally and legally justified in responding to Chamoun's request for aid: Eisenhower's rhetoric worked to (1) establish Eisenhower as the appropriate authority to decide whether intervention was necessary, (2) conflate the Soviets with the threat from Nasser's Arab nationalist movement, (3) portray Lebanon's request for aid as appropriate and the United States as the proper party to respond to such an appeal, and (4) elevate the conflict in Lebanon to the transcendent plane of ideals on which the Cold War was rhetorically fought. These strategies revisited many of the arguments Eisenhower had made over the course of his administration regarding America's role in the Middle East, and he adapted and reconstituted these arguments into a form that authorized his policy decision to intervene. Eisenhower's rhetoric was both principled (Lebanon's right to independence could not be ignored) and pragmatic (it was expedient to send troops to avoid creating misgivings in the minds of other U.S. allies).[60]

How then should Eisenhower's rhetoric in this episode be understood? First, as with all instances of presidential rhetoric, the immediate context must be privileged in any discussion of implications or effect. In that regard it is difficult to argue that, at least domestically, Eisenhower's rhetoric was anything less than successful. The landings and subsequent stationing of troops throughout Lebanon, while leading to a few tense encounters with the Lebanese military, went according to plan. Only one American life was lost because of hostile fire during the occupation, and the final U.S. soldiers withdrew on October 25.[61] And although Eisenhower suffered the lowest approval ratings of his presidency during 1958, his ratings gradually improved after March, and Operation Blue Bat did not significantly harm Ike politically.[62] Interestingly, a pamphlet produced by the United States Information Agency (USIA) instructing U.S. travelers on how to answer questions about their country while abroad saw fit to include an answer for the question, "Wasn't the U.S. guilty of aggression in sending its troops into Lebanon?"[63] The inclusion of this question in the document is telling, for it demonstrates that Americans were perceived by the government to be accepting of Operation Blue Bat, or at least more accepting than foreigners. It is likely that such a perception was not far from the truth, meaning Ike's rhetoric seems to have been at least somewhat effective in limiting the political fallout of the intervention.

Second, Eisenhower's rhetoric surrounding the Lebanon intervention can be seen as a species of imperialist rhetoric (or at least a successor to the imperialist rhetoric of the British). Ike's description of Lebanon as a country buffeted by "civil strife" and whose economy had lapsed into a virtual "standstill" also worked to portray the coastal nation as a hotbed of volatility. As noted earlier one of the major rationales for the Eisenhower Doctrine was the need for the United States to fill the supposed regional power vacuum in order to prevent such instability, which could lead to Communist rule. In that sense Ike's speech can be understood as a kind of imperialist rhetoric: disorder was unacceptable, therefore we will establish order. As Jeff Bass wrote of Edmund Burke, "he was following an organizational strategy based upon the classical rationale for empire, that of establishing order in regions beset by chaos."[64] Such a characterization would appear to fit Eisenhower as well.

Although the American presence in Lebanon (and the Middle East at large) differed greatly from that of the British in 1781 India, Eisenhower's rhetoric nevertheless hit notes that echoed not only the era of imperialism but also the Truman Doctrine. As with Truman, disorder and the potentially calamitous consequences it would bring were unacceptable to Ike because such conditions were the seedbed of Communism. The difference between the two men, however, was the context: because of the shifting political realities on the ground, direct American action was now required to establish order. The fact that Britain was finished as the regional hegemon, combined with the rhetoric of the Eisenhower Doctrine and Suez, worked to transform what had been a case for increased foreign aid into an argument that justified American intervention.

Third, Eisenhower's rhetoric surrounding Operation Blue Bat and the occupation of Lebanon can be viewed, from our present vantage, as having set the argumentative foundation for future American interventions abroad. As mentioned previously Eisenhower's rationale for sending troops to Lebanon—to communicate to American allies that the United States keeps its commitments—would be repeated by Lyndon Johnson and later Richard Nixon in their treatments of Vietnam.[65] Furthermore, it is worth noting the obvious fact that the intervention in Lebanon, while coming after the Korean War, still occurred fairly early in the Cold War. Because of its chronological primacy, then, Eisenhower's rhetoric played an important role in establishing the norms of argument and evidence used by future presidents pursuing their own "limited" interventions abroad. Elements of Ike's rhetoric were adapted and used by presidents throughout the Cold War, from Johnson's use of threat conflation in the 1965 intervention in the Dominican Republic to Reagan's address after the attack on American troops (again) in Lebanon on October 27, 1983.[66] Other elements of Eisenhower's rhetoric, such as the move to elevate conflict to the ground of ideals or the argument that the United States can accomplish the mission of the United Nations, can be seen in the case George W. Bush made for the invasion of Iraq or in the rhetoric of other presidents who have managed conflict in the Middle East.[67]

Overall, Eisenhower's intervention in Lebanon—along with the rhetoric that justified it—is notable for the precedent it set. Executive decision making, employing U.S. troops as peacekeepers and not to win a war, using rhetoric to transform a regional or national crisis into a conflict of ideals—these descriptive features tend to reappear whenever American presidents wish to send troops on limited missions abroad, and to some degree these cases can all trace their origin to Eisenhower's intervention in Lebanon. As David E. Proctor argues, Operation Blue Bat constituted a new form of engagement that he calls "the rescue mission," which "is distinct from declared wars and extended police actions because Americans are not asked to sacrifice economically or socially for this form of military operation."[68] Militarily it was also unique: at a loss for how to describe the marines' experience on the first day of the intervention, a Pentagon spokesperson described Operation Blue Bat as "not war, but like war."[69] The struggle of officials to define or label the intervention testifies to the importance of this episode for foreign-policy rhetoric, particularly given the proliferation of such "rescue missions" in American foreign affairs in the years since Eisenhower.

Perhaps most importantly the intervention in Lebanon neatly merged many of the features of Eisenhower's rhetoric regarding the Middle East into one policy decision and discourse. It is one thing to articulate a new path, purpose, or policy for a country's foreign policy, but quite another to act on that new identity in a militarily significant way. America's role as the regional hegemon was no longer a merely rhetorical stance; in Lebanon Ike's rhetoric was consummated in the material world—the Eisenhower Doctrine was no longer an abstraction but applied. In the process the rhetorical transformation of America's relationship to the Middle East that had begun under Eisenhower was now complete. There was no going back.

Chernus characterizes presidential Cold War rhetoric, including Eisenhower's, as an attempt to grapple with an indissoluble dilemma: if the role of the president is to assure the citizenry that the country is safe, how does one do that in the nuclear age of mutually assured destruction? Because resolution to this conflict would usher in the apocalypse, Chernus calls this style of rhetoric "apocalypse management." This state of perpetual insecurity, Chernus writes, paradigmatically requires "that threats might come from anywhere on the globe. . . . Peace and stability required the United States to control events everywhere."[70] In his decision to intervene in Lebanon in the summer of 1958, Eisenhower can be seen as merely working out the logical implications of this style of rhetoric.

In this chapter I have shown how the rhetoric that Eisenhower used to accomplish various purposes in the Middle East collectively worked to constrain the rhetorical and policy choices available to him when confronted by a new problem in the region: Lebanon. Viewed in light of Zarefsky's definition of presidential rhetoric, Eisenhower's continued redefinition of the Middle East as it pertained to American political reality worked to material effect, namely, Operation Blue Bat. Stated otherwise Ike was a victim of his own words—compelled by the unpalatable constraints of the situation, many of which were creations of his prior rhetoric, he chose intervention over inaction and thereby manifested physically the redefinition of America's stake in the Middle East that occurred rhetorically during his presidency. Although the occupation was short-lived—most American troops were in Lebanon for less than three months—the impact that this episode had on American policy and rhetoric was not. By successfully employing troops on a peacekeeping mission to a small, faraway country, Eisenhower created the template his successors would use to argue for future deployments in the Middle East and around the world. Because "limited" American interventions abroad and the arguments used for doing so show no sign of ceasing—least of all in the Middle East—we still, in a sense, inhabit the Eisenhower era today.

Conclusion

On August 13, 1958, Eisenhower spoke before the United Nations General Assembly for the first time since his famous "Atoms for Peace" address. As in that earlier speech, Eisenhower framed his subject matter under the rubric of "universal" security concerns. Unlike in "Atoms for Peace," however, Eisenhower devoted nearly all of his speech to the ongoing conflicts in the Middle East. Nasser's pan-Arabism was again at high tide with the fall of the Iraqi monarchy, leading to street protests, riots, political upheaval, and whispers of coup attempts across the region. Framing his speech as a discussion of the threats facing the world, Eisenhower proclaimed:

> I recall the moments of clear danger we have faced since the end of the Second World War—Iran, Greece and Turkey, the Berlin blockade, Korea, the Straits of Taiwan.
>
> A common principle guided the position of the United States on all of these occasions. That principle was that aggression, direct or indirect, must be checked before it gathered sufficient momentum to destroy us all—aggressor and defender alike.
>
> It was this principle that was applied once again when the urgent appeals of the governments of Lebanon and Jordan were answered.
>
> I would be less than candid if I did not tell you that the United States reserves, within the spirit of the Charter, the right to answer the legitimate appeal of any nation, particularly small nations.[1]

Thus Eisenhower announced the right of the United States to intervene anywhere on earth as it had in Lebanon, to confront "clear danger" wherever it may rear its head. Visiting what were by now familiar themes, he went on to say that the United States had "no other purpose whatsoever" than to "prevent that crime" of allowing Lebanon and Jordan to fall to external aggression; America acted defensively as a regional insider to the Middle East, not as an external aggressor. Eisenhower even justified the occupation as a preventative intervention meant to head off a potential larger threat, emphasizing how his administration's actions had "checked" aggression before it "gathered sufficient momentum to destroy us all." Stated otherwise Eisenhower's rhetoric outlined an argument for preemptive war—thus articulating the conceptual framework for the George W. Bush Doctrine a near half century in advance.[2]

The rest of the address was devoted to Eisenhower's proposed solutions for the Arab world's economic, technical, political, and security problems. He addressed the issue of Arab nationalism directly, placing limits on American license to intervene and granting that the "peoples of the Arab nations of the Near East clearly possess[ed] the right of determining and expressing their own destiny." He did, however, add a condition this statement: "Other nations should not interfere so long as this expression is found in ways compatible with international peace and security." In qualifying his support for Arab autonomy in the Middle East, Ike worked to link the regional status quo—an arrangement that kept the oil flowing to Europe and the Soviets out of the Middle East—to international peace and security. The message was clear: the United States would give the nations of the Middle East a wide berth, and even concede to Nasser a degree of regional ideological ascendency, within certain bounds. But the moment political developments in the region threatened "international peace and security"—defined in American terms—the United States reserved the right to act. As Operation Blue Bat had shown, Eisenhower would not hesitate to send U.S. troops to the region if he thought they were necessary.

While a noteworthy speech in its own right—Ike did not address the UN General Assembly every day, after all—this address is all the more striking for the dramatic transformation in America's relationship to the Middle East that it signifies. Having come into office talking about the vague need to "win friends" in the Middle East and downplaying his administration's covert role in shaping the region, Eisenhower now devoted an entire speech before the UN General Assembly to the problems of the Middle East.[3] In that speech, moreover, he announced that the United States' would not hesitate to oppose "aggression, direct or indirect" in the region. Few actions could more clearly show just how far American economic, political, and rhetorical investment in the Middle East had come under Ike. Eisenhower's UN address thus aptly symbolizes his presidency as a whole; far from being an afterthought, the Middle East now occupied a prominent place within American politics, a transformation wrought in large part through Ike's use of presidential rhetoric.

The Middle East continually surfaced as a political concern to Eisenhower over the remainder of his presidency, but never again would the region demand the attention it had during the Suez crisis and the Lebanon landing. Events intervened quickly after the UN speech. The simmering Egyptian-Iraqi rivalry rapidly erupted into outright conflict between Nasser and the new Iraqi government of Abd-al-Karim al-Qasim, who styled Baghdad as an alternative revolutionary power center in the Middle East to Cairo. The Soviets ended up backing Qasim, resulting in a significant chill between themselves and the Egyptian government. Nasser again went on the propaganda offensive, but this time attacking Baghdad's "subservience" to the Soviet Union and labeling Qasim's government the "Communist agents of a foreign power."[4] The result of this diplomatic quarrel was to clear the way for a modest rapprochement between Washington and Cairo, allowing the Eisenhower administration to focus on shoring up its regional allies such as Jordan, Iran, and Saudi Arabia through various forms of military and economic aid; American advisors set about making sure there would be no repeat of what happened to the royal family in Baghdad. Eisenhower visited Turkey, Pakistan, Morocco, Afghanistan, Tunisia, India, and Iran on his eleven-nation goodwill tour in late 1959, punctuating the conceptual redefinition of the greater Middle East as an area of primary American political interest. In a stroke of luck for the Eisenhower administration, Qasim ultimately turned against the Iraqi Communist Party in January 1960, leaving the Soviet Union with few direct inroads into Middle Eastern politics as Kennedy came into office a year later.

In sum the United States did not again send troops on a potential combat mission to the Middle East during the Eisenhower presidency. Yet the transformation Eisenhower oversaw in America's relationship to the region was not primarily military in nature but *rhetorical*. Unlike that of some presidents, Ike's legacy in the region was not a specific policy or a Middle Eastern war. Ike's legacy in the Middle East was, and is, the creation of argument fields that serve as sites of rhetorical invention in presidential discourse—arguments fields that have sadly, among their other uses, been deployed by subsequent presidents to justify military conflict. In short Eisenhower fundamentally changed the way U.S. presidents speak about the Middle East, and the effects of this conceptual redefinition—evidenced through the redeployment and adaptations of Ike's arguments—can still be seen in American political discourse at present.

Eisenhower's Arguments

In particular the enduring influence of Eisenhower's rhetoric can be seen in the recurring use of several topoi, he established regarding the Middle East. Specifically, his arguments surrounding unilateralism, covert activity, and ideological conflict persist as common sites of invention in presidential rhetoric concerning the region.

Unilateralism. Eisenhower was the first president to argue that the United States had a unique, leading, and essential role to play in the Middle East: that of advocate for (and enforcer of) peace. This role came with multiple responsibilities—serving as peacemaker and negotiator between the Arabs and the Israelis, working to mediate shared-resource agreements, providing arms and advisors for Western allies in the region, and underwriting much of the economic aid for the countries there. America's most important responsibility, however, was to keep the Middle East free from Communist subversion. Time and time again in the Eisenhower administration's rhetoric, correspondences, and policy decisions, it made clear that its overriding priority was to maintain Soviet containment and prevent Communist breakthrough in the region.

While the Eisenhower administration prosecuted this overarching aim through covert methods for most of Ike's first term, after the Suez crisis this strategy ceased to viably function. To justify his foreign policy in the Middle East, then, Ike was forced to publicly argue—seen most clearly in the Eisenhower Doctrine address and in his speeches defending the landing in Lebanon—for his administration's decisions. These appeals included conflating the mission of the United States with that of the United Nations, framing conflict in the region as taking place at the elevated plane of ideals like freedom (for which the United States was champion), portraying adversaries as a menacing monolith and therefore as meriting a forceful response, and claiming an American right to intervene anywhere to preempt the enemy's schemes. This series of appeals coalesced into an argument for a unilateral American approach to the region, thus justifying the Eisenhower Doctrine, occupation of Lebanon, and other interventionist policies adopted by the Eisenhower administration without the approval of international or regional bodies.

Covert activity. Eisenhower also pioneered the use of covert activity in the Middle East and rhetorical strategies to effectively conceal these activities. He conducted back-channel diplomacy, ordered coups, developed and funded domestic intelligence agencies for regional allies, dispatched secret surrogates to represent him, and disseminated all colors of propaganda across the Middle East. Rhetorically, this approach to the region manifested itself through strategies of misdirection and surreption, as Eisenhower actively sought to deceive friends and foes alike as to American intentions and levels of involvement in the region. These strategies also functioned to mislead the American public about the nature and extent of U.S. investment in the Middle East. Thus the Eisenhower administration, particularly during Ike's first term, developed rhetorical strategies premised on exploiting Americans' misunderstanding of their nation's role in the Middle East to censor knowledge of the full range of U.S. activity in the region.

Ideological conflict. To the Eisenhower administration the Cold War was all-consuming. With the advent of thermonuclear mutually assured destruction, both Eisenhower and Khrushchev quickly realized that this conflict would be waged through words; wielding persuasion they sought alliances, resources, markets, and the denial of these assets for the other. In terms of rhetoric, then, Eisenhower often depicted the Cold War in starkly Manichaean, ideological terms. The United States represented all that was good, peaceful, freedom loving, and friendly, whereas the Soviets were dictatorial, threatening, subversive, conniving, and evil. While a legitimately ideological contest was certainly occurring between competing economic and political systems, Ike's rhetoric worked to frame this conflict as one in which the forces of good were arrayed against those of evil—and the United States, as freedom's champion, held a special responsibility to fight darkness wherever it might appear.

Viewed thus the entire world was divided into two camps competing for global power. Hence, even though few Middle Eastern countries possessed Communist parties of any political significance, the Eisenhower administration interpreted all conflict in the region through a Cold War, friend-or-foe lens. Though no major leaders in the region were Communists, they *might* be Communist sympathizers, or they might be weak willed and therefore susceptible to Communist persuasion, or they might be unfriendly and thereby given to strengthening the Soviets, or they might be inept and thus their tenure could lead to disorder during which Communists might seize power, and so on. Rhetorically, then, Eisenhower depicted the Middle East as a site of total cold war in which the United States must fight the forces of Communism. This rhetoric had two main effects. First, this portrayal provided a warrant for the Eisenhower administration's interventionist policies, as the United States needed to combat Communism in the region. Second, by framing the Middle East in this way, Ike advanced a simplistic understanding of a complicated region. His rhetoric bowdlerized the religious, ethnic, political, and ideological complexities of the Middle East, reducing the region's actors to side characters in the main-stage Cold War drama. The result of this approach was an increasingly interventionist approach to the Middle East with increasingly less accurate portrayals of what was really going on there, as most of the region's actors were primarily concerned not with the Cold War but with Arab nationalism, European imperialism, and the Arab-Israeli conflict.

These three topoi—unilateralism, covert activity, and ideological conflict—though initially developed and applied in reference to the Middle East by Eisenhower, have been deployed and redeployed by subsequent presidents. Virtually all of Ike's appeals for unilateralism, for instance, were replicated by George W. Bush and applied to terrorism in his response to the 9/11 attacks. Indeed, from his "freedom agenda" to his depicting terrorists as a monolith, his U.S.-led "coalition of the willing" as a suitable replacement for the United Nations to his dualistic assertion that "every nation in every region now ha[d] a decision to make: Either you are with us or you are with the terrorists," Bush's arguments surrounding America's role in the greater Middle East were practically copied and pasted from those of Eisenhower.[5] The same arguments were used, with "terrorists" simply replacing "Communists."

Likewise, it is hard not to see shades of rhetorical misdirection in Barrack Obama's treatment of the Middle East. His administration consistently advanced a politically appetizing narrative about its policy approach to the region—choosing to emphasize the Iran nuclear deal or renewed Palestinian-Israeli peace negotiations—all while conducting drone strikes, special operations assassination missions, airstrike campaigns, the arming and organizing of thousands of Syrian militiamen, and military operations involving hundreds of U.S. troops across multiple theatres. Though not deceptive per se, Obama's strategies certainly mirror Ike's in the way his administration drew attention to particular events while deemphasizing others.[6]

And ideologically speaking there is a strong tendency to frame current American conflicts in the Middle East as occurring between two competing views of the world. During the post-9/11 era both President Bush and President Obama went to great lengths to emphasize that the United States was at war not with Arabs, Muslims, or Islam but with "violent extremism" or "radical Islam." Whatever one calls it, the United States has been framed as being at war with an idea—an idea with an insidious foothold across the greater Middle East that must be stopped at all costs. The so-called Islamic State, after all, found success advocating "a political ideology and a worldview" that drew thousands of foreign fighters to its banner; conventional wisdom, as analyst Hassan states, mandates that "understanding the ideological appeal of the Islamic state is crucial to defeating it."[7] Extirpating that belief system and those who hold it (including Al Qaeda's various branches, Boko Haram, Al-Shabaab, Hamas, and countless other groups) has provided a warrant for interventionist policies in the Middle East since 9/11. Such an approach seems unlikely to end soon, as President Trump has labeled the Islamic State "a level of evil that we haven't seen," and on his second day in office he announced, "We're going to end it. It's time. It's time right now to end it."[8] Indeed, far from questioning American military investment in the Middle East, Trump has hitherto loosened the military's rules of engagement, deployed even more troops abroad, graced the region with his inaugural presidential trip, and stringently reaffirmed the United States' commitment to its regional allies.

Without belaboring the point further than I already have, it is easy to find the continued use of Eisenhower's arguments in American presidential discourse surrounding the Middle East today. Almost six decades after Ike left office, it appears that his rhetoric surrounding the Middle East continues to exert an influence on presidential rhetoric, and this impact on presidential discourse—and therefore public perception—can most powerfully be seen in the repeated adaptation and use of Ike's arguments as sites of invention (topoi). Eisenhower's rhetoric, then, profoundly altered the way presidents speak about the Middle

East, which should shape how we view arguments surrounding the region and America's role in it now.

The Eisenhower Era: A Rhetorical Legacy

Of course Eisenhower did not set out to transform the way in which Americans viewed the Middle East. In each of the cases analyzed in this work, his rhetoric was clearly purposed to accomplish whatever instrumental need was demanded by the situation, not to change or question the fundamental nature of American engagement in the Middle East or establish rhetorical topoi for future use. Yet it is hard not to be impressed by the rhetorical distance traveled between his campaign rhetoric and the speech he gave at the United Nations. If there is one lesson to draw from this study, it is that instrumental uses of rhetoric can have powerful constitutive consequences; as the conceptual content of a particular term is reconstituted through discourse, the term then becomes capable of effecting political change. As James Farr elaborates:

> Conceptual change attends political change. . . . To the extent that our concepts constitute the political world, we can say that *conceptual change* attends any *reconstitution* of the political world. In short, our concepts, beliefs, and practices go together and change together. Sometimes these collective practices go together and change together. Sometimes these collective changes find expression in new words. It is as if new worlds are being announced. . . .
>
> Conceptual change, however, need not be signaled only by newly invented names. We find conceptual change whenever we find changes in any of the interrelated features of a concept as outlined above: in its criteria of application, its range of reference, or its attitudinal expressiveness. These changes happen beneath the surface of a vocabulary, as it were. Conceptual change, accordingly, varies from wholesale changes across an entire constellation of words and concepts, to more localized changes in the sense, the reference, or the attitudinal expressiveness of a single concept.[9]

Eisenhower oversaw such a conceptual change in America's treatment of the Middle East. For American policy makers—particularly those involved in intelligence and defense planning—the region had taken priority almost immediately following World War II. Yet this shift in concern was not, as this study has shown, reflected in the presidential rhetoric of Harry Truman. Like many other aspects of American political life, over the course of Ike's presidency he rhetorically reconstituted, or conceptually altered, what the Middle East meant in the context of American political discourse and foreign policy. This rhetoric, in turn, then made possible (even imperative) certain policy decisions regarding the Middle East, exemplified by the intervention in Lebanon. Through Eisenhower's rhetoric the Middle East as a concept in American politics was dramatically reconstituted to signify a region both under threat and of paramount American interest. Ultimately, Ike's discourse created new "conditions of possibility" regarding the region, thus laying the groundwork for the rhetoric and policy of future presidents.[10] In that sense Eisenhower's reconstitution of the Middle East within presidential rhetoric still affects American politics.

This study is not meant to exhaustively catalog and analyze every one of Eisenhower's utterances regarding the Middle East as president. Such a task would, minimally, need also to elaborate more fully on Eisenhower's view of Israel, his Middle East rhetoric after the death of John Foster Dulles in 1959, his utterances surrounding foreign aid and humanitarianism, and his complicated relationships with the American oil industry and the sons of Abdul Aziz ibn Saud. Rather than seeking to accomplish such a feat, this book has aimed to demonstrate the changing ways in which Eisenhower defined the Middle East to the American public and, to a lesser extent, Congress.

As such this book has sought to establish that the Eisenhower presidency enacted a rhetorical revolution regarding America's relationship to the Middle East. Driven by the exigencies of the Cold War and the overarching strategy of containment, Eisenhower at first sought to maintain continuity with previous presidential rhetoric regarding the region, as can be seen in the rhetoric of misdirection surrounding Operation Ajax. This strategy was pushed to its breaking point over the course of Eisenhower's first term, during which his administration prosecuted strategies of rhetorical surreption in its dealings with the Middle East. It was in consideration of these same Cold War concerns that Ike then broke from this rhetorical strategy and articulated a uniquely American responsibility for the Middle East's security and well-being in the Suez crisis speech. This address in turn laid the groundwork for the Eisenhower Doctrine, which was applied to material effect in Lebanon. By 1958, as can be seen in Ike's message to the UN General Assembly, the rhetorical transformation of America's relationship to the Middle East was complete.

While there are certainly a number of perspectives from which to view this study, I believe the findings of this book can especially inform future examinations of discourses concerning the Cold War, Middle East studies, and the field of presidential rhetoric. It is my hope that the work offered here may be used as a starting point for other scholars who wish to investigate Ike's Middle East rhetoric and that it might promote interdisciplinary collaboration among these various fields. Viewed as a whole Eisenhower's rhetoric regarding the Middle East carries manifold implications, of which I will elaborate on two.

First, Eisenhower's rhetoric resembles British imperial rhetoric regarding the Middle East in several regards. To take a specific example, there are similarities between Eisenhower's Suez crisis speech and Eden's first conference speech as leader of the Conservative Party. Eden also confessed worry that "the Middle Eastern situation [was] serious and could be dangerous," noting that Britain had "worked for a long time past by all manner of methods to try to bring about a reduction of tension in that part of the world."[11] Like Eisenhower Eden justified his nation's actions by asserting that they were in the interests of peace. He also seemingly anticipated Eisenhower in his description of the long-term difficulty of achieving such a harmonious state: "We must not be surprised at setbacks. They are inevitable. . . . The processes of diplomacy are slow but behind all this repetition of public and private argument, conciliation may grow and the power of peace prevail." Although Eden, Churchill, and countless other British statesmen historically used the language of national interest to justify their imperial presence in the Middle East, by the 1950s their tone had softened considerably.[12] Eden's Middle East rhetoric in 1955 was not quite so different from Ike's in 1956, and when considering the various topoi typical of imperialist rhetoric—disorder versus order, national interests described as universal values, and the language of paternal responsibility—it becomes difficult not to see traces of imperialism in Ike's rhetoric. These likenesses indicate profitable lines of future scholarly inquiry regarding neo-imperialist themes in American presidential rhetoric about the Middle East.

Second, Eisenhower's later rhetoric, particularly the major premise that it is America's responsibility to maintain order in the Middle East, helped establish a new norm in presidential rhetoric that has lasted from Kennedy to Trump. From the Camp David Accords to the 2003 invasion of Iraq, from Hezbollah to the Islamic State, American presidents post-Eisenhower have consistently spoken of the Middle East as an area of American interest worthy of immense investment of resources. While Ike's is obviously not the only presidency influencing modern American presidential rhetoric on the Middle East, the utterances of the Eisenhower administration worked to authorize an expansion of the United States' direct engagement with the Middle East unlike any other. Subsequent presidents have built on this authorization and adopted his fundamental premise: that America has an essential, leading, and unique role to play in guiding the region. This belief has often been expressed as an enthymeme (unstated premise) and elaborated in terms of defending the region from outside threats or as a determination to employ U.S. influence to bring about an Arab-Israeli peace.

In fact every president since Eisenhower has in some way articulated this very principle. Even before the War on Terror, President Bill Clinton, for instance, defined attacking Saddam Hussein's biological weapons program as being in the "vital interests" of the United States, again depicting America as the executor of UN aims.[13] Clinton also more conspicuously echoed the language of

Eisenhower's Suez crisis speech in his 1994 State of the Union, stating, "We will also work for new progress toward the Middle East peace. . . . There is a long, hard road ahead. And on that road I am determined that I and our administration will do all we can to achieve a comprehensive and lasting peace for all the peoples of the region."[14] He revisited the same metaphor later that year following the Jordan-Israeli peace treaty, emphasizing the United States' essential role in the region: "Israel and Jordan looked to America to help them to make peace. And they and other nations in the Middle East look to America as we travel the difficult road ahead, until we achieve peace throughout the Middle East."[15] As these brief samples from Clinton's presidency make clear, Ike's rhetoric had a lasting and profound effect on the way presidents speak regarding the Middle East.

Resemblances to Ike's rhetoric can also be seen in the speech of other presidents:

John F. Kennedy: (1) "This story is the same in Africa, in the Middle East, and in Asia. Wherever nations are willing to help themselves, we stand ready to help them build new bulwarks of freedom. We are not purchasing votes for the cold war; we have gone to the aid of imperiled nations, neutrals and allies alike." (2) "The great battleground for the defense and expansion of freedom today is the whole southern half of the globe—Asia, Latin America, Africa and the Middle East—the lands of the rising peoples. . . . The adversaries of freedom plan to consolidate their territory—to exploit, to control, and finally to destroy the hopes of the world's newest nations; and they have ambition to do it before the end of this decade. It is a contest of will and purpose as well as force and violence—a battle for minds and souls as well as lives and territory. And in that contest, we cannot stand aside."[16]

Lyndon B. Johnson: (1) "In Africa and the Middle East our energies are engaged with the responsibility that great power brings. Everywhere we seek to serve the common interests of the free." (2) "Now the nations of the Middle East have the opportunity to cooperate with Ambassador Jarring's U.N. mission [to negotiate Arab-Israeli peace after the 1967 War] and they have the responsibility to find the terms of living together in stable peace and dignity, and we shall do all in our power to help them achieve that result."[17]

Richard Nixon: (1) "As you know, the Secretary of State and I have been meeting for the past two hours and a half on various foreign policy matters, but particularly concentrating on the problems of the Mideast. . . . I am gratified that now all three governments to whom we addressed our initiative have responded positively and accepted the U.S. proposal." (2) "We have made it very clear—and this is in the interest of peace in that area—that the balance of power must not be changed and we will keep that commitment."[18]

Gerald R. Ford: "United States policy in the Middle East has two primary objectives. First we seek peace. We have made extraordinary efforts in the last 2 years to help the nations of the Middle East find peace. Much has been achieved. . . . Second, we desire a strong and mutually beneficial relationship with every nation in the Middle East. . . . You [Egyptians] will find Americans deeply concerned over the issues which are important to you—peace and justice in the Middle East—issues which are vital to the future of the whole world."[19]

Jimmy Carter: "Our basic goal is to secure peace, stability, and harmonious relations among the nations of the Middle East. Since becoming President, I and my chief foreign policy advisers have spent more of our time and effort on this subject than any other foreign policy issue. . . . The choice is stark and fundamental. Shall we support and give confidence to those in the Middle East who work for moderation and peace? Or shall we turn them aside, shattering their confidence in us and serving the cause of radicalism?"[20]

Ronald Reagan: (1) "I continue to be cautiously optimistic. I hope that some of the Senators who are opposed will recognize that even more than before it is essential that we show the Middle East that we are prepared to participate there in trying to bring peace and in aligning ourselves with the moderate Arab states, as well as we have with Israel." (2) "The bloodshed we have witnessed in Lebanon over the last several days only demonstrates once again the lengths to which the forces of violence and intimidation are prepared to go to prevent a peaceful reconciliation process from taking place. If a moderate government is overthrown because it had the courage to turn in the direction of peace, what hope can there be that other moderates in the region will risk committing themselves to a similar course? Yielding to violence and terrorism today may seem to provide temporary relief, but such a course is sure to lead to a more dangerous and less manageable future crisis."[21]

George H. W. Bush: (1) "I'm worrying about getting them there and doing what I indicated in our speech in there is necessary: the defense of the Saudis and trying through concerted international means to reverse out this aggression. . . . But a line has been drawn in the sand. The United States has taken a firm position. And I might say we're getting strong support from around the world for what we've done. I've been very, very pleased about that. Large countries and small countries—the world reaction has been excellent. And I would hope that all of this would result in Saddam Hussein or some calmer heads in Iraq understanding that this kind of international behavior is simply unacceptable." (2) "The United States and its coalition allies are committed to enforcing the United Nations resolutions that call for Saddam Hussein to immediately and unconditionally leave Kuwait."[22]

The presidencies of George W. Bush and Barrack Obama, with their attendant ground conflicts in Afghanistan, Iraq, Libya, Syria, and Yemen, attempts at Arab-Israeli peace, and their expanded drone-strike campaigns, have not repudiated the premises of Eisenhower's rhetoric either—although the "War on Terror" and its offspring possess unique rhetorical warrants in their own right. As of this writing, it is still too early to make a definitive judgment on President Donald Trump's Middle East policy and rhetoric.

However, his early utterances as president, with their breathless threats against the Islamic State and other Middle Eastern enemies, make it seem unlikely that Trump will question the premise that the United States has a unique, essential, and leading role to play in the Middle East. Therefore, in a way reminiscent of the rhetorical norms established by Woodrow Wilson, no president after Ike has fundamentally challenged the premises for U.S. engagement in the Middle East introduced during the Eisenhower presidency. If presidential rhetoric truly does "define political reality," then this change constitutes a major rhetorical and political development indeed.[23]

· · ·

More than anything this study complicates simple narratives surrounding Eisenhower, the Cold War, and American imperialism or Orientalism in the Middle East. Ike's rhetoric transformed the way the Middle East is constituted in presidential rhetoric; it has thereby influenced depictions of the region in American media, politics, and culture. If, as Douglass Little contends, "few parts of the world have become as deeply embedded in the U.S. popular imagination as the Middle East," then it is worth studying how these conceptual formations came to be.[24] Yet as this study shows, much of Eisenhower's rhetoric was driven by the immediate needs of the moment as he saw them, not grand designs to subject the Arab world to a neo-imperialist American hegemony. Rhetorical criticism offers a uniquely powerful tool to investigate such matters with nuance, and it is my hope that the analysis offered in this study provides an impetus for future students of rhetoric to conduct similar inquiries. More than the Eisenhower Doctrine, it was the Eisenhower Era that fundamentally altered the way in which presidents speak about the Middle East—and thus laid the groundwork for all that has followed and is still to come. The current time is one in which commentators openly speculate whether the age of American dominance in the Middle East is over.[25] By revisiting the question of how it began, perhaps we can rediscover what that proposition truly entails.

NOTES

All cited references to the Dwight D. Eisenhower Presidential Library Archives (DDE Library) originate from Dwight D. Eisenhower Papers as President, 1953–1961, unless otherwise noted.

Introduction

1. Jon Stewart, *The Daily Show with Jon Stewart*, June 12, 2014.

2. Mather, *Glory of Goodness*, 45.

3. Hale and Loustanau, "U.S.-Middle East Trade."

4. Newspaper clipping, "Eisenhower on Middle East," box 8, Campaign Series, Dwight D. Eisenhower Papers as President, 1953–1961, Dwight D. Eisenhower Presidential Library Archives, Abilene, Kansas (hereafter cited as DDE Library).

5. *Department of State Bulletin*, June 15, 1953, 831, The Hathi Trust Digital Library, http://tinyurl.com/ybm6tech.

6. Spiegel, *Other Arab-Israeli Conflict*, 93.

7. I do not wish to explore questions pertaining to the theoretical foundations of the public sphere in this space, although it is a very significant subject matter within rhetorical studies. For recent examinations of this topic, see Asen, "Critical Engagement," and Randall, "Rhetoric of Violence."

8. Zarefsky, *President Johnson's War on Poverty*, 8.

9. Medhurst, "Rhetorical Leadership and the Presidency," 73.

10. Ceaser, Thurow, Tulis, and Bessette, "Rise of the Rhetorical Presidency," 164.

11. This is not an exhaustive list.

12. Medhurst, "Rhetorical Leadership and the Presidency," 61.

13. Bitzer, "Rhetorical Situation."

14. Medhurst, "Rhetorical Leadership and the Presidency," 61.

15. See Chernus, "Eisenhower and the Soviets."

16. Wilson, "Address at the Shrine Auditorium in Los Angeles, California," September 20, 1919, The American Presidency Project, http://www.presidency.ucsb.edu.

17. Hogan, *Woodrow Wilson's Western Tour*, and Stuckey, *Good Neighbor*.

18. George Washington, "Farewell Address," September 19, 1796, The American Presidency Project, http://www.presidency.ucsb.edu.

19. See Flanagan, "Woodrow Wilson's 'Rhetorical Restructuring,'" and Casey, *Cautious Crusade*.

20. Woodrow Wilson, "Making the World 'Safe for Democracy,'" George Mason University, April 2, 1917, The American Presidency Project, http://www.presidency.ucsb.edu.

21. See Casey, *Cautious Crusade*, 30. Roosevelt, "Quarantine Speech," October 5, 1937; Roosevelt, "The Great Arsenal of Democracy," December 29, 1940; Roosevelt, "Address for Navy and Total Defense Day," October 27, 1941, all at The American Presidency Project, http://www.presidency.ucsb.edu.

22. Franklin D. Roosevelt, "Joint Press Conference with Prime Minister Churchill," December 23, 1941, The American Presidency Project, http://www.presidency.ucsb.edu.

23. U.S.-Soviet Alliance, 1941–1945, Office of the Historian, https://history.state.gov/milestones/1937-1945/us-soviet. See also Knight, "Making of the Soviet Ally."

24. Charland, "Constitutive Rhetoric," and Althusser, *Lenin and Philosophy*, 170–74.

25. Farr, "Conceptual Change and Constitutional Innovation," 18.

26. Quintilian, *Institutes of Oratory*.

27. Mahaffey, *Preaching Politics*, 178–79.

28. Franklin D. Roosevelt, "Inaugural Address," March 4, 1933; Abraham Lincoln, "Address at the Dedication of the National Cemetery at Gettysburg, Pennsylvania," November 19, 1863; John F. Kennedy, "Inaugural Address," January 20, 1961, all at The American Presidency Project, http://www.presidency.ucsb.edu.

29. See Edwards, *Strategic President*.

30. In fairness to Edwards, he has elsewhere noted that modern presidential duties include that of "communicator in chief." Edwards and Wayne, *Presidential Leadership*, 11. See also Medhurst, "Tale of Two Constructs," xi–xxv.

31. Wilson, in this case, was an aberration for heads of state generally. Since the earliest days of the rhetorical discipline, ghostwriters have offered their services to powerful clients willing to pay for them; in Plato's *Gorgias*, for instance, Socrates condemns a number of famous sophists for doing exactly that. In this regard presidents are no different from the wealthier citizens of Athens.

32. Campbell and Jamieson, *Deeds Done in Words*, 17–18.

33. Parry-Giles, *Rhetorical Presidency*, 144.

34. Stuckey, *Good Neighbor*, 7–8.

35. Gaddis, *Strategies of Containment*, 125–27.

36. Dwight D. Eisenhower, "First Inaugural Address," January 20, 1953, The American Presidency Project, http://www.presidency.ucsb.edu.

37. Winslow, *Lebanon*, 118.

38. Bass, "Hearts of Darkness," 432.

39. Medhurst, "Afterword," 267.

40. Black, *Rhetorical Criticism*, 76.

41. Quoted in Newton, *Eisenhower*, 2.

42. Gregg, "Rhetoric of Distancing," 157–88.

43. Maurice Labelle quoted in Soussi, "Legacy of US' 1958 Lebanon Invasion."

44. M. Young, "Of Allies and Enemies," 172.

45. See Shaheen, "Media Coverage"; Frank, "Americans (Still) Don't Understand"; and Lipka, "Muslims and Islam."

Eisenhower Doctrine Address

1. "Special Message to the Congress on the Situation in the Middle East." The American Presidency Project http://www.presidency.ucsb.edu/ws/index .php?pid=11007&st=eisenhower&st1=.

1. The Eisenhower Doctrine

1. Kennan, "George Kennan's Long Telegram"; Kennan [X], "Sources of Soviet Conduct."

2. To get a sense of the rapidity of the shift in relations, consider the following: Stalin's "Election Day Speech," which was interpreted by many Western analysts as a virtual declaration of war, was given February 9, 1946. Kennan's "Long Telegram" was transmitted February 22, 1946. Eleven days later Churchill gave his famous "Iron Curtain" address at Westminster College.

3. Clifford, "American Relations."

4. "A Report to the National Security Council-NSC 68," April 12, 1950, Harry S. Truman Library, https://www.trumanlibrary.org/whistlestop/study_collections /coldwar/documents/pdf/10-1.pdf.

5. Quoted in Medhurst, *Dwight D. Eisenhower*, 31.

6. This term was first used by Dulles in a speech given to the Council on Foreign Relations on January 12, 1954, and became popularized afterward as a shorthand to describe the Eisenhower administration's defense strategy. See "Dulles Speech to the Council on Foreign Relations," January 12, 1954, *Department of State Bulletin* 30, no. 758:108, The Hathi Trust Digital Library, https:// babel.hathitrust.org/cgi/pt?id=msu.31293008121356.

7. Gaddis, *Strategies of Containment*, 162; Eisenhower, "The President's News Conference," March 10, 1954, The American Presidency Project, http://www .presidency.ucsb.edu.

8. Yaqub, *Containing Arab Nationalism*, 2.

9. See Freiburger, *Dawn over Suez*; Watt, *Succeeding John Bull*; Yizhar, "Eisenhower Doctrine"; Takeyh, *Origins of the Eisenhower Doctrine*; and Salami, "Eisenhower Doctrine."

10. Zarefsky, "Presidential Rhetoric," 611.

11. Zarefsky, "Presidential Rhetoric," 611–13.

12. Quoted in Brian, *Elected and the Chosen*, 179.

13. See Lebow, "Woodrow Wilson."

14. Woodrow Wilson, "Letter to Rabbi Stephen S. Wise in New York City," August 31, 1918, *Congressional Record-House*, http://tinyurl.com/ycrbny5w.

15. Hoover and Roosevelt in particular articulated support for Zionism and Judaism in general, despite whatever policy decisions they made that might

appear unfriendly to Jews. See Herbert Hoover, "Message for Jewish Organizations," August 29, 1929, The American Presidency Project, http://www.presidency.ucsb.edu.

16. Indeed, the total Arab population of the United States appears to have been only in the tens of thousands during this era, partially explaining the slant of domestic news coverage. See Haddad, *Not Quite American*, 3–4, 17–18; Christison, *Perceptions of Palestine*, 38–42; Herbert Hoover, "Message to the Zionist Organization of America," November 3, 1932, The American Presidency Project, http://www.presidency.ucsb.edu; Franklin D. Roosevelt, "Greeting to the United Palestine Appeal," February 6, 1937, The American Presidency Project, http://www.presidency.ucsb.edu.

17. Eddy, *F.D.R. Meets Ibn Saud*, 27–33. This was not Roosevelt's first encounter with a representative of the Saudi government, however. See Franklin D. Roosevelt, "Toast to the King of Arabia at a Dinner for the Minister of Foreign Affairs," September 30, 1943, The American Presidency Project, http://www.presidency.ucsb.edu.

18. Franklin D. Roosevelt, "Press and Radio Conference 991," February 19, 1945, Franklin D. Roosevelt Presidential Library & Museum Archives, http://www.fdrlibrary.marist.edu/_resources/images/pc/pc0169.pdf.

19. Indeed, as historian Madawi al-Rasheed writes, "Saudi Arabia was the first area outside the western hemisphere where American political and strategic influence replaced that of Britain." al-Rasheed, *History of Saudi Arabia*, 104.

20. Harry S. Truman, "The President's Special Conference," May 13, 1947; Truman, "The President's News Conference," January 15, 1948, both at The American Presidency Project, http://www.presidency.ucsb.edu.

21. Harry S. Truman, "The President's News Conference," September 5, 1946; Truman, "Statement by the President on Palestine," June 5, 1947; Truman, "Statement by the President on Israel," October 24, 1948, all at The American Presidency Project, http://www.presidency.ucsb.edu.

22. All quotations from the Truman Doctrine speech are from Harry S. Truman, "Special Message to the Congress on Greece and Turkey: The Truman Doctrine," March 12, 1947, The American Presidency Project, http://www.presidency.ucsb.edu.

23. Quoted in Clarke, *Last Thousand Days*, 464–503.

24. Bostdorff, *Proclaiming the Truman Doctrine*, 99–102.

25. Bitzer, "Rhetorical Situation," 6.

26. Quoted in Briggs, *Making American Foreign Policy*, 99.

27. Yaqub, *Containing Arab Nationalism*, 89–97.

28. "Defense of Formosa, Pescadores," *Congressional Quarterly*, 1956, Office of the Historian, https://history.state.gov/historicaldocuments/frus1955-57v02/d56.

29. Wander, "Rhetoric of American Foreign Policy," 432.

30. O'Gorman argues that Ike theologically flattened the Abrahamic religions in his project of promoting a generalized spirituality identifiable with American

liberalism set in contrast to atheistic Communism. In his words, "Eisenhower here made topography, the Middle East, a kind of text, and then this text yet a mere sign: Mecca and Jerusalem were 'places on the map,' yet they were more than this. On a register of the ultimate, they were symbols of a spiritual truth, that of the supremacy of spirit. . . . Thus, Islam, Christianity, and Judaism— blithely conflated and reduced to symbols of the spiritual—validated the essentially metaphysical thrust of Eisenhower's American liberalism." O'Gorman, *Spirits of the Cold War*, 220–21.

31. Dwight D. Eisenhower, "Message to Congress on Mid-East," box 19, Speech Series, DDE Library.

32. "It is logical that the United States should do whatever it is able to do to assist in the return of normal economic health in the world, without which there can be *no political stability and no assured peace*" (emphasis mine). Marshall, "Marshall Plan Speech."

33. Quoted in Immerman, *John Foster Dulles*, 157.

34. Chernus, *Apocalypse Management*, 229.

35. On Ike and Korea, see Medhurst, "Text and Context," and Medhurst, *Dwight D. Eisenhower*, 38–44. Regarding his 1956 campaign, see "Football/Peace Commercial," The Living Room Candidate, http://www.livingroomcandidate .org/commercials/1956.

36. It is worth noting here that this speech was given several years before the U-2 incident with Francis Gary Powers and well before the Watergate scandal. As such both the presidency and Eisenhower were held in a high esteem difficult to imagine today. Again Eisenhower never had negative approval ratings during his two terms in office, and an average of 49 percent of Democrats said they approved of the job Ike was doing. See Gao, "Presidential Job Approval Ratings."

37. For the rhetorical importance of narrative, see Levasseur and Gring-Pemble, "Not All Capitalist Stories"; Gring-Pemble, "'Are We Going"; Lucaites and Condit, "Re-constructing Narrative Theory"; and Green, Strange, and Brock, *Narrative Impact*.

38. Fisher, "Narration," 6.

39. Robert Taft, "Republican Fund-Raising Dinner in Milwaukee, Wisconsin," *Congressional Record*, June 9, 1951.

40. Stuckey, *Good Neighbor*, 16.

41. On this point it is worth noting that in his edits of the penultimate draft of the speech Eisenhower questioned whether the phrase "Words alone are not enough" was necessary, thus reinforcing the claim that Ike conceived of the situation in the Middle East as principally a rhetorical problem. Dwight D. Eisenhower, "Jan. 4, 1957 Draft," box 19, Speech Series, DDE Library.

42. Quotes taken from Yaqub, *Containing Arab Nationalism*, 111–12.

43. Dean Acheson, "Speech on the Far East," January 12, 1950, Central Intelligence Agency, https://www.cia.gov/library/readingroom/docs/1950-01-12.pdf.

44. Aronson, *From Sideshow to Center Stage*.

45. One of the earlier drafts of the speech (draft 11, dated to January 2, 1957) produced by John Foster Dulles included multiple references explaining Britain and France's historic and contemporary roles in the region; these references were reduced to a sentence by Dulles's next complete draft, at least according to what is available in the archives (draft 13, dated to January 3, 1957). That sentence was then crossed out, indicated that Eisenhower sought to virtually omit any reference to Britain and France in his speech. Earlier drafts explained even more fully the historic and economic ties between Europe and the Middle East, which were also cut. John Foster Dulles, "Middle East Message to Congress etc. January 5, 1957," box 2, Presidential Correspondence and Speeches Series, DDE Library.

2. Operation Ajax

1. Steve Kroft, "President Rouhani," *60 Minutes*, September 20, 2015.

2. Knowledge of American involvement in the coup has been public information since at least the publication of Kermit Roosevelt's memoir-style account, *Countercoup*, and was widely known in Iran soon after the shah's restoration. See Malcolm Byrne, "Introduction," in Gasiorowski and Byrne, *Mohammad Mossadeq*, xiii.

3. Wilford, *America's Great Game*, 160–61.

4. In using this label, I am expounding on others' scholarly work on misdirective or trickster rhetoric. See Martin, "Rhetoric of Misdirection"; Best, "Rhetorical Misdirection"; Markel, "Rhetoric of Misdirection"; and Arthos, "Shaman-Trickster's Art of Misdirection."

5. For background on the U.S. deliberation on this point, see Handy, "Patrick J. Hurley and China," 54–61.

6. Indeed, the October 29, 1944, *New York Times* article headline reporting the crisis literally read "Iran's Oil Problem Revived by Russia . . . Country in British Sphere of Influence, but Americans Also Are Involved." J. H. Carmical, "Iran's Oil Problem Revived by Russia," *New York Times*, October 29, 1944.

7. Truman, "The President's News Conference," March 14, 1946, and Harry S. Truman, "The President's News Conference," March 8, 1946, The American Presidency Project, http://www.presidency.ucsb.edu.

8. Quoted in Bostdorff, *Proclaiming the Truman Doctrine*, 29.

9. Indeed, Stalin and Molotov viewed the indigenous Tudeh Party with annoyance and started a new Soviet-backed puppet Communist Party in Iran, the Iranian Azerbaijan Party (ADN). See Zubok and Pleshakov, *Inside the Kremlin's Cold War*, 120–25.

10. For more on the relationship between Reza Shah and the Majlis, see Frye, *Persia*, 90–104.

11. See Azimi, *Iran*, 37, and Katouzian, *Mussadiq*.

12. See Azimi, *Iran*, 35–265, and Katouzian, "Mosaddeq's Government in Iranian History," 1–3.

13. See Azimi, "Reconciliation of Politics and Ethics."

14. Pahlavi, *Mission for My Country*, 90–91.

15. Dwight D. Eisenhower, "Convention Hall, Philadelphia" Address, September 4, 1952, box 1, Speech Series, DDE Library.

16. "NSC 136/1," November 20, 1952, Office of the Historian, https://history.state.gov/historicaldocuments/frus1952-54v10/d240.

17. Harry S. Truman, "Special Message to the Congress on Greece and Turkey: The Truman Doctrine," March 12, 1947, The American Presidency Project, http://www.presidency.ucsb.edu.

18. John Foster Dulles, "Christian Responsibility for Peace," May 4, 1948, quoted in Bowie and Immerman, *Waging Peace*, 63.

19. Ambrose, *Eisenhower: The President*, 107.

20. John Foster Dulles, "Thoughts on Soviet Policy and What to Do About It," *Life*, June 3, 1946.

21. Quoted in N. B. Young, *Documentary History*, 10:86.

22. Quoted in Bury, *Eisenhower*, 52.

23. Quoted in Osgood, *Total Cold War*, 46.

24. Dwight D. Eisenhower, "Address by Republican Nominee for President at San Francisco," October 8, 1952, box 2, Speech Series, DDE Library.

25. Medhurst, "Introduction," in *Eisenhower's War of Words*, 1.

26. See Brooks, "When the Cold War."

27. LaFeber, *America, Russia*, 147.

28. Central Intelligence Agency, "Probable Developments in Iran through 1953," NIE-75, November 13, 1952, Central Intelligence Agency, https://www.cia.gov/library/readingroom/docs/CIA-RDP79R00904A000100030011-8.pdf.

29. It is unclear how much oversight Eisenhower exercised over Operation Ajax; however, the plan had to be approved by Eisenhower before it could be put into effect. As Ambrose notes, "Eisenhower participated in none of the meetings that set up Ajax; he received only oral reports on the plan; and he did not discuss it with his Cabinet or the NSC. Establishing a pattern he would hold to throughout his Presidency, he kept his distance and left no documents behind that could implicate the President in any projected coup. But in the privacy of the Oval Office, over cocktails, he was kept informed by Foster Dulles, and he maintained a tight control over the activities of the CIA." Ambrose, *Eisenhower: Soldier and President*, 111.

30. Wilber, *Overthrow, March 1954*, National Security Archive, http://nsarchive.gwu.edu/NSAEBB/NSAEBB28/; Katouzian, "CIA Documents"; K. Roosevelt, *Countercoup*.

31. See Dwight D. Eisenhower, box 4, NSC Series, DDE Library.

32. For more on misdirection as a strategy in magic, see Lamont and Wiseman, *Magic in Theory*, 28–82.

33. Martin, "Rhetoric of Misdirection," 209–10.

34. Arthos, "Shaman-Trickster's Art of Misdirection"; Levine, *Black Culture*; Hardin, "Trickster in History."

35. Markel, "Rhetoric of Misdirection."

36. Stuckey, *Defining Americans*, 5.

37. Excerpts taken from Eisenhower, *Mandate for Change*, 160, and Norouzi, "Eisenhower-Mossadegh Cables."

38. Quoted in Arash, "Eisenhower-Mossadegh Cables."

39. Ambrose, *Ike's Spies*, 196.

40. Dwight D. Eisenhower, "Inaugural Address," January 20, 1953, The American Presidency Project, http://www.presidency.ucsb.edu.

41. Dwight D. Eisenhower, "Address at Annual Dinner of the American Society of Newspaper Editors," April 21, 1956, The American Presidency Project, http://www.presidency.ucsb.edu.

42. For examples, see Dwight D. Eisenhower, "The President's News Conference," August 11, 1954; Eisenhower, "Remarks and Address at Dinner of the National Conference on the Foreign Aspects of National Security," February 25, 1958; Eisenhower: "Remarks at the President's Birthday Breakfast," October 14, 1958, all at The American Presidency Project, http://www.presidency.ucsb.edu.

43. Dwight D. Eisenhower, "Exchange of Messages between the President and Prime Minister Mossadegh on the Oil Situation and the Problem of Aid to Iran," July 9, 1953, Mohammad Mossadegh, http://www.mohammadmossadegh.com/biography/dwight-d-eisenhower/cables/.

44. Kennett Love, "Mossadegh Is Seen Facing a Dilemma," *New York Times*, July 11, 1953.

45. "Iran Seems Stunned by Eisenhower Note," *New York Times*, July 12, 1953.

46. Eisenhower, "Exchange of Messages," July 9, 1953.

47. In later retellings Ike framed the choice as one between wisdom (stewarding America's resources) versus unwisdom (pouring more money into a failing and untrustworthy regime). Eisenhower, *Mandate for Change*, 162.

48. Eisenhower, "Exchange of Messages," July 9, 1953.

49. See Gregg, "Rhetoric of Distancing," 157–88.

50. Dwight D. Eisenhower, "The President's News Conference," March 5, 1953, The American Presidency Project, http://www.presidency.ucsb.edu.

51. See Dwight D. Eisenhower, "Remarks at the Governors' Conference, Seattle, Washington," August 4, 1953, and Eisenhower, "The President's News Conference," December 2, 1953, both at The American Presidency Project, http://www.presidency.ucsb.edu.

52. Bose and Greenstein, "Hidden Hand."

53. Arthur Krock, "Impressions of the President," *New York Times Magazine*, June 23, 1957.

54. Srodes, *Allen Dulles*, 457.

55. F. S. Saunders, *Cultural Cold War*, 2.

56. The CIA History states, "There can be no doubt whatsoever that this [propaganda] campaign . . . reached a very large audience and . . . directly influ-

enced their thinking in a most positive way." The CIA was also able to plant an article in the August 10 issue of *Newsweek* titled "Iran: Reds . . . Taking Over." Gasiorowski, "1953 Coup d'État against Mossadeq," 245.

57. Osgood, *Total Cold War*, 137.

58. "Mohammed Mossadeq, Man of the Year," *TIME*, January 7, 1952, cover.

59. Bill, "Politics of Intervention," 265.

60. All quotations from this report are taken from Risen, "C.I.A. Tried."

61. Bennett and Waltz, *Counterdeception Principles*, 63.

62. Ambrose, *Eisenhower: The President*, 320.

63. Greenstein, *Hidden-Hand Presidency*, 57–65.

64. See Immerman, "Eisenhower and Dulles," and Greenstein, *Hidden-Hand Presidency*, 87–90.

65. Quoted in Hoopes, *Devil and John Foster Dulles*, 184.

66. "Mr. Dulles' Return," *New York Times*, May 30, 1953.

67. "Text of Secretary Dulles' Report on Near East Trip," *New York Times*, June 2, 1953.

68. File of Henderson, Loy W.-Ambassador to Iran, March 11, 1954, Evaluation of Chiefs of Mission (2), box 1, Personnel Series, John Foster Dulles Papers, DDE Library.

69. Osgood, *Total Cold War*, 137–38.

70. Henderson, for instance, helped frame the new aid package as being directed against the threat of internal and external Communism. See Robert C. Doty, "Iran's Need of Aid Held Key to Policy," *New York Times*, August 26, 1953.

71. See Ceccarelli, "Polysemy"; Solomon and McMullen, "*Places in the Heart*"; Condit, "Rhetorical Limits of Polysemy"; Pearce, "Rhetorical Polysemy"; Rosteck and Frentz, "Myth and Multiple Readings"; Asen, "Reflections on the Role"; and Hasian, "Anne Frank."

72. K. Roosevelt, *Countercoup*, ix.

73. Quoted in A. S. Cooper, *Oil Kings*, 147.

74. See Dwight D. Eisenhower: "Annual Message to the Congress on the State of the Union," January 5, 1956; Eisenhower, "The President's News Conference," July 27, 1955; Eisenhower: "Special Message to the Congress on the Mutual Security Program," April 20, 1955, all at The American Presidency Project, http://www.presidency.ucsb.edu.

75. "NSC 136/1," November 20, 1952, Office of the Historian, https://history.state.gov/historicaldocuments/frus1952-54v10/d240.

3. From Baghdad to Cairo

1. Dwight D. Eisenhower, "A Chance for Peace," April 16, 1953, The American Presidency Project, http://www.presidency.ucsb.edu.

2. "World Reaction to President Eisenhower's Foreign Policy Address," April 21, 1953, Confidential File, Subject Series, DDE Library. See also Ivie, "Dwight D. Eisenhower's 'Chance for Peace,'" 227–43.

3. Eisenhower, "Inaugural Address," January 20, 1953, The American Presidency Project, http://www.presidency.ucsb.ed.

4. See Chernus, *Eisenhower's Atoms for Peace*, and Osgood, *Total Cold War*.

5. Cited in Osgood, *Total Cold War*, 162.

6. See Medhurst, "Eisenhower's 'Atoms for Peace' Speech," 204–20; Osgood, *Total Cold War*, 161–67; and Chernus, *Eisenhower's Atoms for Peace*, 112–17.

7. Medhurst, "Introduction," in *Eisenhower's War of Words*, 1–2.

8. Barghoorn, *Soviet Foreign Propaganda*, 111–14.

9. See Zubok and Pleshakov, *Inside the Kremlin's Cold War*, 203–9, and Osgood, *Total Cold War*, 355–58.

10. See Yaqub, *Containing Arab Nationalism*, 31–32.

11. Cited by Dawisha, in *Arab Nationalism in the Twentieth Century*, 147.

12. See Morris, *Israel's Border Wars*.

13. See Yergin, *Prize*, 168–261, 478.

14. Letter, Dwight D. Eisenhower to Winston Churchill, March 19, 1956, quoted in Spiegel, *Other Arab-Israeli Conflict*, 56.

15. Quoted in William Blum, *Killing Hope*, 84–85.

16. Ginat, *Soviet Union and Egypt*, 172–82.

17. Dwight D. Eisenhower, "The President's News Conference," July 28, 1954, The American Presidency Project, http://www.presidency.ucsb.edu.

18. Diary of the President, March 8, 1956, Office of the Historian, https://history.state.gov/historicaldocuments/frus1955-57v15/d177.

19. Waggoner, "Academic Adultery," 211.

20. On surreptitious rhetoric, see also Billig and Marinho, "Manipulating Information and Manipulating People," 158–74.

21. Parry-Giles, *Rhetorical Presidency*, 186.

22. See Louis, "Tragedy of the Anglo-Egyptian Settlement."

23. See Doran, *Ike's Gamble*.

24. Dwight D. Eisenhower, "The President's News Conference," June 30, 1954, The American Presidency Project, http://www.presidency.ucsb.edu.

25. "Text of Secretary Dulles' Report on Near East Trip," *New York Times*, June 2, 1953.

26. Dwight D. Eisenhower, "The President's News Conference," January 19, 1955, The American Presidency Project, http://www.presidency.ucsb.edu.

27. S/S-NSC files, lot 63 D 351, "NSC 129 Memoranda," *Foreign Relations of the United States* (hereafter cited as *FRUS*), April 24, 1952.

28. S/P—NSC files, lot 61 D 167, "Near East (NSC 155)," *FRUS*, July 14, 1953.

29. NSC 155.

30. NSC 155, emphasis in original.

31. See Wilford, *America's Great Game*, 133–59.

32. Copeland, *Game of Nations*, 88.

33. Heikal, *Cutting the Lion's Tail*, 42.

34. Quoted in Wilford, *America's Great Game*, 153.

35. Jalal, "Towards the Baghdad Pact," 409–33.

36. Hammond, *Cold War and Détente*, 89.

37. Hurewitz, "Historical Context," 28.

38. Jasse, "Baghdad Pact," 142.

39. Sanjian, "Formulation of the Baghdad Pact," 226–66.

40. "NSC 162/2: A Report to the National Security Council by the Executive Secretary on Basic National Security Policy," October 30, 1953, Federation of American Scientists, https://fas.org/irp/offdocs/nsc-hst/nsc-162-2.pdf.

41. Dwight D. Eisenhower, "Annual Message to the Congress on the State of the Union," January 5, 1956. Eisenhower, "The President's News Conference," April 4, 1956; Eisenhower, "The President's News Conference," March 21, 1956, all at The American Presidency Project, http://www.presidency.ucsb.edu.

42. C. L. Sulzberger, "Plugging the Last Gap in Free World Defenses," *New York Times*, January 29, 1955.

43. For more on the Baghdad Pact, see Persson, *Great Britain*; Ovendale, *Britain, the United States*; Podeh, *Quest for Hegemony*; and Sanjian, *Turkey and Her Arab Neighbors*.

44. Barr, *Line in the Sand*, 283–359.

45. Quoted in Blum, *Killing Hope*, 85.

46. See NSC reports of January 9, 1956, and January 16, 1956, quoted in Blum, *Killing Hope*, 85.

47. Quoted in A. Roosevelt, *For Lust of Knowing*, 445.

48. John Foster Dulles, "Press Conference," October 16, 1956, Steeley G. Mudd Manuscript Library, Princeton University, Princeton, New Jersey. See also Eveland, *Ropes of Sand*, 224.

49. Wilford, *America's Great Game*, 245–70.

50. Callanan, *Covert Action*, 102–3, and Blum, *Killing Hope*, 87–88.

51. P. J. Rabinowitz, "'Betraying the Sender'," 205. See also C. E. Morris, "Pink Herring," 228–44.

52. Dwight D. Eisenhower, "The President's News Conference," August 21, 1957, The American Presidency Project, http://www.presidency.ucsb.edu.

53. Quoted in Gerson, *American Secretaries of State*, 25.

54. Diary of the President, March 13, 1956, quoted in Spiegel, *Other Arab-Israeli Conflict*, 55.

55. For an excellent overview of the history of negotiations between Arabs and Jews over Palestine, including this period, see Caplan's four-volume *Futile Diplomacy*.

56. Caplan, *Futile Diplomacy*, 4:33.

57. Memorandum of Conversation, FRUS, January 27, 1955.

58. Dwight D. Eisenhower, "Statement by the President on Eric Johnston's Mission to the Near East," October 16, 1953, The American Presidency Project, http://www.presidency.ucsb.edu.

59. Quoted in Caplan, *Futile Diplomacy*, 4:126.

60. Quoted in Caplan, *Futile Diplomacy*, 4:92–94.

61. John Foster Dulles, "The Middle East," August 26, 1955, Steeley G. Mudd Manuscript Library, Princeton University, Princeton, New Jersey.

62. Media quotes taken from State Department report of reactions to Dulles's speech, "Further Reactions to Secretary Dulles' August 26 Statement on Israel-Arab Settlement (as of August 31)," box 1, John Foster Dulles Papers, Subject Series, DDE Library.

63. John Foster Dulles, "An Address by John Foster Dulles before the Council on Foreign Relations New York, N.Y., August 26, 1955," box 1, John Foster Dulles Papers, Subject Series, DDE Library.

64. Hahn, *Caught in the Middle East*, 185–86.

65. Quoted in Hahn, *United States, Great Britain, and Egypt*, 186.

66. Nye, *Is the American Century Over?*, 3. See also Nye, *Future of Power*.

67. Podeh, *Quest for Hegemony*, 99–100.

68. Quoted in Ewald, *Eisenhower the President*, 119–10.

69. Henry Byroade, "The Middle East in New Perspective April 9, 1954," Steeley G. Mudd Manuscript Library, Princeton University, Princeton, New Jersey.

4. Lion's Last Roar, Eagle's First Flight

1. Eden, *Full Circle*, 465–654.

2. Thorpe, *Eden*, xvii, 557.

3. Quoted in Louis Menand III, "Nukes of Hazard," *New Yorker*, September 30, 2013.

4. To see the way Eisenhower's 1956 presidential campaign used this claim, see "Football/Peace Commercial," The Living Room Candidate, http://www.livingroomcandidate.org/commercials/1956.

5. On Glubb's dismissal, see Massad, *Colonial Effects*.

6. Sanjian, "Formulation of the Baghdad Pact," 226–66.

7. Alteras, *Eisenhower and Israel*, 146.

8. Spiegel, *Other Arab-Israeli Conflict*, 65.

9. Eisenhower's 1956 letter to Richard Leo Simon: "We are rapidly getting to the point that no war can be won. War implies a contest: when you get to the point that contest is no longer involved and the outlook comes close to the destruction of the enemy and suicide for ourselves—an outlook that neither side can ignore—then arguments as to the exact amount of available strength as compared to somebody else's are no longer the vital issues." Reprinted by David Broder, "Negotiate or Die—Eisenhower," *Washington Post*, September 7, 1983.

10. Zubok and Pleshakov, *Inside the Kremlin's Cold War*, 184–86.

11. USSR Ministry of Foreign Affairs, *SSR I Arabskie strany, 1917–1960 qq. Dokumenty i materialy* (Moscow: Gospolitizdat, 1961), 116–20. Translation by Dmytryshyn and Cox in *Soviet Union and the Middle East*, 24–25.

12. Though Eisenhower made this point most emphatically in his second inaugural address, he had stated this sentiment numerous times beforehand.

See Dwight D. Eisenhower, "Remarks to the 63d Continental Congress of the National Society of the Daughters of the American Revolution," April 22, 1954, The American Presidency Project, http://www.presidency.ucsb.edu.

13. Gregg, "Rhetoric of Distancing," 157–88.

14. Gregg, "Rhetoric of Distancing," 184.

15. Gregg, "Rhetoric of Distancing," 169.

16. C. L. Cooper, Lion's Last Roar, 65.

17. Hurewitz, "Historical Context," 352.

18. Eden actually found out about the nationalization while dining with the Iraqi royal family and Iraqi president Nuri as-Said. He phoned Eisenhower, saying, "Our influence and yours throughout the Middle East will, we are convinced, be finally destroyed. . . . We must be ready, in the last resort, to use force to bring Nasser to his senses." Quoted in Bowie, "Eisenhower, Dulles, and the Suez Crisis," 197. See also Wall, France, the United States.

19. Quoted in Kyle, "Britain and the Crisis," 123.

20. Quoted in Spiegel, Other Arab-Israeli Conflict, 72.

21. Bose and Greenstein, "Hidden Hand," 195. Regarding the "missile gap controversy": some in the media, fueled by hysterical anti-Communists and partisan Democrats, alleged that the United States was far behind the Soviet Union in ballistic missile technology. Eisenhower knew that such claims were false because of top-secret U-2 spy plane photographs gathered by the CIA. He chose not to reveal the source of his information for diplomatic reasons, however, so the allegations continued until the U-2 program was exposed in 1960.

22. Fullick and Powell, Suez, 620–34.

23. See Campbell, "Soviet Union," 233–53.

24. Gyorkei, Soviet Military Intervention in Hungary, 401.

25. Medhurst, "Rhetoric and Cold War," 19–20.

26. Dwight D. Eisenhower, "TV Report to the Nation 10/31/56," box 19, DDE Library; see also Eisenhower, "Radio and Television Report to the American People on the Developments in Eastern Europe and the Middle East," October 31, 1956, The American Presidency Project, http://www.presidency.ucsb.edu.

27. Pratt, "Analysis of Three Crises Speeches," 199.

28. Gregg, "Rhetoric of Distancing," 164.

29. Medhurst, Dwight D. Eisenhower, 55–62.

30. This use of language, as mentioned previously, is examined more fully in Gregg's "The Rhetoric of Distancing" review.

31. Dwight D. Eisenhower, "TV Report to the Nation October 31, 1956," box 19, DDE Library.

32. Ivie, "Cold War Motives," 71–72. For prior Cold War rhetoric, see Hinds and Windt, Cold War as Rhetoric.

33. Eisenhower, "TV Report to the Nation October 31, 1956."

34. See Bury, Eisenhower.

35. Rabinowitch, "New Year's Thoughts," 3. See also Schrecker, *Many Are the Crimes*, xviii.

36. As Ira Chernus writes, "The purity and innocence of America was a fundamental premise of Eisenhower's discourse; it legitimated every American policy and maneuver in the incipient cold war. . . . Purity, in his discourse, meant not an absence of sin but a voluntary refusal to act upon sinful impulses." Chernus, *General Eisenhower*, 113.

37. Ivie, "Images of Savagery," 286.

38. Ivie, "Cold War Motives," 72–74.

39. Ivie, "Cold War Motives," 74.

40. Ivie, "Images of Savagery," 287–88.

41. By overcoming the devilish enemy, Ivie argues, America proves worthy of its exceptionalism and thus reinforces its own mythic character. Ivie, "Fighting Terror," 233.

42. Eisenhower, "TV Report to the Nation October 31, 1956."

43. Eisenhower, "TV Report to the Nation October 31, 1956."

44. Said, *Orientalism*, 55.

45. Said, *Orientalism*, 56

46. Said, *Orientalism*, 293.

47. Klein, *Cold War Orientalism*, 21.

48. Levey, *Israel and the Western Powers*, 19–20.

49. While I am relying primarily on Said's original work for this discussion, there obviously exists a multiplicity of interpretations of Orientalism and its validity as a scholarly paradigm. However, all I wish to demonstrate here is the clear presence of Orientalism within Eisenhower's rhetoric and its implications in his characterization of Egypt in the Suez Crisis. For a summary and dissection of postcolonialism within a communication framework, see Lal, "Politics and Culture."

50. Cain, "Economics," 39.

51. Eisenhower, "TV Report to the Nation October 31, 1956."

52. B. Morris, *Israel's Border Wars*, 22.

53. Drachman and Shank, *Presidents and Foreign Policy*, 70.

54. Eisenhower, "TV Report to the Nation October 31, 1956."

55. Perelman and Olbrechts-Tyteca, *New Rhetoric*, 325.

56. Gregg, "Rhetoric of Distancing," 181.

57. Dwight D. Eisenhower, "Press Conference of June 22, 1952," box 1, Speech Series, DDE Library, and Eisenhower, "Press Conference of June 24, 1952," box 1, Speech Series, DDE Library.

58. Cole, "Avoiding the Quagmire," 369.

59. Eisenhower, "TV Report to the Nation October 31, 1956."

60. America's relationship to the United Nations was also complicated by the Korean War. See MacQueen, *Humanitarian Intervention*, 20.

61. Campbell and Jamieson, *Presidents Creating the Presidency*, 224.

62. Chomsky, "Advance Agent," 415–32.

63. Harry S. Truman, "Special Message to the Congress on Greece and Turkey: The Truman Doctrine," March 12, 1947, The American Presidency Project, http://www.presidency.ucsb.edu.

64. Eisenhower, "TV Report to the Nation October 31, 1956."

65. O'Gorman, "Eisenhower and the American Sublime," 55.

66. Eisenhower, "TV Report to the Nation 10/31/56."

67. Bass, "Appeal to Efficiency," 110.

68. Ike ordered the Sixth Fleet to shadow the European landing parties, passed a UN resolution condemning the actions of America's allies, and withheld much-needed energy and monetary supplies to the Europeans (now that the Suez Canal was blocked by Nasser) until they fully complied. The British almost liquidated their dollar reserve.

69. Gyorkei and Neff, *Warriors at Suez*, 407–23.

70. Dwight D. Eisenhower, "Speech on the U.S. Role in the Middle East (Eisenhower Doctrine)," January 5, 1957, Council on Foreign Relations, http://www.cfr.org/middle-east-and-north-africa/president-eisenhowers-speech-us-role-middle-east-eisenhower-doctrine-1957/p24130.

71. I am using "consubstantial" in a loosely Burkean sense in that Ike depicted America and the United Nations as remaining individual loci of motives yet identative in their purposes in the Middle East. Burke, *Rhetoric of Motives*.

5. The Doctrine Applied

1. Seeking to circumvent congressional reluctance to impose sanctions on Israel, which Eisenhower and Dulles attributed to the influence of the Zionist lobby in Washington, Eisenhower went before the public on February 20 and argued that Israel threatened not only international order, but the very mission of the United Nations:

"Should a nation which attacks and occupies foreign territory in the face of United Nations disapproval be allowed to impose conditions on its own withdrawal? If we agreed that armed attack can properly achieve the purposes of the assailant, then I fear we will have turned back the clock of international order.

"If the United Nations once admits that international disputes can be settled by using force, then we will have destroyed the very foundation of the organization and our best hope of establishing world order. The United Nations must not fall. I believe that in the interests of peace the United Nations has no choice but to exert pressure upon Israel to comply with the withdrawal resolutions."

See Dwight D. Eisenhower, "Radio and Television Address to the American People on the Situation in the Middle East," February 20, 1957, The American Presidency Project, http://www.presidency.ucsb.edu.

2. Dann, *King Hussein*, 48–67; Lunt, *Hussein of Jordan*, 36–43; Ashton, *King Hussein of Jordan*, 61–64.

3. U.S. Embassy, Damascus, to Department of State, tel. 2779, May 17, 1957, record group 59, National Archives and Records Administration, College Park, Maryland.

4. Yaqub, *Containing Arab Nationalism*, 205.

5. Many consider the assassination of Nasib al-Matni, publisher and owner of the *Telegraph*, to be the event that officially sparked the Revolt of the Pashas, as the insurgency against Chamoun's rule became known. See Petron, *Struggle over Lebanon*, 50–55.

6. "Discussion at the 358th Meeting of the National Security Council, Thursday, March 13, 1958," box 9, NSC Series, DDE Library. For an account of this exchange, see Lenczowski, *American Presidents*, 57–61.

7. Memorandum of conversation, Eisenhower, John Foster Dulles and congressional leaders, *FRUS*, July 14, 1958.

8. Memorandum of conversation, Eisenhower and John Foster Dulles, *FRUS*, May 13, 1958; "Discussion at the 370th Meeting of the National Security Council, Thursday, June 26, 1958," box 9, NSC Series, DDE Library; Memorandum of conversation, John Foster Dulles, Hammarskjold, and Henry Cabot Lodge, July 7, 1958, box 1, General Correspondence and Memoranda Series, John Foster Dulles Papers, DDE Library.

9. "Discussion at the 369th Meeting of the National Security Council, Thursday, June 19, 1958," box 9, NSC Series, DDE Library.

10. Quoted in Macdonald, *Rolling the Iron Dice*, 166–67.

11. Quoted in Donovan, *U.S. & Soviet Policy*, 102.

12. Dulles and Eisenhower quoted in Yaqub, *Containing Arab Nationalism*, 215.

13. John Foster Dulles's Remarks at Cabinet Friday, July 18, 1958, box 11, Cabinet Series, DDE Library.

14. In 1945 Eisenhower wrote, "In this war, which was Total in every sense of the word, we have seen many great changes in military science. It seems to me that not the least of these was the development of psychological warfare as a special and effective weapon. . . . Without doubt, psychological warfare has proved its right to a place of dignity in our military arsenal." Quoted in Osgood, *Total Cold War*, 49.

15. Little, "His Finest Hour?," 53.

16. Memorandum of conversation, Eisenhower and John Foster Dulles, *FRUS*, July 14, 1958.

17. The United States was so invested in Chamoun, in fact, that the CIA helped rig the 1957 elections that put him in power. Wilbur Eveland, a CIA operative and confidant of Chamoun, has described in detail how American money helped propel Chamoun to victory. Eveland, *Ropes of Sand*, and Wilson, "Eisenhower Doctrine," 25–27.

18. John Foster Dulles's Remarks at Cabinet Friday, July 18, 1958.

19. Quoted in Yaqub, *Containing Arab Nationalism*, 223.

20. Medhurst, "Rhetorical Leadership and the Presidency," 60.

21. While this concept has been articulated by numerous presidents, Benjamin Harrison said that exact phrase in his address "The Development of the National Constitution" at Stanford University. See Harrison, *Views of an Ex-President*, 29.

22. Eisenhower and John Foster Dulles also hedged on American military superiority preventing the Soviets from escalating the conflict. During the July 18 cabinet meeting, both acknowledged that their actions in Lebanon could lead to a global war with the Soviet Union, to which they argued that "the United States [was] *now* in a very strong position, perhaps stronger than in years to come when Russia has operational missiles." If there was to be a fight over the Middle East, so to speak, better to have it now than later. Minutes of Cabinet Meeting, box 11, Cabinet Series, DDE Library.

Regarding Ike's coordination with Britain, Macmillan, in fact, did his best to convince Eisenhower to send troops to Amman as well. In trying to get Ike to deploy troops to Jordan and Lebanon, Macmillan hoped to broaden the American mission to such a degree that offensive action against Nasser or the new leaders of Iraq might be contemplated. As Macmillan said in a phone conversation in the late afternoon of July 14, 1958, "I think we have got to see it together, dear friend. There is no good in being in that place and sitting there a few months and the whole rest being in flames. As soon as we start we have to face it—we have probably got to do a lot of things." Eisenhower, citing the need for congressional approval for any larger action than Operation Blue Bat, steadfastly refused to get sucked in to a larger mission. See Report of Telephone Call between the President and Prime Minister Macmillan, box 40, International Series, DDE Library.

23. See Smith, *Eisenhower in War and Peace*, xiii; for authors' associations of "gunboat diplomacy" with Eisenhower, see E. N. Saunders, *Leaders at War*, 86; Worley, *Shaping U.S. Military Forces*, 168; Ambrose, *Eisenhower: Soldier and President*, 469; Patterson, *Grand Expectations*, 423; and Hagan, *This People's Navy*, 350.

24. Letter from Mrs. John Beardsley, in folder 122 EE (6), box 884, General Files Series, DDE Library.

25. Memorandum of conversation, Eisenhower and John Foster Dulles, FRUS, May 13, 1958.

26. "Timetable of Events of Week of July 14–19 in Connection with Mid East," box 40, International Series, DDE Library.

27. Cherwitz and Zagacki, "Consummatory versus Justificatory Crisis Rhetoric," 316.

28. The idea of America responding in retaliation to an attack on the homeland, its embassies, or other interests is included in their definition and therefore not perfectly applicable to Eisenhower's rhetoric; justificatory rhetoric for them takes place in a situation in which "presidential discourse was from the beginning part of a larger, overt military retaliation taken by the government." Cherwitz and Zagacki, "Consummatory versus Justificatory Crisis Rhetoric," 308.

Implicit in my argument concerning Ike's audience here is Lloyd Bitzer's definition of what constitutes a "rhetorical" audience or situation. The international community and the American public, more than any other audience (including Congress), were the parties being hailed who were capable of acting in such a way as to positively modify the rhetorical exigence. See Bitzer, "Rhetorical Situation."

29. "Timetable of Events of Week of July 14–19."

30. Edwards, Valenzano, and Stevenson, "Peacekeeping Mission," 339.

31. Minutes of Cabinet Meeting, July 18.

32. Campbell and Jamieson, *Deeds Done in Words*, 107.

33. Dwight D. Eisenhower, "Special Message to the Congress on the Sending of United States Forces to Lebanon," July 15, 1958, The American Presidency Project, http://www.presidency.ucsb.edu.

34. Eisenhower, "Special Message to the Congress," July 15, 1958.

35. I have used two sources for this address: Dwight D. Eisenhower, "Lebanese Statement," box 26, Speech Series, DDE Library, and Eisenhower, "Statement by the President following the Landing of United States Marines at Beirut," July 15, 1958, The American Presidency Project, http://www.presidency.ucsb.edu.

36. Considering, for instance, that Nasser himself cracked down heavily on Communist influence within the borders of Egypt and Syria, and that Lebanon was a U.S. ally, there is very little evidence to suggest that Communist influence in Lebanon was a significant political threat to either the regime or its nationalist opponents. In fact Nasser viciously persecuted Communism within the United Arab Republic's borders and upon the union of Syria and Egypt forced the Syrian Communist Party to dissolve.

37. Yaqub, *Containing Arab Nationalism*, 225.

38. To get a sense of how Eisenhower worded the address: up to this point in the speech, he had used "we" fourteen times, and the only prior usage of "I" was in the sentence "I should now like to take a few minutes to explain the situation in Lebanon."

39. Eisenhower, "Lebanese Statement," July 15, 1958.

40. Eisenhower, "Statement by the President following the Landing," July 15, 1958.

41. Ivie and Giner, "Hunting the Devil," 581.

42. Ivie, "Images of Savagery," 287.

43. Eisenhower, "Lebanese Statement," July 15, 1958.

44. Eisenhower, "Special Message to the Congress," July 15, 1958.

45. Wander, "Rhetoric of American Foreign Policy," 340

46. Wander, "Rhetoric of American Foreign Policy," 342.

47. Eisenhower, "Special Message to the Congress," July 15, 1958.

48. Dwight D. Eisenhower, "Special Message to the Congress on the Situation in the Middle East," The American Presidency Project, http://www.presidency.ucsb.edu/ws/index.php?pid=11007&st=eisenhower&st1=.

49. Chirindo and Neville-Shepard, "Obama's 'New Beginning,'" 221.

50. Eisenhower, "Lebanese Statement," July 15, 1958.

51. Eisenhower, "Lebanese Statement," July 15, 1958.

52. Eisenhower, "Special Message to the Congress," July 15, 1958.

53. Eisenhower, "Special Message to the Congress," July 15, 1958.

54. Chernus, *Apocalypse Management*, 11.

55. Dwight D. Eisenhower, "Message to the United States Forces in Lebanon and the Mediterranean Area," box 26, DDE Library.

56. "Text of Khrushchev Message on Summit Parley," *New York Times*, July 20, 1958; "Text of Eisenhower's Reply to Khrushchev on Summit Talk," *New York Times*, July 23, 1958; "Eisenhower's Letter to Khrushchev about Summit Talk," *New York Times*, July 26, 1958.

57. Quoted in Saivetz, "Soviet Union and the Middle East," 239.

58. Dwight D. Eisenhower, "Letter to Nikita Khrushchev, Chairman, Council of Ministers, U.S.S.R.," July 22, 1958; Eisenhower, "Letter to Nikita Khrushchev, Chairman, Council of Ministers, U.S.S.R.," July 25, 1958, both at The American Presidency Project, http://www.presidency.ucsb.edu.

59. Eisenhower, "Letter to Nikita Khrushchev," July 22, 1958.

60. Travis J. Cram identifies this combination of idealism and pragmatism in Reagan's rhetoric, writing, "The central implication is that principle and pragmatism (at least for Reagan) are not necessarily opposite modes or rhetorical impulses, but instead can additively work together to ground a president's symbolic worldview." Such a statement, I hold, could also be applied to Eisenhower in this rhetorical instance. See Cram, "'Peace.'"

61. Spiller, *"Not War but like War,"* 1.

62. "Presidential Approval Ratings—Gallup Historical Statistics and Trends," Gallup.com, http://news.gallup.com/poll/116677/presidential-approval-ratings-gallup-historical-statistics-trends.aspx.

63. Osgood, *Total Cold War*, 247.

64. Bass, "Perversion of Empire," 211.

65. Campbell, *Great Silent Majority*.

66. Johnson: Lyndon B. Johnson, "Radio and Television Report to the American People on the Situation in the Dominican Republic," May 2, 1965, The American Presidency Project, http://www.presidency.ucsb.edu, and Bass, "Appeal to Efficiency." While this was a complicated rhetorical situation, elements of threat conflation, destabilization, and other features of Ike's rhetoric can be seen in Reagan's speech of October 27. Reagan: Ronald Reagan, "Address to the Nation on Events in Lebanon and Grenada," October 27, 1983, The American Presidency Project, http://www.presidency.ucsb.edu; Birdsell, "Ronald Reagan"; and Klope, "Defusing a Foreign Policy Crisis."

67. These themes can be seen most clearly in Bush's March 17, 2003, address to the nation regarding Iraq. Bush: George H. W. Bush, "Address to the Nation on Iraq," March 17, 2003, The American Presidency Project, http://www.presidency.ucsb.edu.

68. Proctor, "Rescue Mission," 246.

69. Jack Raymond, "U.S. Forges Move to Back Marines," *New York Times*, July 16, 1958, front page.

70. Chernus, *Apocalypse Management*, 11.

Conclusion

1. Dwight D. Eisenhower, "Address to the Third Special Emergency Session of the General Assembly of the United Nations," August 13, 1958, The American Presidency Project, http://www.presidency.ucsb.edu.

2. See Dunmire, "9/11 Changed Everything," 195–222, and Suzuki and Niitsuma, "Argumentative Analysis," 87–93.

3. Dwight D. Eisenhower, "Press Conference held at the Brown Palace Hotel," June 24, 1952, box 1, Speech Series, DDE Library.

4. Barrett, *Greater Middle East*, 120.

5. George W. Bush, "Transcript of President Bush's Address to a Joint Session of Congress," CNN, September 20, 2001.

6. David Samuels, "Through the Looking Glass with Ben Rhodes," *New York Times Magazine*, May 8, 2016.

7. Hassan, "Sectarianism of the Islamic State."

8. Donald Trump, "Remarks at CIA Headquarters in Langley, Virginia," January 21, 2017, The American Presidency Project, http://www.presidency.ucsb.edu.

9. Farr, "Conceptual Change and Constitutional Innovation," 21–22.

10. See James Jasinki's summation of Farr's work in relation to other formulations of constitutive rhetoric. Jasinki, *Sourcebook on Rhetoric*, 106.

11. Eden, "Leader's Speech, 1955," May 26, 1955, British Political Speech Online Archives, http://www.britishpoliticalspeech.org/speech-archive.htm?speech=105.

12. Indeed, the transformation in Eden's rhetoric alone is striking, seen most notably in comparing his 1955 speech with his 1946 address before Parliament discussing the British stake in Egypt. For the latter, see Eden, *Freedom and Order*, 398–405.

13. William J. Clinton, "Address to the Nation Announcing Military Strikes on Iraq," December 16, 1998, The American Presidency Project, http://www.presidency.ucsb.edu.

14. William J. Clinton, "Address before a Joint Session of the Congress on the State of the Union," January 25, 1994, The American Presidency Project, http://www.presidency.ucsb.edu.

15. William J. Clinton, "Remarks on Returning from the Middle East," October 29, 1994, The American Presidency Project, http://www.presidency.ucsb.edu.

16. John F. Kennedy, "Special Message to the Congress on Urgent National Needs," May 25, 1961, and Kennedy, "Annual Message to the Congress on the State of the Union," January 14, 1963, both at The American Presidency Project, http://www.presidency.ucsb.edu.

17. Lyndon B. Johnson, "Remarks Broadcast on the 30th Anniversary of V-E Day," May 7, 1965, and Johnson, "Annual Message to the Congress on the State

of the Union," January 17, 1968, both at The American Presidency Project, http://
www.presidency.ucsb.edu.

18. Richard M. Nixon, "The President's News Conference," May 8, 1970, and
Nixon, "Remarks to Reporters Announcing Acceptance by Middle East Nations
of United States Cease-Fire Proposal," July 31, 1970, both at The American Presidency Project, http://www.presidency.ucsb.edu.

19. Gerald Ford, "Remarks of Welcome to President Anwar el-Sadat of Egypt,"
October 27, 1975, The American Presidency Project, http://www.presidency
.ucsb.edu.

20. James E. Carter, "Middle East Arms Sales Letter to Members of Congress,"
May 12, 1978, The American Presidency Project, http://www.presidency.ucsb.edu.

21. Ronald Reagan, "Question-and-Answer Session with Reporters on Middle East Issues," October 12, 1981, and Reagan, "Statement on the Situation in
Lebanon," February 7, 1984, both at The American Presidency Project, http://
www.presidency.ucsb.edu.

22. George H. W. Bush, "The President's News Conference," August 8, 1990,
and Bush, "Remarks on the Persian Gulf Conflict," February 22, 1991, both at
The American Presidency Project, http://www.presidency.ucsb.edu.

23. Zarefsky, "Presidential Rhetoric," 611.

24. Little, *American Orientalism*, 9.

25. In fact the November/December 2015 issue of *Foreign Affairs* was dedicated to questioning America's role in the Middle East. See Rose, "Post-American
Middle East."

BIBLIOGRAPHY

Abrahamian, Ervand. *The Coup: 1953, the CIA, and the Roots of Modern U.S.-Iranian Relations*. New York: New Press, 2013.

Abu-Jaber, Faiz S. *American-Arab Relations from Wilson to Nixon*. New York: University Press of America, 1979.

Acheson, Dean. "Speech on the Far East," January 12, 1950." Teaching American History. http://teachingamericanhistory.org/library/document/speech-on-the-far-east/.

al-Rasheed, Madawi. *A History of Saudi Arabia*. Cambridge: Cambridge University Press, 2002.

Alteras, Isaac. *Eisenhower and Israel: U.S.-Israeli Relations, 1953–1960*. Gainesville: University of Florida Press, 1993.

Althusser, Louis. *Lenin and Philosophy and Other Essays*. Translated by Ben Brewster. New York: Monthly Review Press, 1971.

Ambrose, Stephen E. *Eisenhower: Soldier and President*. New York: Simon & Schuster, 2014.

———. *Eisenhower: The President*. New York: Simon & Schuster, 1984.

———. *Ike's Spies: Eisenhower and the Espionage Establishment*. Jackson: University Press of Mississippi, 1991.

Amirahmadi, Hooshang, ed. *The United States and the Middle East: A Search for New Perspectives*. Albany: State University of New York Press, 1993.

Aronson, Geoffrey. *From Sideshow to Center Stage: U.S. Policy toward Egypt, 1946–1956*. Boulder CO: Lynne Rienner, 1986.

Arthos, John, Jr. "The Shaman-Trickster's Art of Misdirection: The Rhetoric of Farrakhan and the Million Men." *Quarterly Journal of Speech* 87 (2001): 41–60.

Asen, Robert. "Critical Engagement through Public Sphere Scholarship." *Quarterly Journal of Speech* 101 (2015): 132–44.

———. "Reflections on the Role of Rhetoric in Public Policy." *Rhetoric & Public Affairs* 13 (2010): 121–44.

Ashton, Nigel J. *Eisenhower, Macmillan and the Problem of Nasser: Anglo-American Relations and Arab Nationalism, 1955–59*. New York: St. Martin's Press, 1996.

———. *King Hussein of Jordan: A Political Life*. New Haven CT: Yale University Press, 2008.

Axelrod, Alan. *Eisenhower on Leadership: Ike's Enduring Lessons in Total Victory Management*. San Francisco: Jossey-Bass, 2010.

Azimi, Fakhreddin. *Iran: The Crisis of Democracy 1941–1953: From the Exile of Reza Shah to the Fall of Mossadiq*. New York: I. B Tauris, 1989.

———. "The Reconciliation of Politics and Ethics, Nationalism and Democracy: An Overview of the Political Career of Dr Muhammad Musaddiq." In Bill and Louis, *Musaddiq, Iranian Nationalism and Oil*, 47–68.

Badeau, John S. *The American Approach to the Arab World*. New York: Harper & Row, 1968.

Baker, Raymond William. *Egypt's Uncertain Revolution under Nasser and Sadat*. Cambridge, MA: Harvard University Press, 1978.

Banani, Amin. *The Modernization of Iran 1921–1941*. Stanford CA: Stanford University Press, 1961.

Barghoorn, Frederick Charles. *Soviet Foreign Propaganda*. Princeton NJ: Princeton University Press, 2015.

Barr, James. *A Line in the Sand: The Anglo-French Struggle for the Middle East, 1914–1948*. New York: W. W. Norton, 2012.

Barrett, Roby C. *The Greater Middle East and the Cold War: U.S. Foreign Policy under Eisenhower and Kennedy*. London: I. B. Tauris, 2007.

Bass, Jeff D. "The Appeal to Efficiency as Narrative Closure: Lyndon Johnson and the Dominican Crisis, 1965." *Southern Speech Communication Journal* 50 (1985): 103–20.

———. "Hearts of Darkness and Hot Zones: The Ideologeme of Imperial Contagion in Recent Accounts of Viral Outbreaks." *Quarterly Journal of Speech* 85 (1998): 430–47.

———. "The Perversion of Empire: Edmund Burke and the Nature of Imperial Responsibility." *Quarterly Journal of Speech* 81 (1995): 208–27.

Bennett, Michael, and Edward Waltz. *Counterdeception Principles and Applications for National Security*. Boston: Artech House, 2007.

Best, Lindon Layton. "Rhetorical Misdirection: Of Public Policy and Duplicitous Rhetoric." Master's thesis, University of Manchester, 2012.

Bill, James A. "America, Iran, and the Politics of Intervention, 1951–1953." In Bill and Louis, *Mussadiq, Iranian Nationalism, and Oil*, 261–95.

Bill, James A., and William Roger Louis, eds. *Mussadiq, Iranian Nationalism, and Oil*. Austin: University of Texas Press, 1988.

Billig, Michael, and Cristina Marinho. "Manipulating Information and Manipulating People: Examples from the 2004 Portuguese Parliamentary Celebration of the April Revolution." *Critical Discourse Studies* 11 (2014): 158–74.

Birdsell, David S. "Ronald Reagan on Lebanon and Grenada: Flexibility and Interpretation in the Application of Kenneth Burke's Pentad." *Quarterly Journal of Speech* 73 (1987): 267–79.

Bitzer, Lloyd. "The Rhetorical Situation." *Philosophy and Rhetoric* 1 (1968): 1–14.

Black, Edwin. *Rhetorical Criticism: A Study in Method*. Madison: University of Wisconsin Press, 1978.

Blum, William. *Killing Hope: U.S. Military and CIA Interventions since World War II*. London: Zed Books, 2003.

Bose, Meena, and Fred Greenstein. "The Hidden Hand vs. the Bully Pulpit: The Layered Political Rhetoric of President Eisenhower." In *The Presidency and Rhetorical Leadership*, edited by Glen Dorsey, 184–99. College Station: Texas A&M University Press, 2002.

Bostdorff, Denise. "The Evolution of a Diplomatic Surprise: Richard M. Nixon's Rhetoric on China, 1952–July 15, 1971." *Rhetoric & Public Affairs* 5 (2002): 31–56.

———. *Proclaiming the Truman Doctrine: The Cold War Call to Arms*. College Station: Texas A&M University Press, 2008.

Bowie, Robert R. "Eisenhower, Dulles, and the Suez Crisis." In Louis and Owen, *Suez 1956*, 189–214.

Bowie, Robert R., and Richard H. Immerman. *Waging Peace: How Eisenhower Shaped an Enduring Cold War Strategy*. Oxford: Oxford University Press, 1998.

Brian, Denis. *The Elected and the Chosen: Why American Presidents Have Supported the Jews and Israel; From George Washington to Barrack Obama*. Jerusalem: Gefen, 2012.

Briggs, Philip J. *Making American Foreign Policy: President-Congress Relations from the Second World War to the Post–Cold War Era*. New York: Rowman & Littlefield, 1994.

Brooks, Jeffrey. "When the Cold War Did Not End: The Soviet Peace Offensive of 1953 and the American Response." Kennan Institute Occasional Papers Series 278. 2000. Wilson Center. https://www.wilsoncenter.org/sites/default/files/op278_when_cold_war_did_not_end_brooks_2000.pdf.

Bryson, Thomas A. *American Diplomatic Relations with the Middle East, 1784–1975: A Survey*. Metuchen NJ: Scarecrow Press, 1977.

Burke, Kenneth. *A Rhetoric of Motives*. Berkeley: University of California Press, 1969.

Bury, Helen. *Eisenhower and the Cold War Arms Race*. London: I. B. Taurus, 2014.

Cain, P. J. "Economics and Empire: The Metropolitan Context." In *The Oxford History of the British Empire*, edited by Andrew Porter, 3:31–52. Oxford: Oxford University Press, 1999.

Callanan, James. *Covert Action in the Cold War: U.S. Policy, Intelligence and CIA Operations*. New York: I. B. Tauris, 2010.

Campbell, John C. "The Soviet Union, the United States, and the Twin Crises: Hungary and Suez." In Louis and Owen, *Suez 1956*, 233–56.

Campbell, Karlyn Kohrs. *The Great Silent Majority: Nixon's 1969 Speech on Vietnamization*. College Station: Texas A&M University Press, 2014.

Campbell, Karlyn Kohrs, and Kathleen Hall Jamieson. *Deeds Done in Words*. Chicago: University of Chicago, 1990.

————. *Presidents Creating the Presidency*. Chicago: University of Chicago Press, 2008.

Caplan, Neil. *Futile Diplomacy*. Vol. 1, *Early Arab-Zionist Negotiation Attempts, 1913–1931*. London: Frank Cass, 1983.

————. *Futile Diplomacy*. Vol. 2, *Arab-Zionist Negotiations and the End of the Mandate*. London: Frank Cass, 1986.

————. *Futile Diplomacy*. Vol. 3, *The United Nations, the Great Powers, and Middle East Peacemaking, 1948–1954*. London: Frank Cass, 1997.

————. *Futile Diplomacy*. Vol. 4, *Operation Alpha and the Failure of Anglo-American Coercive Diplomacy in the Arab-Israeli Conflict, 1954–1956*. London: Frank Cass, 1997.

Casey, Steve. *Cautious Crusade: Franklin D. Roosevelt, American Public Opinion, and the War against Nazi Germany*. New York: Oxford University Press, 2002.

Ceaser, James W., Glen E. Thurow, Jeffrey Tulis, and Joseph M. Bessette. "The Rise of the Rhetorical Presidency." *Presidential Studies Quarterly* 11 (1981): 158–71.

Ceccarelli, Leah. "Polysemy: Multiple Meanings in Rhetorical Criticism." *Quarterly Journal of Speech* 84 (1998): 398–99.

Charland, Maurice. "Constitutive Rhetoric: The Case of the *Peuple Quebecois*." *Quarterly Journal of Speech* 73 (1987): 133–50.

Chernus, Ira. *Apocalypse Management: Eisenhower and the Discourse of National Insecurity*. Stanford CA: Stanford University Press, 2008.

————. "Eisenhower and the Soviets, 1945–1947: Rhetoric and Policy." *Rhetoric & Public Affairs* 2 (1999): 59–82.

————. *Eisenhower's Atoms for Peace*. College Station: Texas A&M University Press, 2002.

————. *General Eisenhower: Ideology and Discourse*. East Lansing: Michigan State University Press, 2002.

Cherwitz Richard A., and Kenneth S. Zagacki. "Consummatory versus Justificatory Crisis Rhetoric." *Western Journal of Speech Communication* 50 (1986): 307–24.

Chirindo, Kundai, and Ryan Neville-Shepard. "Obama's 'New Beginning'": U.S. Foreign Policy and Comic Exceptionalism." *Argumentation and Advocacy* (2015): 215–30.

Chomsky, Daniel. "Advance Agent of the Truman Doctrine: The United States, the *New York Times*, and the Greek Civil War." *Political Communication* 17 (2000): 415–32.

Christison, Kathleen. *Perceptions of Palestine: Their Influence on U.S. Middle East Policy*. Berkeley: University of California Press, 1999.

Churchill, Winston. "Winston Churchill's Iron Curtain Speech." *The History Guide: Lectures on Twentieth Century Europe*. http://www.historyguide.org/europe/churchill.html.

Clarke, Peter. *The Last Thousand Days of the British Empire: Churchill, Roosevelt, and the Birth of the Pax Americana*. New York: Bloomsbury, 2010.

Clevenger, Theodore, Jr., and Eugene Knepprath. "A Quantitative Analysis of Logical and Emotional Content in Selected Campaign Addresses of Eisenhower and Stevenson." *Western Speech* 30 (1966): 144–50.

Clifford, Clark. "American Relations with the Soviet Union" ["Clifford-Elsey Report"], September 24, 1946. Conway Files, Truman Papers, Truman Presidential Library. https://www.trumanlibrary.org/whistlestop/study_collections/coldwar/documents/pdf/4-1.pdf.

Cohn, Lora. "An Unconventional Leader: Eisenhower's Agricultural Policy Leadership as a Preemptive President." *Conference Papers—National Communication Association* (January 2008).

Cole, Timothy. "Avoiding the Quagmire: Alternative Rhetorical Constructs for Post–Cold War American Foreign Policy." *Rhetoric & Public Affairs* 2 (1999): 367–93.

Condit, Celeste M. "The Rhetorical Limits of Polysemy," *Critical Studies in Mass Communication* 6 (1989): 103–22.

Cooper, Andrew Scott. *The Oil Kings: How the U.S., Iran, and Saudi Arabia Changed the Balance of Power in the Middle East.* New York: Simon & Schuster, 2011.

Cooper, Chester L. *The Lion's Last Roar: Suez, 1956.* San Francisco: Harper & Row, 1971.

Copeland, Miles. *The Game of Nations: The Amorality of Power Politics.* New York: Simon & Schuster, 1969.

Cram, Travis J. "'Peace, Yes, but World Freedom As Well': Principle, Pragmatism, and the End of the Cold War." *Western Journal of Communication* 79 (2015): 367–86.

Dann, Uriel. *King Hussein and the Challenge of Arab Radicalism: Jordan, 1955–1958.* Oxford: Oxford University Press, 1989.

Davison, Lawrence. "Historical Ignorance and Popular Perception: The Case of U.S. Perceptions of Palestine, 1917," *Middle East Policy* 3 (1994): 125-147.

Dawisha, Adeed. *Arab Nationalism in the Twentieth Century: From Triumph to Despair.* Princeton NJ: Princeton University Press, 2016.

"Defense of Formosa, Pescadores." In *Congressional Quarterly Almanac 1955,* 11th ed., 277–80. Washington DC: Congressional Quarterly, 1956. http://library.cqpress.com/cqalmanac/cqal55-1353305.

DeNovo, John A. *American Interests and Policies in the Middle East: 1900–1939.* Minneapolis: University of Minnesota Press, 1963.

Dmytryshyn, Basil, and Frederick Cox. *The Soviet Union and the Middle East: A Documentary Record of Afghanistan, Iran, and Turkey 1917–1985.* Princeton NJ: Kingston Press, 1987.

Donovan, John. *U.S. & Soviet Policy in the Middle East: 1957–1966.* New York: Facts on File, 1974.

Doran, Michael. *Ike's Gamble: America's Rise to Dominance in the Middle East.* New York: Free Press, 2016.

Drachman, Edward, and Alan Shank. *Presidents and Foreign Policy.* Albany: State University of New York Press, 1997.

Dunmire, Patricia L. "'9/11 Changed Everything': An Intertextual Analysis of the Bush Doctrine." *Discourse & Society* 20 (2009): 195–222.

Eberly, Susan K. "The Eisenhower Doctrine: A Study of United States Middle East Policy in the Years 1957–58." Master's thesis, American University, 1965.

Eddy, William A. *F.D.R. Meets Ibn Saud.* Washington DC: America-Mideast Educational & Training Services, 1954.

Eden, Anthony. *Freedom and Order: Selected Speeches, 1939–1946.* Boston: Houghton Mifflin, 1948.

——. *Full Circle: The Memoirs of Anthony Eden.* Boston: Houghton Mifflin, 1960.

Edwards, George C., III. *The Strategic President: Persuasion and Opportunity in Presidential Leadership.* Princeton NJ: Princeton University Press, 2009.

Edwards, George C., III, and Joseph Wayne. *Presidential Leadership: Politics and Policy Making.* 5th ed. New York: Worth, 1999.

Edwards, Jason A., Joseph M. Valenzano III, and Karla Stevenson. "The Peacekeeping Mission: Bringing Stability to a Chaotic Scene." *Communication Quarterly* (2011): 339–58.

Eisenhower, Dwight D. *Mandate for Change: The White House Years, 1953–1953.* New York: Doubleday, 1963.

——. "Special Message to the Congress on the Situation in the Middle East," January 5, 1957. Gerhard Peters and John T. Woolley, The American Presidency Project. http://www.presidency.ucsb.edu/ws/?pid=11007.

——. *Waging Peace: The White House Years, 1956–1961.* New York: Doubleday, 1965.

Eveland, Wilbur Crane. *Ropes of Sand: America's Failure in the Middle East.* New York: W. W. Norton, 1980.

Ewald, William Bragg, Jr. *Eisenhower the President: Crucial Days, 1951–1960.* Eaglewood Cliffs NJ: Prentice-Hall, 1981.

Farmanfarmaian, Manucher, and Roxane Farmanfarmaian. *Blood and Oil: Memoirs of a Persian Prince.* New York: Random House, 1997.

Farr, James. "Conceptual Change and Constitutional Innovation." In *Conceptual Change and the Constitution,* edited by Terence Ball and J. A. Pocock, 24–49. Lawrence: University Press of Kansas, 1988.

Federer, William J. *Treasury of Presidential Quotations.* St. Louis: Amerisearch, 2004.

Finer, Herman. *Dulles over Suez: The Theory and Practice of His Diplomacy.* Chicago: Quadrangle Books, 1964.

Fisher, Walter R. "Narration as a Human Communication Paradigm: The Case of Public Moral Argument." *Communication Monographs* 51 (1984): 1–22.

Flanagan, Jason C. "Woodrow Wilson's 'Rhetorical Restructuring': The Transformation of the American Self and the Construction of the German Enemy." *Rhetoric & Public Affairs* 7 (2004): 115–48.

Frank, Mitchell. "Americans (Still) Don't Understand the Middle East: This Man Wants to Help." *Chicago Policy Review*, July 28, 2015.

Freiberger, Stephen. *Dawn over Suez: The Rise of American Power in the Middle East, 1953–1957*. Chicago: Ivan R. Dee, 1992.

Frye, Richard. *Persia*. New York: Routledge, 2011.

Fullick, Roy, and Geoffrey Powell. *Suez: The Double War*. London: Hamish Hamilton, 1979.

Gaddis, John Lewis. *Strategies of Containment: A Critical Appraisal of American National Security Policy during the Cold War*. Oxford: Oxford University Press, 1982.

Gao, George. "Presidential Job Approval Ratings from Ike to Obama." Pew Research Center. www.pewresearch.org/fact-tank/2015/02/16/presidential -job-approval-ratings-from-ike-to-obama/.

Gasiorowski, Mark J. "The 1953 Coup d'État against Mossadeq." In Gasiorowski and Byrne, *Mohammad Mossadeq*, 227–60. Syracuse NY: Syracuse University Press, 2004.

Gasiorowski, Mark J., and Malcolm Byrne, eds. *Mohammad Mossadeq and the 1953 Coup in Iran*. Syracuse NY: Syracuse University Press, 2004.

Gerson, Louis. *The American Secretaries of State and Their Diplomacy*. Lawrence: University of Kansas Press, 1964.

Ghods, M. Reza. *Iran in the Twentieth Century: A Political History*. Boulder CO: Lynee Rienner, 1989.

Ginat, Rami. *The Soviet Union and Egypt, 1945–1955*. London: Frank Cass, 1993.

Green, Melanie C., Jeffrey J. Strange, and Timothy C. Brock, eds. *Narrative Impact: Social and Cognitive Foundations*. Mahwah NJ: Lawrence Erlbaum, 2002.

Greenstein, Fred I. *The Hidden-Hand Presidency: Eisenhower as Leader*. Baltimore: Johns Hopkins University Press, 1994.

Gregg, Richard B. "The Rhetoric of Distancing: Eisenhower's Suez Crisis Speech, 31 October 1956." In Medhurst, *Eisenhower's War of Words: Rhetoric and Leadership*, 157–87.

Gring-Pemble, Lisa M. "'Are We Going to Now Govern by Anecdote?': Rhetorical Constructions of Welfare Recipients in Congressional Hearings, Debates, and Legislation, 1992–1996." *Quarterly Journal of Speech* 87 (2001): 341–65.

Groisser, Philip L., ed. *The United States and the Middle East*. Albany: State University of New York Press, 1982.

Guhin, Michael A. *John Foster Dulles: A Statesman and His Times*. New York: Columbia University Press, 1972.

Gyorkei, Jeno. *Soviet Military Intervention in Hungary, 1956*. Budapest: Central European University Press, 1999.

Gyorkei, Jeno, and Donald Neff. *Warriors at Suez: Eisenhower Takes America into the Middle East in 1956*. Brattleboro VT: Amana Books, 1988.

Haddad, Yvonne Yasbeck. *Not Quite American? The Shaping of Arab and Muslim Identity in the United States*. Waco TX: Baylor University Press, 2004.

Hagan, Kenneth J. *This People's Navy: The Making of American Sea Power.* New York: Simon and Schuster, 1992.

Hahn, Peter L. *Caught in the Middle East: U.S. Policy toward the Arab-Israeli Conflict, 1945–1961.* Chapel Hill: University of North Carolina Press, 2006.

———. *The United States, Great Britain, and Egypt, 1945–1956: Strategy and Diplomacy in the Early Cold War.* Chapel Hill: University of North Carolina Press, 1991.

Hale, Peter B., and Cherle A. Loustanau. "U.S.-Middle East Trade." In *Business and the Middle East: Threats and Prospects,* edited by Robert A. Kilmarx and Yonah Alexander, 161–177. New York: Pergamum Press, 1982.

Handy, Robert T. "Patrick J. Hurley and China, 1944–1945." Master's thesis, Portland State University, 1971.

Hardin, Michael. "The Trickster in History: The Heirs of Columbus and the Dehistorization of Narrative." *MELUS* 23 (1998): 25–45.

Harrison, Benjamin. *Views of an Ex-President.* Indianapolis: Bowen-Merrill, 1901.

Hasian, Marouf, Jr. "Anne Frank, Bergen-Belsen, and the Polysemic Nature of Holocaust Memories." *Rhetoric & Public Affairs* 4 (2001): 349–74.

Hassan, Hassan. "The Sectarianism of the Islamic State: Ideological Roots and Political Context." June 13, 2016. Carnegie Endowment for International Peace. http://carnegieendowment.org/2016/06/13/sectarianism-of-islamic-state-ideological-roots-and-political-context-pub-63746.

Heikal, Mohammad H. *Cutting the Lion's Tail: Suez through Egyptian Eyes.* New York: Arbor House, 1987.

Hinds, Lynn Boyd, and Theodore Otto Windt Jr. *The Cold War as Rhetoric: The Beginnings, 1945–1950.* New York: Praeger, 1991.

Hixson, Walter. *Parting the Curtain: Propaganda, Culture, and the Cold War, 1945–1961.* New York: Palgrave Macmillan, 1997.

Hogan, J. Michael. *Woodrow Wilson's Western Tour: Rhetoric, Public Opinion, and the League of Nations.* College Station: Texas A&M University Press, 2006.

Hoopes, Townsend. *The Devil and John Foster Dulles.* Boston: Little, Brown, 1973.

Hurewitz, J. C. "The Historical Context." In Louis and Owen, *Suez 1956,* 19–30.

———. *Middle East Dilemmas: The Background of United States Policy.* New York: Harper & Brothers, 1953.

Immerman, Richard. "Eisenhower and Dulles: Who Made the Decisions?" *Political Psychology* 1 (1979): 21–38.

———. *John Foster Dulles and the Diplomacy of the Cold War.* Princeton NJ: Princeton University Press, 1992.

———. *John Foster Dulles: Piety, Pragmatism, and Power in U.S. Foreign Policy.* Wilmington DE: SR Books, 1999.

Ivie, Robert L. "Cold War Motives and the Rhetorical Metaphor: A Framework of Criticism." In Medhurst, Ivie, Wander, and Scott, *Cold War Rhetoric,* 71–80.

———. "Eisenhower's 'Chance for Peace': Quest or Crusade?" *Rhetoric & Public Affairs* 1 (1998): 227–43.

————. "Fighting Terror by Rite of Redemption and Reconciliation." *Rhetoric & Public Affairs* 10 (2007): 221–48.

————. "Images of Savagery in American Justifications for War." *Communication Monographs* 47 (1980): 279–94.

Ivie, Robert L., and Oscar Giner. "Hunting the Devil: Democracy's Rhetorical Impulse to War." *Presidential Studies Quarterly* 37 (2007): 580–98.

Jalal, Ayesha. "Towards the Baghdad Pact: South Asia and the Middle East Defence in the Cold War." *International History Review* (1989): 409–33.

Jasinki, James. *Sourcebook on Rhetoric: Key Concepts in Contemporary Rhetorical Studies.* London: Sage, 2001.

Jasse, Richard L. "The Baghdad Pact: Cold War or Colonialism?" *Middle Eastern Studies* 27 (1991): 140–56.

Johnson, Paul. *Eisenhower: A Life.* New York: Penguin, 2014.

Joyce, Miriam. *Anglo-American Support for Jordan: The Career of King Hussein.* New York: Palgrave Macmillan, 2008.

Kaplan, Edward. *To Kill Nations: American Strategy in the Air-Atomic Age and the Rise of Mutually Assured Destruction.* Ithaca NY: Cornell University Press, 2015.

Katouzian, Homa. "The CIA Documents and the 1953 Coup in Iran." In *The CIA Documents on the 1953 Coup and the Overthrow of Dr. Mussadiq of Iran,* edited by Gholamreza Vatandoust, 41–62. Tehran: Rasa, 2000.

————. "Mossaddeq's Government in Iranian History: Arbitrary Rule, Democracy, and the 1953 Coup." In Gasiorowski and Byrne, *Mohammad Mossadeq,* 1–27.

————. *Mussadiq and the Struggle for Power in Iran.* London: I. B. Tauris, 1990.

Kennan, George. "George Kennan's 'Long Telegram,'" February 22, 1946. NSA Archive. http://nsarchive.gwu.edu/coldwar/documents/episode-1 /kennan.htm.

Kennan, George [X]. "The Sources of Soviet Conduct," July 1947." Society for Historians of American Foreign Relations. https://shafr.org/teaching/classroom -documents/the-x-article.

Klein, Christina. *Cold War Orientalism: Asia in the Middlebrow Imagination, 1945– 1961.* Los Angeles: University of California Press, 2003.

Klieman, Aaron S. *Soviet Russia and the Middle East.* Baltimore: Johns Hopkins University Press, 1970.

Klope, David C. "Defusing a Foreign Policy Crisis: Myth and Victimage in Reagan's 1983 Lebanon/Grenada Address." *Western Journal of Speech Communication* 50 (1986): 336–49.

Knight, Claire. "The Making of the Soviet Ally in British Wartime Popular Press." *Journalism Studies* 14 (2013): 476–90.

Krock, Arthur. "Impressions of the President—and the Man." *New York Times Magazine,* June 23, 1957.

Kroft, Steve. "President Rouhani." CBS News, *60 Minutes,* September 20, 2015. http://www.cbsnews.com/news/iran-president-hassan-rouhani-nuclear-deal -60-minutes/.

Kuniholm, Bruce Robellet. *The Origins of the Cold War in the Near East*. Princeton NJ: Princeton University Press, 1980.

Kyle, Keith. "Britain and the Crisis, 1955–1956." In Louis and Owen, *Suez 1956*, 103–30.

———. *Suez: Britain's End of Empire in the Middle East*. New York: I. B. Tauris, 2011.

LaFeber, Walter. *America, Russia, and the Cold War, 1945–1990*. New York: McGraw-Hill, 1991.

Lal, Vinay. "The Politics and Culture of Knowledge after Postcolonialism: Nine Theses." *Continuum: Journal of Media & Cultural Studies* 26 (2012): 191–205.

Lamont, Peter, and Richard Wiseman. *Magic in Theory: An Introduction to the Theoretical and Psychological Elements of Conjuring*. Hatfield, UK: University of Hertfordshire Press, 2005.

Lebow, Richard Ned. "Woodrow Wilson and the Balfour Declaration." *Journal of Modern History* 40 (1968): 501–23.

Leffler, Melvyn P., ed. *Origins of the Cold War: An International History*. New York: Routledge, 1994.

Lenczowski, George. *American Presidents and the Middle East*. Durham NC: Duke University Press, 1990.

Lesch, David W., ed. *The Middle East and the United States: A Historical and Political Reassessment*. Boulder CO: Westview, 1996.

Levasseur, David G., and Lisa M. Gring-Pemble. "Not All Capitalist Stories Are Created Equal: Mitt Romney's Bain Capital Narrative and the Deep Divide in American Economic Rhetoric." *Rhetoric & Public Affairs* 15 (2015): 1–38.

Levey, Zach. *Israel and the Western Powers, 1952–1960*. Chapel Hill: University of North Carolina Press, 1997.

Levine, L. W. *Black Culture and the Black Consciousness: Afro-American Folk Thought from Slavery to Freedom*. New York: Oxford University Press, 1977.

Lipka, Michael. "Muslims and Islam: Key Findings in the U.S. and around the World." July 22, 2016. Pew Research Center. http://www.pewresearch.org/fact-tank/2017/08/09/muslims-and-islam-key-findings-in-the-u-s-and-around-the-world/.

Little, Douglass. "1949–1958, Syria: Early Experiments in Covert Action." *Press for Conversion!* 51 (2003): 12–13.

———. *American Orientalism: The United States and the Middle East since 1945*. Chapel Hill: University of North Carolina Press, 2002.

———. "His Finest Hour? Eisenhower, Lebanon, and the 1958 Middle East Crisis." *Diplomatic History* 20 (1996): 27–54.

Louis, William Roger. *British Empire in the Middle East, 1945–51: Arab Nationalism, the United States and Postwar Imperialism*. Oxford: Oxford University Press, 1984.

———. *Ends of British Imperialism: The Scramble for Empire, Suez, and Decolonization*. London: I. B. Tauris, 2007.

————. "The Tragedy of the Anglo-Egyptian Settlement of 1954." In Louis and Owen, *Suez 1956*, 43–71.

Louis, William Roger, and Roger Owen, eds. *Suez 1956: The Crisis and Its Consequences*. Oxford: Clarendon Press, 1989.

Lowry, Dennis, and Mohammad Abu Naser. "From Eisenhower to Obama: Lexical Characteristic of Winning versus Losing Presidential Campaign Commercials." *Journalism & Mass Communication Quarterly* 87 (2010): 530–47.

Lucaites, John Louis, and Celeste M. Condit, "Re-constructing Narrative Theory: A Functional Perspective." *Journal of Communication* 35 (1985): 90–108.

Lunt, James. *Hussein of Jordan: Searching for a Just and Lasting Peace*. New York: William Morrow, 1989.

Macdonald, Scot. *Rolling the Iron Dice: Historical Analogies and Decisions to Use Military Force in Regional Contingencies*. Westport CT: Greenwood, 2000.

MacQueen, Norrie. *Humanitarian Intervention and the United Nations*. Edinburgh: University of Edinburgh Press, 2011.

Mahaffey, Jerome Dean. *Preaching Politics: The Religious Rhetoric of George Whitefield and the Founding of a New Nation*. Waco TX: Baylor University Press, 2007.

Majd, Mohammad Gholi. *From Qajar to Pahlavi: Iran, 1919–1930*. New York: University Press of America, 2008.

Markel, Mike. "The Rhetoric of Misdirection in Corporate Privacy-Policy Statements." *Technical Communication Quarterly* 14 (2005): 197–214.

Marshall, George C. "The Marshall Plan Speech," June 5, 1947. Marshall Foundation. http://marshallfoundation.org/marshall/the-marshall-plan/marshall-plan-speech/.

Martin, Michael. "The Rhetoric of Misdirection: Dietrich Bonhoeffer's Response to the Gestapo's Investigation." *Journal of Communication and Religion* 28 (2005): 206–23.

Massad, Joseph. *Colonial Effects: The Making of National Identity in Jordan*. New York: Columbia University Press, 2001.

Mather, Cotton. *The Glory of Goodness: The goodness of God celebrated; in remarkable instances and improvements thereof: and more particularly in the redemption remarkably obtained for the English captives, which have been languishing under the tragical, and the terrible and the most barbarous cruelties of Barbary*. Boston: Printed by T. Green, for Benjamin Eliot, 1703.

Medhurst, Martin J. "Afterword: Rhetorical Perspectives on the Cold War." In Martin and Brands, *Critical Reflections on the Cold War*, 266–69.

————. *Dwight D. Eisenhower: Strategic Communicator*. Westport CT: Greenwood Press, 1993.

————. "Eisenhower's 'Atoms for Peace' Speech: A Case Study in the Strategic Use of Language." *Communication Monographs* 54 (1987): 204–20.

————, ed. *Eisenhower's War of Words: Rhetoric and Leadership*. East Lansing: Michigan State University Press, 1994.

———. "Reconceptualizing Rhetorical History: Eisenhower's Farewell Address." *Quarterly Journal of Speech* 80 (1994): 195–218.

———. "Rhetorical Leadership and the Presidency: A Situational Taxonomy." In *The Values of Presidential Leadership*, edited by Terry L. Price and J. Thomas Wren, 59–84. New York: Palgrave Macmillan, 2007.

———. "Rhetoric and Cold War: A Strategic Approach." In Medhurst, Ivie, Wander, and Scott, *Cold War Rhetoric*, 19–28.

———. "A Tale of Two Constructs: The Rhetorical Presidency versus Presidential Rhetoric." In *Beyond the Rhetorical Presidency*, edited by Martin J. Medhurst, xi–xxv. College Station: Texas A&M University Press, 1996.

———. "Text and Context in the 1952 Presidential Campaign: Eisenhower's "I Shall Go to Korea" Speech." *Presidential Studies Quarterly* 30 (2000): 464–84.

Medhurst, Martin J., and H. W. Brands, eds. *Critical Reflections on the Cold War: Linking Rhetoric and History*. College Station: Texas A&M University Press, 2000.

Medhurst, Martin J., Robert L. Ivie, Phillip Wander, and Robert L. Scott. *Cold War Rhetoric: Strategy, Metaphor, Ideology*. 2nd ed. Easting Lansing: Michigan State University Press, 1997.

Medvedev, Roy. *Khrushchev*. Garden City NY: Anchor, 1983.

Medvedev, Roy A., and Zhores A. Medvedev. *Khrushchev: The Years in Power*. New York: Columbia University Press, 1976.

Melanson, Richard A., and David Mayers. *Reevaluating Eisenhower: American Foreign Policy in the 1950s*. Champaign: University of Illinois Press, 1987.

Menand, Louis. "Nukes of Hazard." *New Yorker*, September 30, 2013. http://www.newyorker.com/magazine/2013/09/30/nukes-of-hazard.

Merkley, Paul. *The Politics of Christian Zionism*. London: Frank Cass, 1998.

"Mohammed Mossadegh." *Time*, January 7, 1952, cover. http://content.time.com/time/covers/0,16641,19520107,00.html.

Morris, Benny. *Israel's Border Wars, 1949–1956*. Oxford: Clarendon Press, 1993.

Morris, Charles E., III. "Pink Herring and the Fourth Persona: J. Edgar Hoover's Sex Crime Panic." *Quarterly Journal of Speech* 88 (2002): 228–44.

Newton, Jim. *Eisenhower: The White House Years*. New York: Anchor, 2011.

Nichols, David A. *Eisenhower 1956: The President's Year of Crisis; Suez and the Brink of War*. New York: Simon & Schuster, 2011.

Nijim, Basheer K., ed. *American Church Politics and the Middle East*. Belmont MA: Association of Arab-American University Graduates, 1982.

Norouzi, Arash. "The Eisenhower-Mossadegh Cables: Complete Exchange of Messages." The Mossadegh Project. June 26, 2011. http://www.mohammadmossadegh.com/biography/dwight-d-eisenhower/cables/.

Nye, Joseph S., Jr. *Is the American Century Over?* Cambridge: Polity, 2015.

———. *The Future of Power*. New York: Public Affairs, 2011.

O'Gorman, Ned. "Eisenhower and the American Sublime." *Quarterly Journal of Speech* 94 (2008): 44–72.

————. *Spirits of the Cold War: Contesting Worldviews in the Classical Age of American Security Strategy*. East Lansing: Michigan State University Press, 2011.

Osgood, Kenneth. *Total Cold War: Eisenhower's Secret Propaganda Battle at Home and Abroad*. Lawrence: University of Kansas Press, 2006.

Ovendale, Ritchie. *Britain, the United States, and the Transfer of Power in the Middle East, 1945-1962*. London: Leicester University Press, 1996.

Pahlavi, Mohammed Reza Shah. *Mission for My Country*. London: Hutchinson, 1961.

Papastratis, Procopis. *British Policy towards Greece during the Second World War, 1941–1944*. Cambridge: Cambridge University Press, 1984.

Parry-Giles, Shawn. *The Rhetorical Presidency, Propaganda, and the Cold War, 1945–1955*. London: Praeger, 2002.

Patterson, James T. *Grand Expectations: The United States, 1945–1974*. Oxford: Oxford University Press, 1996.

Pearce, Kimber Charles. "Rhetorical Polysemy in Mary Baker Eddy's 'Christian Science in Tremont Temple.'" *Journal of Communication and Religion* 23 (2000): 73–94.

Perelman, Chaïm, and L. Olbrechts-Tyteca. *The New Rhetoric: A Treatise on Argumentation*. Notre Dame IN: University of Notre Dame Press, 1969.

Perry, Mark. *Partners in Command: George Marshall and Dwight Eisenhower in War and Peace*. New York: Penguin, 2007.

Perry, Pam. *Eisenhower: The Public Relations President*. New York: Lexington Books, 2014.

Persson, Magnus. *Great Britain, the United States, and the Security of the Middle East: The Formation of the Baghdad Pact*. Lund: Lund University Press, 1998.

Petron, Tabitha. *The Struggle over Lebanon*. New York: Monthly Review Press, 1987.

Plato. *Gorgias*. Translated by W. C. Hembold. Upper Saddle River NJ: Prentice Hall/Library of Liberal Arts, 1997.

Podeh, Elie. *The Quest for Hegemony in the Arab World: The Struggle over the Baghdad Pact*. Leiden: E. J. Brill, 1995.

Pratt, James. "An Analysis of Three Crisis Speeches." *Western Speech* 34 (1970): 194–203.

Proctor, David E. "The Rescue Mission: Assigning Guilt to a Chaotic Scene." *Western Journal of Speech Communication* 51 (1987): 245–55.

Quintilian. *Institutes of Oratory*. Translated by Harold Edgeworth Butler. Cambridge MA: Harvard University Press, 1920.

Rabinowitch, Eugene. "New Year's Thoughts." *Bulletin of the Atomic Scientists* 14 (1958): 3.

Rabinowitz, Peter J. "'Betraying the Sender': The Rhetoric and Ethics of Fragile Texts." *Narrative* 2 (1994): 201–13.

Rahnema, Ali. *Behind the 1953 Coup in Iran: Thugs, Turncoats, Soldiers, and Spooks*. Cambridge: Cambridge University Press, 2015.

Randall, David. "The Rhetoric of Violence, the Public Sphere, and the Second Amendment." *Philosophy and Rhetoric* 49 (2016): 125–48.

Risen, James. "C.I.A. Tried, with Little Success, to Use US Media in Coup." *New York Times*, April 15, 2000. http://www.nytimes.com/library/world/mideast /041600iran-cia-media.html.

Roosevelt, Archie. *For Lust of Knowing: Memoirs of an Intelligence Officer*. New York: Little, Brown, 1988.

Roosevelt, Kermit. *Countercoup: The Struggle for the Control of Iran*. New York: McGraw-Hill, 1979.

Rose, Gideon. "The Post-American Middle East: What's Inside." *Foreign Affairs* 94 (2015): xi.

Rosteck, Thomas, and Thomas S. Frentz. "Myth and Multiple Readings in Environmental Rhetoric: The Case of *An Inconvenient Truth*." *Quarterly Journal of Speech* 95 (2009): 1–19.

Rottinghaus, Brandon, and Justin Vaughn. "New Ranking of U.S. Presidents Puts Lincoln at No. 1, Obama at 18; Kennedy Judged Most Overrated." *Washington Post*, February 16, 2015.

Said, Edward. *Orientalism*. New York: Vintage Books, 1979.

Saivetz, Carol R. "The Soviet Union and the Middle East, 1956–1958." In *A Revolutionary Year: The Middle East in 1958*, edited by William Roger Louis and Roger Owen, 221–24. London: I. B. Tauris, 2002.

Salami, George Raymond. "The Eisenhower Doctrine: A Study in Alliance Politics," PhD diss., Catholic University of America, 1974.

Salibi, Kamal. *The Modern History of Jordan*. London: I. B. Tauris, 1993.

Samuels, David. "The Aspiring Novelist Who Became Obama's Foreign-Policy Guru: How Ben Rhoades Rewrote the Rules of Diplomacy for the Digital Age." *New York Times Magazine*, May 8, 2016.

Sanjian, Ara. "The Formulation of the Baghdad Pact." *Middle Eastern Studies* 33 (1997): 226–66.

———. *Turkey and Her Arab Neighbors, 1953–1958: A Study in the Origins and Failure of the Baghdad Pact*. Wiltshire, UK: Archive Editions, 2001.

Saunders, Bonnie F. *The United States and Arab Nationalism: The Syrian Case, 1953–1960*. Westport CT: Greenwood, 1996.

Saunders, Elizabeth Nathan. *Leaders at War: How Presidents Shape Military Interventions*. Ithaca NY: Cornell University Press, 2011.

Saunders, Francis Stonor. *The Cultural Cold War: The CIA and the World of Arts and Letters*. New York: New Press, 2001.

Schrecker, Ellen. *Many Are the Crimes*. Princeton NJ: Princeton University Press, 1998.

Scott, David K. "The Eisenhower/Khrushchev Rhetorical Compact: Toward a Model of Cooperative Public Discourse." *Southern Communication Journal* 68 (2003): 287–306.

Shaheen, Jack G. "Media Coverage of the Middle East: Perception and Foreign Policy." *Annals of the American Academy of Political and Social Science* 482 (1985): 160–75.

Shaked, Haim, and Itamar Rabinovich, eds. *The Middle East and the United States: Perceptions and Policies.* London: Transaction Books, 1980.

Smith, Jean Edward. *Eisenhower in War and Peace.* New York: Random House, 2013.

Solomon, Martha, and Wayne J. McMullen. "*Places in the Heart*: The Rhetorical Force of an Open Text." *Western Journal of Communication* 55 (1991): 339–53.

Soussi, Alasdair. "Legacy of US' 1958 Lebanon Invasion." *Al Jazeera English,* July 15, 2013. http://www.aljazeera.com/indepth/features/2013/07/201371411160525538.html.

Spiegel, Steven. *The Other Arab-Israeli Conflict: Making America's Middle East Policy, from Truman to Reagan.* Chicago: University of Chicago Press, 1985.

Spiegel, Steven, Mark Heller, and Jacob Goldberg. *The Soviet-American Competition in the Middle East.* Los Angeles: University of California Center for International and Strategic Affairs, 1988.

Spiller, Roger J. "*Not War but like War*": American Intervention in Lebanon." Leavenworth Papers 3. January 1981. Combat Studies Institute, U.S. Army Command and General Staff College, Fort Leavenworth, Kansas. http://usacac.army.mil/cac2/cgsc/carl/download/csipubs/spiller2.pdf.

Srodes, James. *Allen Dulles: Master of Spies.* Washington: Regnery, 1999.

Stephens, Robert. *Nasser: A Political Biography.* New York: Simon & Schuster, 1971.

Stuckey, Mary E. *Defining Americans: The Presidency and National Identity.* Lawrence: University Press of Kansas, 2004.

———. *The Good Neighbor: Franklin D. Roosevelt and the Rhetoric of American Power.* East Lansing: Michigan State University Press, 2013.

Suleiman, Michael W. *U.S. Perceptions of Palestine: From Wilson to Clinton.* Normal IL: Association of Arab-American University Graduates, 1995.

Suzuki, Takeshi, and Aya Niitsuma. "Argumentative Analysis of President Bush's War against Terrorism after 9/11." In *Critical Problems in Argumentation,* edited by Charles Arthur Willard, 87–93. Washington DC: National Communication Association, 2005.

Taft, Robert A. "Republican Fund-Raising Dinner in Milwaukee, Wisconsin." June 9, 1951. *Congressional Record,* 82nd Cong., 1st Sess., vol. 97, pt. 13, pp. A3462–A3464.

Takeyh, Ray. *The Origins of the Eisenhower Doctrine: The U.S., Britain, and Nasser's Egypt, 1953–57.* London: Macmillan, 2000.

Taubman, William. *Khrushchev: The Man and His Era.* New York: W. W. Norton, 2003.

Thomas, Evan. *Ike's Bluff: President Eisenhower's Secret Battle to Save the World.* New York, Little, Brown, 2012.

Thorpe, D. R. *Eden: The Life and Times of Anthony Eden, First Earl of Avon, 1897–1977*. London: Chatto & Windus, 2003.

Tomlinson, Jim. "The Decline of the Empire and the Economic 'Decline' of Britain." *Twentieth Century British History* 14 (2003): 201–21.

Troen, Selwyn Ilan, and Moshe Shemesh, eds. *The Suez-Sinai Crisis 1956: Retrospective and Reappraisal*. London: Frank Cass, 1990.

Tulis, Jeffrey. *The Rhetorical Presidency*. Princeton NJ: Princeton University Press, 1987.

Urofsky, Michael. *American Zionism*. Lincoln: University of Nebraska Press, 1975.

Waggoner, Catherine Egley. "Academic Adultery: Surreptitious Performances of the Professor/Mother." *Women's Studies in Communication* 31 (2008): 209–12.

Wall, Irwin M. *France, the United States, and the Algerian War*. Berkeley: University of California Press, 2001.

Wander, Phillip. "The Rhetoric of American Foreign Policy." *Quarterly Journal of Speech* 70 (1984): 339–61.

Watt, Donald Cameron. *Succeeding John Bull: Britain in America's Place, 1900–1975*. Cambridge: Cambridge University Press, 1984.

Wilber, Donald. *Overthrow of Premier Mosaddeq of Iran: November 1952–August 1953*. NSA Archive, George Washington University. http://nsarchive.gwu.edu/NSAEBB/NSAEBB28/.

Wilford, Hugh. *America's Great Game: The CIA's Secret Arabists and the Shaping of the Modern Middle East*. New York: Basic Books, 2013.

Wilson, David Nason. "The Eisenhower Doctrine and Its Implementation in Lebanon—1958." Master's thesis, University of Texas at Austin, 2003.

Winslow, Charles. *Lebanon: War and Politics in a Fragmented Society*. New York: Routledge, 1996.

Wolf, John Berchrans. "An Interpretation of the Eisenhower Doctrine, Lebanon 1958." PhD diss., American University, 1967.

Worley, Duane Robert. *Shaping U.S. Military Forces: Revolution or Relevance in a Post–Cold War World*. Westport CT: Greenwood, 2006.

Wynbrandt, James. *A Brief History of Saudi Arabia*. New York: Facts on File, 2010.

Yaqub, Salim. *Containing Arab Nationalism: The Eisenhower Doctrine and the Middle East*. Chapel Hill: University of North Carolina Press, 2004.

Yergin, Daniel. *The Prize: The Epic Quest for Oil, Money and Power*. London: Free Press, 2009.

Yeşilbursa, Behçet Kemal. *The Baghdad Pact: Anglo-American Defence Policies in the Middle East, 1950–1959*. London: Frank Cass, 2005.

Yizhar, Michael. "The Eisenhower Doctrine: A Case Study of American Foreign Policy Formulation and Implementation." PhD diss., New School for Social Research, 1968.

Young, Marilyn J. "Of Allies and Enemies: Old Wine in New Bottles or New Wine in an Old Jug?" In *The Prospect of Presidential Rhetoric*, edited by

James Arnt Aune and Martin J. Medhurst, 160–81. College Station: Texas A&M University Press, 2008.

Young, Nancy Beck, ed. *Documentary History of the Dwight D. Eisenhower Presidency*. Vol. 10, CIA *Intervention in Iran and the Nationalization of the Iranian Oil Industry*. Bethesda MD: LexisNexis, 2009.

Zagacki, Kenneth. "Eisenhower and the Rhetoric of Postwar Korea." *Southern Communication Journal* 60 (1995): 233–45.

Zarefsky, David. "Presidential Rhetoric and the Power of Definition." *Presidential Studies Quarterly* 34 (2004): 607–19.

———. *President Johnson's War on Poverty: Rhetoric and History*. Tuscaloosa: University of Alabama Press, 1986.

Zubok, Vladislav, and Constantine Pleshakov. *Inside the Kremlin's Cold War: From Stalin to Khrushchev*. Cambridge MA: Harvard University Press, 1996.

INDEX

In this index, DDE is used for Dwight
David Eisenhower

Abadan oil refinery, 42, 46, 49
Abdullah I (king of Jordan), 78–79
Acheson, Dean, 37
AIOC (Anglo-Iranian Oil Company), 42,
  46, 49, 55
Ajax, Operation. *See* Operation Ajax
Albright, Madeline, 42
al-Fadl, Abu, 87
Algeria, 79
Alpha, Project (peace talks), 95–100
al-Qasim, Abd-al-Karim, 169, 170
al-Quwatli, Shukri, 92
al-Rasheed, Madawi, 186n19
Althusser, Louis, xxii
Ambrose, Stephen, 48
American public: addressed during Operation Blue Bat, 145, 148, 150–53, 156–
  58; addressed in the Suez crisis speech,
  114–16; circumvention through rhetorical surreption, 101; Eisenhower Doctrine
  attempting to persuade, 31–36; impact
  of misdirection on, 69–70; influence of
  presidential rhetoric on, xvi–xvii, xxi–xxiii;
  misdirected through media, 60–64; misdirected through surrogates, 66; during
  Operation Ajax, 47, 60–64, 66; perceptions of the Middle East, xiii–xiv, xv–xvi,
  xxxv; rhetoric aimed at persuading, xix–
  xxi, 33–36; shifts in rhetoric toward, xv
Anderson, Robert, 99
Anglo-Iranian Oil Company (AIOC), 42,
  46, 49, 55
"apocalypse management" (rhetorical
  style), 165

Arab-Israeli conflict: factors behind, 119;
  impact on U.S.-Arab relations, 73, 81–82,
  86; increases in, 79; Orientalist explanations for, 120–21; portrayed in Suez
  crisis speech, 118–21; and the Project
  Alpha talks, 95–100. *See also* Suez crisis
Arab League Collective Security Pact, 89
argument fields, xxiii–xxv, 170–75
Aristotle, xvii, xxiv
Aronson, Geoffrey, 37–38
Arthos, John, Jr., 53–54
as-Said, Nuri, 90, 100, 102, 107, 147,
  195n18
"Atoms for Peace" address, 76, 167

Baghdad Pact, 89–92, 101, 102, 107,
  109–10, 111
Balfour Declaration, 19–20
Baltic countries, 4, 32
Bass, Jeff, xxix, 163
Ben Gurion, David, 97, 99, 122
Bennett, Michael, 64
Beria, Lavrentiy, 50–51
bin Laden, Osama, xvii, xxii
Bitzer, Lloyd, 23, 199n28
Black, Edwin, xxx
Blue Bat, Operation. *See* Operation Blue Bat
Bonhoeffer, Dietrich, 53
Bose, Meena, 60, 113
Britain: and the Arab-Israeli conflict, 96–
  100; and the Baghdad Pact, 88–92, 107;
  dependency on oil, 79–80; in the Eisen-
  hower Doctrine, 38, 188n45; impact of
  Suez crisis on, 105, 132; impact of sur-
  reptitious strategies on, 102–3; impe-
  rialistic rhetoric of, 177–78; imperial
  paradigm of, 19–20, 70, 82–83, 87–88,

Britain *(continued)*
120–21; in the Iranian oil dispute, 46,
52, 55, 58–59, 70–71; Middle Eastern
military bases, 84–85, 89, 111; occupying
Iran, 43–45; during Operation Ajax, 56–
57; during Operation Blue Bat, 199n22;
portrayed in Suez crisis speech, 121–23,
125–28, 130–32; portrayed in the Truman Doctrine, 125–26; pre-Eisenhower
rhetoric on, 20–23; relations with Jordan, 79, 145, 147; role in containment
strategy, 49, 70, 109–10; role in Iraq, 73;
role in Palestine, 19–20; role in the Middle East, 19–23, 85–86, 89–90, 103, 107;
in Soviet rhetoric, 51, 109–10; during
the Suez crisis, xxviii–xxix, 111–13; U.S.
replacing as hegemon, x, xxviii–xxix, 103
Bulganin, Nikolai, 116
bully pulpit, xvi–xvii, xix
Burke, Edmund, 163
Bush, George H. W., 181
Bush, George W., xiii, xvii, 164, 168, 173, 181
Byrnes, James, 44–45
Byroade, Henry, 104

Campbell, Karlyn Kohrs, xxvi
Carter, James Earl "Jimmy," Jr., 180
Castro, Fidel, 77
Central Intelligence Agency (CIA). *See* CIA
(Central Intelligence Agency)
Chamoun, Camille, 138, 140–43, 147, 153,
198n5, 198n17
"Chance for Peace" speech, 74
Charland, Maurice, xxii
Chehab, General Fuad, 140
Chernus, Ira, xix, 29–30, 75, 159, 165,
196n36
Childs, Marquis, xxxi
China, 26, 92
Chirindo, Kundai, 157
Christianity, 3–4, 187n30
Churchill, Winston, 20, 23, 44, 68, 73,
80, 185n2
CIA (Central Intelligence Agency): advis-
ing Nasser's Egypt, 86–88; under Allen
Dulles, 61–62; during DDE's first term,
106; in the New Look, 16; in Operation

Ajax, 42, 61–64, 190n56; propaganda
campaigns, 62–63, 190n56; rigging
Lebanese elections, 198n17; Syrian coup
attempts, 92–95, 137
Civil War, xxiii
classical rhetoric, xvii–xviii, xxiii–xxiv
Clifford-Elsey report, 14–15
Clinton, Hillary, xxv
Clinton, William "Bill," 178–79
Cold War: Arab nonalignment during, 17,
80; CIA's role in, 61–62; during DDE's
first term, 14, 106–7; DDE's impact on,
164; dualistic rhetoric in, 29, 75, 116–
18, 172; global nature of, 142; ideological nature of, 14–15, 172–73; impact of
Suez crisis on, 132–33; Middle East as
front in, 38, 77–78, 80, 172–73; "missile
gap" controversy, 195n21; under Nikita
Khrushchev, 108–10; presidential rhetoric portraying, 152–54, 165; psychological
nature of, 50–51, 108, 142, 198n14; rapid
shift in relations during, 185n2; rhetorical escalation of, 74–75; rhetorical nature
of, 50–51, 62, 75–77; Soviet occupation
of Iran, 44–45; strategic use of rhetoric
during, 113–14; transcendent rhetoric in,
160–61; during the Truman administration, 47–48. *See also* containment policy
Cole, Timothy, 123
Communism: conflated with Arab
nationalism, 152–54; containment strategy addressing, xxvii–xxix, 14–15, 88–
89; during DDE's first term, 106–7; in
dualistic rhetoric, 28–29, 75, 172–73; in
Egypt, 87, 200n36; in the Eisenhower
Doctrine, 2, 3, 4–10, 32–34, 129–30, 131–
32; in Iran, 47–51, 188n9; in Lebanon,
xxix, 200n36; in the Suez crisis speech,
117–18; Syria's neutralist policy toward,
92; Truman Doctrine addressing, 21–
23; viewed as threat to Middle East, 29,
32–34, 41, 47–51, 171
Congress (U.S.): and the 1956 election,
115; addressed in the Suez crisis speech,
114–16; approving Middle East Resolution, 36–37; DDE justifying Operation
Blue Bat to, 149–50, 153–54, 155, 159;

Eisenhower Doctrine addressing, 6–8, 10–11, 24–31; impact of presidential rhetoric on, xvi–xvii; during occupation of Lebanon, 145; role in Operation Blue Bat, 144–45, 148

Containing Arab Nationalism (Yaqub), 17

containment policy: alliance logic of, 27; basic premise of, 14; Britain's role in, 49, 70, 109–10; dualistic rhetoric of, 28; under the Eisenhower administration, xxvii–xxix, 48–49, 88–89, 112; in the Eisenhower Doctrine, xxviii, 14, 16–17, 32, 37, 157; justifying Operation Blue Bat, 139, 142, 145; in the Middle East, 81, 128, 171; in the New Look, 16; and psychological warfare, 76, 142; rhetorical surreption limiting, 102–3

Cooper, Chester, 105

Copeland, Miles, 86–87

corporatist rhetoric of misdirection, 54

Countenance, Operation, 43–45

Countercoup (Roosevelt), 52, 188n2

coups (military): in Egypt, 78, 84; in Iraq, 143–44, 147; in Syria, 92–95, 137. *See also* Operation Ajax

covert strategies: of Allen Dulles' CIA, 61–62; in the Arab-Israeli conflict, 96–100; circumventing public opinion, xxi; constraints requiring, 51; during DDE's first term, 171; in the Doolittle Report, 41; polysemy in, 94–95; as rhetorical invention, 171–72; surreptitious rhetoric concealing, 95; in Syria, 92–95

Cram, Travis J., 201n60

The Daily Show (TV show), xiii

distancing rhetoric, 54–60, 114–15, 189n29

Doolittle Report (1954), 41

dualism: in current conflicts, 174; in DDE's rhetoric, 28–30, 33, 75, 118, 186n30; in George W. Bush's arguments, 173

Dulles, Allen Welsh, 52, 61–62, 94, 139

Dulles, John Foster: and the Baghdad Pact, 89; on British-Egyptian conflict, 84–85; on containment strategies, xxvii–xxviii; countering Soviet propaganda,

110; as DDE's surrogate, 65–66; death of, 176; drafts of Eisenhower Doctrine speech, 188n45; foreign relations successes, 74; on French-Israeli relations, 107; on "kissing triangles" system, 98; Middle Eastern tours of, xv; in Middle East Resolution debates, 36; on neutrality, 80; and the New Look, 16; and Operation Ajax, 52, 189n29; and Operation Blue Bat, 140–43, 146, 199n22; and Operation Straggle, 93, 94–95; in Project Alpha talks, 96–97, 98–99; rhetorical polysemy of, 94–95; during the Suez crisis, 111–13; surreptitious methods used by, 83, 100; on threat of Communism, 29; on U.S.-Arab relations, 73, 81; on war in the nuclear age, 48; and the Yalta agreement, 33

Eastern Europe, 4, 74, 116–18

economic aid: addressed in the Eisenhower Doctrine, 7; combating Communism, 191n70; Syria's rejection of, 92; in the Truman Doctrine, 21–22; withheld from Iran, 49, 57–59

Economist, 69

Eden, Anthony: and the Baghdad Pact, 91; imperialistic rhetoric of, 177; and Operation Ajax, 57, 68; and Project Alpha, 96; and the Suez crisis, 105–6, 111, 112–13, 122, 195n18; transformation in rhetoric of, 202n12; working for peace, 105

Edwards, George C., III, xxv, 184n30

Edwards, Jason A., 148

Egypt: addressed in the Eisenhower Doctrine, 5; CIA advisors sent to, 86–88; Communism in, 87, 200n36; conflict with Britain, 84–85, 111; conflict with Iraq, 169; factors behind conflicts in, 119; impact of Suez crisis on, 132; nationalist movement in, 78, 84, 111; nonalignment under Nasser, 17, 80; portrayed in Suez crisis speech, 119–21, 196n49; and Project Alpha, 97–100; relations with Soviet Union, 136, 169; in the UAR, 137, 147. *See also* Suez crisis

Eichelberger, Jim, 86

Eisenhower, Dwight E. (DDE): 1952 presidential campaign, xv, 15–16; 1956 presidential campaign, 105, 113, 115; approval ratings, 162, 187n36; events during first term, 74–75, 106–7; on facing war, 135; first inaugural address, xxviii, 55; interactions with Mossadegh, 54–59; leadership style, xviii–xix, 64–65; legacy of, xiv–xv, 170, 174–75; military ethos of, ix–x, xviii–xix, 115–16, 150, 151–52; public images of, ix, 115; reputation of, 30–31, 151–52; trustworthiness of, 30–31

Eisenhower: Captive Hero (Childs), xxxi

Eisenhower Doctrine: addressing Congress, 6–8, 10–11, 24–31; addressing the American public, 31–36; assumptions in, 132; audiences of, 24; constraints created by, 39, 143; containment in, xxviii, 14, 16–17, 32, 157; effects of, 36–40; exigences addressed by, 23–24; failures of, 136–38; full text of address, 1–11; imperialistic rhetoric in, 163; justifying occupation of Lebanon, 138–39, 140, 144–46, 150–51; limited Arab support for, 136; nationalism addressed in, 17; opposition to, 25; problematic features of, 38–39; references to Europe, 3, 38, 188n45; as rhetorical invention, xxv; rhetorical significance of, 18–23, 34–35; Suez crisis speech as foundation of, 129–32; UN portrayed as inadequate in, 130; U.S. assumption of responsibility in, x, xxix, 40, 131–32. *See also* Middle East Resolution

Elsey, George, 41

England. *See* Britain

Estonia, 4

Europe: addressed in the Eisenhower Doctrine, 3, 38, 188n45; dependency on oil, 27, 79–80, 96; imperialism of, 28, 51, 102–3, 131–32, 173; satellite states, 4, 32

Eveland, Bill, 93

Eveland, Wilbur, 198n17

exceptionalism, 157–58, 196n41

executive authority, 149–52

al-Fadl, Abu, 87

Farouk I (king of Egypt), 20, 78

Farr, James, xxii, 175

Fisher, Walter, 32

Ford, Gerald R., 180

foreign policy: bilateral engagement, 90–91, 169–70; Communism's impact on, 74; contradictions implicit in, 109–10; DDE's legacy in, xiv–xv; failures of, 136; under Franklin Roosevelt, 34; of friendly impartiality, 80–82, 90–92, 103, 107, 121, 122; growing interventionism in, 103–4, 127; impact of Eisenhower Doctrine on, 25, 37–38; impact of Suez crisis on, 123, 133; impacts of surreption on, 100–104; impacts on reelection, 115; Middle East as priority, xxiii, 37–38, 85–86; Operation Ajax's impact on, 69–71; Operation Blue Bat's impact on, 166; presidential rhetoric influencing, xix–xxi, 30, 135–36, 164–65; Project Alpha talks signifying shifts in, 98–100; rhetorical transformation of, 126–28; shifts in under DDE, xxvii–xxix, 98–100, 176–77; under Truman administration, 47–48; use of surrogates in, 65–66. *See also* containment policy; Middle East Resolution

Formosa Straits Resolution (1955), 26

France: and the Baghdad Pact, 107; in the Eisenhower Doctrine speech, 38, 188n45; impact of Suez crisis on, 132; impact of surreptitious strategies on, 102–3; lessening influence of, 85–86; portrayed in Suez crisis speech, 125–28, 131–32; relations with Israel, 79, 107, 111; role in containment, 109–10; during the Suez crisis, xxviii–xxix, 111, 113, 121–23; U.S. displacing in Middle East, x

Free Officers Movement, 78, 84, 111, 147

Fulbright, J. William, 25, 139

Gaddis, John Lewis, 16

Germany, xx

Gettysburg Address, xxiii

ghostwriters, xxvi, 184n31

Giner, Oscar, 152

Glubb, John, 107

"good neighbor" metaphor, 34, 59

Gorgias (Plato), 184n31
Graham, Billy, 14
Great Awakening, xxiv
Great Britain. *See* Britain
Greece, 21–22, 125
Greenstein, Fred, 60, 113, 115
Gregg, Richard, 59, 110

Hammarskjöld, Dag, 139–40
Hansen, Hans-Christian, 108
Hardin, Michael, 53–54
Harrison, Benjamin, 199n21
Hashemite monarchies, 78, 144
Hassan, Hassan, 174
Hearst, William Randolph, xix
Heikal, Muhammad, 87
Henderson, Loy, 49, 65, 66–67, 191n70
Hoover, Herbert, 185n15
Humphrey, Hubert, 25
Hungary: addressed in the Eisenhower
     Doctrine, 4, 5; addressed in the Suez
     crisis speech, 116–18; protests in, 113;
     Soviet occupation of, 30, 32, 113
Hussein, Saddam, 178
Hussein I (king of Jordan), 79, 137, 146, 147

Ibn Saud, Abdul Aziz (king of Saudi Ara-
     bia), 20
ideological conflict (topos), 172–73, 174
Ilyan, Mikhail, 93
imperialism: Arab resentment of, 20, 78–
     79, 102, 118, 123; British paradigm, 19–
     20, 70, 82–83, 87–88, 120–21; in Cold
     War rhetoric, 77; impact on contain-
     ment, 131–32; in the Middle East, 28; in
     Soviet rhetoric, 51, 102–3, 109–10; U.S.
     experience with, 120; U.S. incongruities
     regarding, 102–3
imperialistic rhetoric, 162–63, 177–78,
     202n12
independence: in contrasting strategies,
     117–18; in DDE's inaugural address,
     xxviii; in Eisenhower Doctrine address,
     5–7, 33, 35–36; as rhetorical strategy, 35–
     36; as transcendent ideal, 158–60
India, 79, 88
instability (topos), 29–30
interventionist policies: articulated to the

UN, 167–68; in the Eisenhower Doc-
     trine, xxviii–xxix, 37; need for defending,
     145–46; precedent set by Operation Blue
     Bat, 163–65; pre-Eisenhower, 18, 21–22;
     rhetorical justifications for, 127–28, 149–
     61, 172–73. *See also* Operation Blue Bat
invention, rhetorical: American Middle
     Eastern depictions as, xiv; and argument
     fields, xxiii–xxiv, 170, 174–75; contrast-
     ing techniques, 117–18; covert activity
     (topos), 171–72; Eisenhower Doctrine as
     act of, xxv; ideological conflict (topos),
     172–73, 174; unilateralism (topos), 170–71
Iran: Abadan oil refinery, 42, 46, 49; Allied
     occupation of, 43–45; anti-American sen-
     timent in, 42, 69; and the Baghdad Pact,
     89–91, 107; Cold War conflict in, 44–45,
     48–51; Communism viewed as threat to,
     41; control of oil in, 28; DDE's polyva-
     lent rhetoric concerning, 67–68; DDE's
     press conferences regarding, 60–61; eco-
     nomic aid withheld from, 49, 57–59;
     under the Majlis, 45–46; under Moham-
     med Mossadegh, 46; nuclear program,
     41–42; Operation Ajax's impact on, 69–
     70; political turmoil in, 43–46; during
     the Truman administration, 46–48. *See
     also* Operation Ajax
Iranian Azerbaijan Party (ADN), 188n9
Iraq: and the Baghdad Pact, 89–91, 102,
     107; Britain's role in, 73; conflict with
     Egypt, 102, 169; Islamic State in, xiii;
     military coups in, 143–44, 147, 152;
     nationalist movements in, 78
Islam, 3–4, 187n30
Islamic State (IS), xiii, 174
Israel: addressed in the Eisenhower Doc-
     trine, 8; and the Baghdad Pact, 107;
     during the Clinton administration, 179;
     conflicts with Palestine, 79, 81–82; DDE
     condemning role in Suez crisis, 121–23,
     197n1; in DDE's impartiality policy, 81–
     82; impact of Suez crisis on, 132; por-
     trayed in Suez crisis speech, 120–21,
     125–28; and the Project Alpha talks, 95–
     100; relations with France, 107; during
     the Suez crisis, xxviii–xxix, 94, 111, 113,

Israel (*continued*)
136; during the Truman administration, 21; U.S. support of, 73, 86, 95–96, 109, 121; during the Wilson administration, 19–20
Ivie, Robert L., 117, 152, 196n41

Jamieson, Kathleen Hall, xxvi
Johnson, Lyndon B., 142, 163, 164, 179–80
Johnston, Eric, 97
Jordan: British troops sent to, 145, 147, 199n22; impact of Eisenhower Doctrine on, 136–37; nationalist movements in, 78–79; political conflicts in, 136–37, 146, 152; relations with Israel, 179; U.S. role in, 167–68
Judaism, 3–4, 185n15, 187n30
justificatory rhetoric: audiences for, 147–48, 199n28; effects of, 161–66; establishing executive authority, 149–52; for military force, 148–49; right to independence trope, 154–58; threat conflation, 152–54; transcendent ideals, 158–61

Kabbani, Colonel, 94
Kennan, George, 14, 44, 185n2
Kennedy, John F., 179
Khrushchev, Nikita, 77, 102–3, 108–10, 136, 160–61, 172
Kirkpatrick, Ivone, 111–12
"kissing triangles" system, 98
Korean War, 15, 37, 61, 74, 145
Krock, Arthur, 60
Kroft, Steve, 41–42

LaFeber, Walter, 51
Latvia, 4
League of Nations, xix, 156–57
Lebanon: and the Baghdad Pact, 89–91; CIA covert operations in, 198n17; civil war in, 138; Communism as threat to, xxix, 200n36; impact of Eisenhower Doctrine on, 37, 146; imperialist rhetoric describing, 162–63; political conflict in, 138, 139–40, 198n5; U.S. role in, 167–68. *See also* Operation Blue Bat
Lenin, Vladimir, 13
Levine, L. W., 53–54

Lewis, John L., xix
Life magazine, xxvii–xxviii
Lincoln, Abraham, xxii–xxiii
The Lion's Last Roar (Cooper), 105
Lithuania, 4
Little, Douglass, 142, 182
"Long Telegram" (Kennan), 14, 185n2
Love, Kenneth, 64
Lumumba, Patrice, 77

Macmillan, Harold, 145, 199n22
Mahaffey, Jerome Dean, xxiv
Majlis (Iranian parliamentary body), 45–46
Malenkov, Georgi, 50–51
Mandate for Change (Eisenhower), 56
Mansfield, Mike, 25, 36, 151
Mansfield Amendment, 36–37, 146, 151
Markel, Mike, 54
Marshall, George, 29, 187n32
Martin, Michael, 53
Mather, Cotton, xiii
al-Matni, Nasib, 147, 198n5
McCarthy, Joseph, 116
Medhurst, Martin J., xvi, xvii–xviii, xxx, 30, 50, 76–77, 113–14, 144
media: CIA's manipulation of, 62; coverage of Iranian coup, 62–64; DDE's manipulation of, 60–61, 66; downplaying U.S. role in Middle East, 98–99; impact on American public, xvi; role in psychological warfare, 76
Middle East: American perceptions of, xiii–xiv, xv–xvi, 31–32; anti-American sentiment in, 42, 69; Britain's role in, 19–23, 48, 107; as Cold War theater, 172–73; Communism as threat to, 16–17; DDE's 1959 goodwill tour to, 169–70; during DDE's first term, 107–10; DDE's legacy in, xiv–xv, xxxiv; in the Eisenhower Doctrine, 1–10; growing importance to U.S., xxii, 27–28, 37–38, 85–86; impact of Eisenhower Doctrine on, 37–38, 40; impact of Suez crisis on, 132–33; impacts of surreption on, 100–104; map of, *xxxviii*; Operation Ajax's impact on, 69–71; political turmoil in, 75, 77–80; portrayed

as instable, 29–30; presidential rhetoric on, xiii, xxxiv–xxxv, 18–23; regional defense agreements in, 88–92; resentment of imperialism in, 123; shifts in U.S. policy toward, xxiii, xxviii–xxx; simplistic framings of, 28–30, 32–33, 173; Soviet propaganda campaigns in, 108–10; in Suez crisis speech, 118–21, 124–28; during the Truman administration, 47–48; U.S. changing role in, xxviii–xxix, 103–4, 129–30, 169; U.S. regional hegemony in, x, xxix, 131–32, 136, 157–58, 165, 178–82; U.S. rhetorical changes in, 165, 176–77. *See also* foreign policy

Middle East Resolution: DDE's proposal, 23; justifying Operation Blue Bat, 138, 144–46, 150–51; Mansfield Amendment to, 36–37, 146, 151; need for congressional approval, 24–25; passage of, 36; rhetorical nature of, 34–35, 187n41; Senate debating of, 36; Suez crisis speech as foundation, 132. *See also* Eisenhower Doctrine

military (U.S.): addressed in the Eisenhower Doctrine, 7–8, 9–10; under Donald Trump, 174; during Operation Blue Bat, 138, 140, 145–47, 149–51, 155–56, 159–60, 162, 164, 199n22

misdirection, rhetorical, xxviii, 43, 177; distancing rhetoric, 54–60, 114–15, 189n29; effects of, 68–71; manipulation of the media, 60–64; in Operation Ajax, 51–54; polyvalence, 67–68; subverting power hierarchies, 53–54; surreption as continuation of, 83–84; through covert activity, 171–72; used by Barack Obama, 173; use of surrogates, 64–67

"missile gap" controversy, 195n21
"Mission Accomplished" speech, xiii, xvii
Mollet, Guy, 111, 122
Molotov, Vyacheslav, 44, 188n9
Morse, Wayne, 25
Mossadegh, Mohammed, 41, 42, 46, 51, 52–53, 54–59, 62–64, 67–68
Musketeer, Operation, 113
Mutual Security Act (1954), 8

Naguib, Mohammad, 78
narrative frame (rhetorical strategy), 31–36, 127–28
Nasser, Gamal Abdel: on American "stupid moves," 135; anti-American propaganda of, 100; and the Arab-Israeli conflict, 99; and the Baghdad Pact, 90, 107, 111; and the CIA, 86–87; coming to power, 78; on Communism, 200n36; and conflict in Lebanon, 139; Czech arms deal, 108; DDE's portrayals of, 121; and Egyptian-Iraqi conflict, 169; nonalignment policy of, 17, 80; pan-Arab nationalism of, 78, 132, 137; and Project Alpha, 97; relations with Soviet Union, 80, 111, 136; and the Suez crisis, 111; and the UAR, 94, 137; on Western imperialism, 102

National Front (political party), 46
nationalism, 78–79; conflated with Soviet threat, 152–54, 167–68; constructive use of, 73; in the Eisenhower Doctrine, 17; in Iraqi coup, 144; in Lebanon, 138; nonalignment of, 17, 80; Suez crisis affirming, 132; and the UAR, 137; U.S. policy regarding, 86

national security: American conceptions of, 112; basic doctrine of Eisenhower administration, 90; British conceptions of, 112; importance of Middle East to, 80, 85–86; and Operation Blue Bat, 142–43, 159

National Security Council (NSC), 92, 135, 139–40; NSC 68, 15; NSC 129/1, 85; NSC 136/1, 47, 70; NSC 155/1, 85–86, 88; NSC 162/2, 90

NATO (North Atlantic Treaty Organization), 88, 108

neutrality, 17, 28, 49, 55, 80, 91–92
Neville-Shepard, Ryan, 157
New Look policy, 16, 76, 80, 88, 142
Newsweek, 63, 66, 76, 191n56
New York News, 99
New York Times, 57, 63, 64, 66, 95, 188n6
Nitze, Paul, 15
Nixon, Richard, 64–65, 163, 180
Nkrumah, Kwame, 77

North Atlantic Treaty Organization (NATO), 88, 108

NSC (National Security Council). *See* National Security Council (NSC)

Nye, Joseph, 101

Obama, Barack, xvii, xix, xxi–xxii, 173, 181

O'Gorman, Ned, 28, 126, 186n30

oil: addressed in the Eisenhower Doctrine, 2–3; American business investment in, 20, 70–71; colonialism in, 28; economic importance of, 96; European dependency on, 27, 79–80, 96; and the Iranian coup, 42, 46, 49, 70–71; nationalization of Iran's, 52

Operation Ajax: American media's role in, 62–64; American public's knowledge of, 53–54, 69–70, 188n2; compared to Operation Blue Bat, 143; distancing rhetoric during, 54–60, 189n29; impacts of, 42–43, 68–71; international news accounts of, 63–64; main events of, 52–53; manipulation of media during, 60–64; planning of, 56–57; propaganda campaign during, 62–63; rhetorical surrogates during, 65–67; rhetoric of misdirection in, 51–54, 83

Operation Blue Bat: context of, 139–44; effects of, 161–66; Eisenhower Doctrine manifested in, 135–36, 144–46; executive authority justifying, 149–52; imperialistic rhetoric justifying, 162–63; military assumptions during, 199n22; precedent set by, 158, 163–65, 166; right to independence justifying, 154–58; role of Congress in, 144–45, 148; threat conflation justifying, 152–54; timeline of, 146–47; transcendent ideals justifying, 158–61

Operation Countenance, 43–45

Operation Musketeer, 113

Operation Straggle, 92–95

Operation Wappen, 94, 137, 146

Orientalism, 118–21, 196n49

Orientalism (Said), 118–19

Osgood, Kenneth, 62, 75

Pahlavi, Mohammed Reza Shah, xv, 42, 44, 45–46, 52–53, 63, 69

Pahlavi, Reza Shah, 44

Pakistan, 79, 88, 89–91, 102, 107

Palestine: addressed in the Eisenhower Doctrine, 8; addressed in the Suez crisis speech, 120–21; British control of, 19–20; conflicts with Israel, 79, 81–82, 120–21; DDE's approach to, 81–82; Jewish settlement in, 19–20; and nationalism in Jordan, 78–79; during the Truman administration, 21

Parry-Giles, Shawn J., xxvii, 83–84

"passing" (rhetorical strategy), 94–95

"Peace through Deeds" (UN resolution), 156

persuasive strategies (rhetorical): continuity theme, 25–27; directed toward American public, xix–xxi, 31–36; directed toward Congress, 24–31; emphasizing trustworthiness, 30–31; theme of necessity, 27–28; through narrative construction, 31–36

Plato, xvii, 184n31

Poland, 116–18

polysemy, 67, 94–95

polyvalence, 67–68

Powers, Francis Gary, 187n36

Pratt, James, 114

Preaching Politics (Mahaffey), xxiv

presidential rhetoric: on American purity, 196n36; apocalypse management, 165; argument fields in, xxiii–xxv, 170, 174–75; audiences for, 144–48; censoring function of, 121; during the Cold War, 75–77; constitutive function of, xxi–xxiii; constraints created by, 46–48, 138–39, 143, 165–66; damage control function of, 144; effects of, 128–32, 162–66; Eisenhower Doctrine's impact on, 17; functions of, xvii–xix, xvii–xxv, xxi–xxiii, 54, 115–18, 121, 144; impact of Suez crisis on, 106, 132–33; impact on policy, x, 30, 38, 135–36, 164–65; impact on political reality, xvi–xxv, 18, 36; justifying military force, 148; limits of, xxi, xxv–xxvi; major shifts in, 128–32; Orientalism in, 119, 196n49; precedent set by DDE, 164, 173–75, 178–82; pre-Eisenhower, 18–23; regarding the Middle East, xxxiv–

xxxv; as response to exigences, xviii; strategic function of, xvii–xix. *See also* rhetorical strategy

presidents: bully pulpit of, xvi–xvii, xix; as "communicators in chief," 184n30; rhetorical leadership of, xviii–xix; rhetorical power of, xxi–xxv; use of ghostwriters, xxvi

press conferences, 60–61, 65, 93–95

Proctor, David E., 164

Project Alpha peace talks, 95–100

propaganda campaigns: of the CIA, 62–63, 190n56; during the Cold War, 75–77; during Operation Ajax, 62–64; during Operation Blue Bat, 153–54; power of, xx–xxi; of the Soviet Union, 77, 102–3, 108–10

prophetic dualism, 28, 154

Providence Journal, 98

psychological warfare, xxiii, 16, 50–51, 62–63, 75–77, 142, 198n14

Qajar Dynasty (Iran), 45

al-Qasim, Abd-al-Karim, 169, 170

Qibya (West Bank settlement), 79

Quintilian, xxiii

al-Quwatli, Shukri, 92

Rabinowitz, Peter, 94–95

al-Rasheed, Madawi, 186n19

Reagan, Ronald, 164, 180–81, 201n60

religions: addressed in the Eisenhower Doctrine, 3–4; changes in U.S., 13–14; Middle East's significance to, 27–28; rhetorical flattening of, 186n30

Republican Party, 24–25, 115

rhetoric: audiences for, 144–46, 199n28; classical, xvii–xviii, xxiii–xxiv; constitutive consequences of, 175–76; dualistic, 28–30, 33, 75, 116–18, 154, 172–74; effects of, 128–32; exigences addressed by, xviii, 23; five canons of, xxiii–xxiv; impacts on policy, 38, 132–33; rhetorical criticism, xxx–xxxi; strategic use of, ix–x, xv, 52, 110–11, 113–14; time depictions, 118–19. *See also* presidential rhetoric; rhetorical strategy

rhetorical criticism, xxx–xxxi

rhetorical leadership, xvi, xviii–xix

The Rhetorical Presidency (Tulis), xvi

rhetorical strategy: during the Cold War, 75–77; continuity theme, 34–35; contradictions in, 159; emphasizing trustworthiness, 30–31; of established precedent, 25–27; impact of Suez crisis on, 106; independence trope, 35–36; metaphors of savagery, 117; of narrative construction, 31–36, 127–28; strategic ambiguity, 60, 91, 153; in Suez crisis speech, 123–25; theme of necessity, 27–28; transcendent theme, 126–28. *See also* justificatory rhetoric; misdirection, rhetorical; persuasive strategies (rhetorical)

romantic tropes, 118

Roosevelt, Archie, 92–93

Roosevelt, Franklin D.: "good neighbor" metaphor, 34; on the Middle East, 18, 20; supporting Zionism, 185n15; at the Tehran Conference, 44; use of rhetoric, xix, xx, xxii, xxvi; and the Yalta agreement, 33

Roosevelt, Kermit, 52, 68, 188n2

Rouhani, Hassan, 41–42, 69

Russell, Francis, 97–98

Russell, Richard, 25

Said, Edward, 118–19

as-Said, Nuri, 90, 100, 102, 107, 147, 195n18

Sarraj, Abd al-Hamid, 94

Saudi Arabia, 20, 186n19

Saunders, Francis Stonor, 62

scholarly revisionism, xxxi

SEATO (Southeast Asia Treaty Organization), 88

Selassie, Haile (emperor of Ethiopia), 20

Senate (U.S.), 36–37

"shaman-trickster" figure, 54

Shuckburgh, Evelyn, 97–98

Simon, Richard Leo, 194n9

60 Minutes (TV news show), 41–42

Socrates, 184n31

Southeast Asia Treaty Organization (SEATO), 88

Soviet Union: American perceptions of, xx–xxi; and the Baghdad Pact, 107; conflated with Arab nationalism, 152–54;

Soviet Union (continued)
  containment strategy addressing, xxvii–
    xxix, 14–15, 88–89; during DDE's first
    term, 106–7; dualistic rhetoric regard-
    ing, 28–29, 75, 172–73; in the Egyptian-
    Iraqi rivalry, 169, 170; in the Eisenhower
    Doctrine, 2–3, 4–5, 30, 32–34, 39; impact
    on U.S. foreign policy, 74; interest in
    UAR, 139; under Nikita Khrushchev,
    108–10; occupation of Hungary, 30,
    113; and Operation Ajax, 67, 68; during
    Operation Blue Bat, 160–61; portrayed
    in Suez crisis speech, 116–18; post-Stalin
    strategies of, 50–51; propaganda cam-
    paigns of, 77, 102–3, 108–10; relations
    with Egypt, 136, 169; relations with Iran,
    43–45, 52, 57; relations with Syria, 92;
    during the Suez crisis, 122–23; as threat
    to Middle East, 32–34, 47–51, 79, 171,
    172–73; in the UN, 33, 122–23, 130
Spiegel, Steven, xv
Stalin, Joseph, xx, 13, 33, 44, 50, 185n2,
    188n9
Stassen, Harold, 89
Stevenson, Adlai, 113, 115
Stevenson, Karla, 148
Stewart, Jon, xiii
Straggle, Operation, 92–95
Streibert, Theodore, 76
Stuckey, Mary, xxvii, 54
Suez Canal: addressed in the Eisenhower
    Doctrine, 2, 3; British military at, 84–85,
    111; nationalization of, 111
Suez crisis: contextualization of, 94, 106–
    10; DDE condemning attack, 121–23;
    ending of, 136; events leading to, 111–13,
    195n18; events of, 106, 197n68; impacts
    of, 105–6, 132–33; Israeli plan, 113
Suez crisis speech (DDE's), 113–28;
    addressing Congress, 114–16; address-
    ing the American public, 114–16; chang-
    ing U.S. responsibility in, 124–30;
    compared to Truman Doctrine, 125–26;
    contextual frame of, 128–29; Europe
    portrayed in, 130–32; as foundation for
    Eisenhower Doctrine, 129–32; Oriental-
    ism in, 118–21; rhetorical strategies of,

xxviii–xxix, 114–15, 123–25; significance
    of, 128–33; tensions in rhetoric, 110–11
surreptitious rhetoric (strategy): and the
    Baghdad Pact, 88–92; DDE's break
    from, xxix, 177; in dealings with Egypt,
    84–88; defined, 82; limits of, 82–83,
    100–103, 112; during Operation Strag-
    gle, 92–95; during Project Alpha talks,
    95–100; purposes of, 83–84; during
    the Suez crisis, 112–13; through covert
    activity, 171–72
surrogacy (rhetorical), xxvi–xxvii, 64–67,
    97–99
Syria: attempted coups in, 92–95, 137;
    and the Baghdad Pact, 89–91; oppo-
    sition to Communism in, 200n36; in
    the UAR, 137, 147; U.S. covert action in,
    92–95, 146

Taft, Robert, 13, 33
Talal I (king of Jordan), 79
Tehran Conference (1943), 44
Tennent, Gilbert, xxiv
Thorpe, D. R., 105
threat conflation, 152–54
Time magazine, 66
Tripartite Agreement (1950), 79, 107, 111
Troutbeck, John, 73
Truman, Harry S.: on Britain's role, 20–
    23, 125–26; defense spending under,
    15–16; neutral policy of, 49, 55; oppos-
    ing Communism, 13, 29, 41, 163; rheto-
    ric regarding Iran, 44, 46–48; rhetoric
    regarding Middle East, xiv–xv, 13, 18;
    supporting Israel, 66; and the Yalta
    agreement, 33
Truman Doctrine, xv, 21–23, 26–27, 29,
    125–26, 163
Trump, Donald, xvii, 174, 181–82
Tudeh Party, 44, 51, 188n9
Tulis, Jeffrey, xvi
Turkey: and the Baghdad Pact, 89–91,
    107; in the Truman Doctrine, 21–22, 125

U-2 program, 187n36, 195n21
UAR (United Arab Republic), 94, 137, 139,
    140, 147, 153, 200n36
unilateralism, 170–71, 173

United Arab Republic (UAR), 94, 137, 139, 140, 147, 153, 200n36

United Nations (UN): and the Arab-Israeli conflict, 96; DDE's "Atoms for Peace" speech to, 76; DDE's August 1958 speech to, 167–69; in the Eisenhower Doctrine, 5, 7, 8, 39; and Iran's nuclear program, 41–42; and Lebanon political tensions, 147; on occupation of Lebanon, 139–40; and Operation Ajax, 44–45; and Operation Blue Bat, 149–50, 155; portrayed in Suez crisis speech, 124–25, 130–31; Soviet veto power in, 33, 130; during the Suez crisis, 122–23, 136; as supporting U.S. policy, 124–25, 161; U.S. as stand-in for, 30, 34, 130–31, 155–57

United States Information Agency (USIA), 62, 76, 162

Universal Pictures, 76

USIA (United States Information Agency), 62, 76, 162

U.S. Mutual Security Act (1955), 92

Valenzano, Joseph M., III, 148

Vietnam War, 163

"Voice of the Arabs" radio program, 78

Waggoner, Catherine Egley, 82

Waltz, Edmund, 64

Wander, Phillip, 28

Wappen, Operation, 94, 137, 146

Warsaw Treaty, 4

Washington, George, xx

Whitefield, George, xxiv

Wilber, Donald, 52

Wilford, Hugh, 43

Wilson, Woodrow, xix, xx, 18–20, 182, 184n31

Wise, Stephen, 19–20

Woodhouse, C. M., 52

World War I, xx

World War II, xviii–xix, xx, xxii, xxvi, 35

Yalta Conference (1945), 20, 32–33

Yaqub, Salim, 17

Yemen, 79

Young, Marilyn J., xxxiv

Zarefsky, David, xvi, 18, 165

Zionism, 19–20, 73, 185n15, 197n1